P9-BYO-277

Long Fuse, Big Bang

Long Fuse, BIG BANG

Achieving Long-term Success
Through Daily Victories

ERIC HASELTINE

HYPERION

NEW YORK

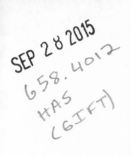
Copyright © 2010 Eric Haseltine

All rights reserved. No part of this book may be used or
reproduced in any manner whatsoever without the written
permission of the Publisher. Printed in the United States of
America. For information address Hyperion, 114 Fifth
Avenue, New York, New York, 10011.

Library of Congress Cataloging-in-Publication Data
has been applied for.

ISBN: 978-1-4013-2363-9

Hyperion books are available for special promotions,
premiums, or corporate training. For details contact
the HarperCollins Special Markets Department in the
New York office at 212-207-7528, fax 212-207-7222,
or e-mail spsales@harpercollins.com.

Book design by Karen Minster

FIRST EDITION

10   9   8   7   6   5   4   3   2   1

THIS LABEL APPLIES TO TEXT STOCK

We try to produce the most beautiful books possible, and we are
also extremely concerned about the impact of our manufacturing
process on the forests of the world and the environment as a whole.
Accordingly, we've made sure that all of the paper we use has been
certified as coming from forests that are managed to ensure the
protection of the people and wildlife dependent upon them.

FOR STACEY

Hard work pays off in the future,
laziness pays off now

—Steven Wright

Wes Neff and Bill Leigh of the Leigh Bureau were the first to suggest that I turn the long fuse, big bang concept into a book, and provided key guidance and support throughout all phases of the project. Don Conti was a fabulous writing coach, as was my editor, Brenda Copeland. Max Krasnow brought me up to date on current theories of evolutionary psychology and introduced me to the idea that the human brain has a playbook, written into our nervous systems over millions of years of evolution, that guides much of our behavior. If *Long Fuse, Big Bang* contains inaccurate descriptions of evolutionary psychology, the errors are mine, not Max's. Thanks also to my good friends Steve and Nancy, who loaned me their young daughters, Tessa and Sydney, for an afternoon's discussion of Toontown Online. Mike Goslin, who worked with me at Disney, helped set my memory straight on how Toontown Online actually came into being. Bobby Baldridge, a long time Wal-Mart employee, helped me understand the company's unique culture, and David Hartshorn introduced me to the strange and wonderful story of how the tiny island nation of Tonga became a major player in the commercial satellite business. Finally, the book would not have been possible without the patient cooperation and helpful suggestions from the visionaries that I interviewed for the different case studies. These include Alan Kay, Bran Ferren, Bill Haseltine, Prasad Nimmagadda, George Helimeyer, Don Burke, Sean Dennehey, Carol Fenster, Amy Kruse, and last but not least, Dr. XX. I can't tell the world who you are, but the world has benefited mightily from your presence in it.

CONTENTS

Why You Shouldn't Buy This Book

As one part of your brain processes the words of this introduction—converting black symbols on a white page into meaning—another part of your brain is urging you to put the book down and focus on something more pressing. Get back to work on the budget due tomorrow. Answer emails growing stale in your inbox. Get off your rear and update that résumé.

Even if you've already bought the book, odds are that the constant tug of here-and-now demands will stop you from finishing it. Most people who buy business books, even best sellers, never read them—much less complete them—because something more pressing always comes along.

That's where *Long Fuse, Big Bang* comes in. This book—yes, the very one you are holding in your hands—contains new and important ideas on how to generate explosive results in your professional world. But because none of these ideas requires urgent action, your first-things-first brain will compel you to park the book on a shelf where you'll get to it *later*. But in all likelihood *later* will never come, because your brain won't let it. Take it from me, a neuroscientist: left to its own devices, your brain will forever forsake important pursuits in order to handle more urgent ones.

Don't feel too sheepish about being shortsighted, though, because evolution has hardwired our brains to have temporal myopia, the tendency to focus only on the immediate future. For instance, I don't know any executives—including some Fortune 500 CEOs—who think they spend as much time as they ought to fostering long-term, game-changing advances in their businesses. These leaders lament that the constant need to react to emergencies interrupts and derails their efforts at transformative change. You can't focus on tomorrow, so the thinking goes, without sacrificing today.

But this thinking is wrong.

It's an unconscious holdover from a time—hundreds of thousands of years in our past—when our environments were so filled with immediate peril and our life expectancies so short (around twenty years) that focusing exclusively on surviving *right here, right now* made sense.

That was then and this is now.

Long Fuse, Big Bang shows how, in the modern world, where life expectancies are long and physical perils rare (at least for people who buy books), it's possible not only to build a strong tomorrow without sacrificing today, but to actually *increase* the number of here-and-now victories by pursuing distant wins.

The first step is to learn how ancient survival scripts compel us to focus all attention on immediate threats and opportunities, creating a false sense of urgency. Armed with this insight, we can prevent our brains from getting in the way of progress. But *Long Fuse, Big Bang* doesn't stop after showing how to neutralize your brain as an enemy: the book goes on to illustrate— through case studies of successful long fuse thinkers—how to turn our brains into *major allies* in the pursuit of major progress.

Some of these case studies come from my strange and varied career as a brain scientist, aerospace manager, Disney executive, and recently, one of America's most senior intelligence officers. Other stories are drawn from history, or visionary leaders such as Sam Walton, Lou Gerstner, or Jean Monnet, who, without realizing it, perfected the application of neuroscience to achieve big bang results.

And you can do the same if you only convince your got-to-have-it-all-right-now brain to put off instant gratification long enough to start the first chapter. Turning this page will be like lighting a match; one that ignites a long fuse to big bang results in your not too distant future.

Long Fuse, Big Bang

The Ancient Script

CAPABILITIES AND INTENTIONS

Flying low and fast to thwart insurgents' surface-to-air missiles, our Blackhawk headed south over the desert toward Hillah, the site of ancient Babylon. I adjusted the five-point harness that held me in the helicopter, twisting in my seat to get a better look at the barren terrain below. The Blackhawk's doors were open, filling the cabin with a frigid, howling wind that made conversation impossible. But the openings gave our gunners an unobstructed field of fire and afforded me a panoramic view of Iraq. I surveyed the landscape and thought about the war.

I was an intelligence officer on a three-week visit "downrange," as we called combat zones, to help defeat the growing threat of improvised explosive devices, also known as roadside bombs or simply IEDs. The number and sophistication of IED attacks had been climbing since the previous March, and Coalition casualties were mounting. I led a team of scientists researching new ways to cope with the constant improvements insurgents were making to these devices. But gazing at the ancient land below, I wondered whether historic forces would limit my team to temporary successes. The local population had fought occupying powers on and off for more than two thousand years, and the current insurgents showed little sign of quitting. Moreover, tactics for using IEDs had been improving since the early nineteenth century, when guerrillas in Spain first buried roadside kegs of gunpowder, to attack Napoleon's convoys. Since that time, insurgents from Northern Ireland to Lebanon had successfully used IEDs to harass and sometimes expel larger, better equipped occupying armies.

One of the lessons resistance fighters had learned since Napoleon's occupation of Spain was that by changing the time, place, or method of attack, they could keep defenders off balance. Extremists in Iraq seemed to have absorbed this lesson quickly. Early in the war Coalition Forces were able to spot IEDs from signs of recent digging, so insurgents got smarter, hiding their bombs in roadside trash, hollowed-out cement curbs, and even dead animals.

"It's not these latest IEDs we're up against," I thought. "It's two thousand years of culture and two hundred years of learning about how to use IEDs." Clearly, my team and others trying to defeat these resistance fighters were locked in a spiraling contest of move, countermove, and counter-countermove for as long as the war lasted. What we needed, I realized, was not an endless series of quick, temporary fixes, but fundamental and enduring changes to the way the IED game was played, changes that would tip the odds in our favor. As our helicopter flew over a small settlement of earthen huts, I saw a woman wearing a deep purple burka, feeding goats in a fenced yard. The vivid color of the woman's clothes stood in stark contrast to the pale desert around her. She looked up, smiled, and waved as we sped past. "Looks like they don't all hate us," I thought. And then it struck me: What if my scientists were taking the wrong approach? What if others here didn't want to kill us? Wouldn't that be a better answer to IEDs than any technology my team could develop?

Intelligence organizations everywhere have two basic goals: to understand the intentions and the capabilities of foreign powers. What are foreign actors trying to achieve and what tools do they have to achieve it? My scientists had been focusing on the capabilities of new IEDs, not the overarching intentions of the extremists who used them. If there was a way to understand the motivations of different individuals who funded, assembled, planted, and triggered the bombs, perhaps we could persuade them not to attack our convoys in the first place. Then, my scientists wouldn't get dragged into an endless circle of defeating insurgent IED technology, only to have the insurgents adapt to our adaptations . . . and so on and so on.

Others in the Intelligence Community—sixteen different agencies that include CIA, NSA, and intelligence groups of the armed services—had been exploring questions of insurgent intent from geopolitical and economic points of view. These officers concluded that insurgents used IEDs for a variety of reasons, ranging from advancing jihadist ideology to simply earning a living. But I was unaware of any significant work on the behavioral science of the struggle against insurgents or Islamic extremists that would lay bare these motives, never mind help us to understand them.

As the purple-robed woman shrank to a dot behind us, I recalled the social psychology and anthropology I had studied while getting a PhD in Physiological Psychology—the study of how the brain feels, perceives, learns, and thinks. What did science know about human perception and motivation and how to change deeply entrenched attitudes? What causes people to choose violence in the first place? Is it possible to persuade people to abandon violence once they have embraced it? This last question led me to think about the history book I had just finished reading on Iraq, Mesopotamia, and the Middle East. This region had been occupied by the Persians, Alexander the Great, the Parthians, the Turks, and finally the British after World War I. What had these powers learned about discouraging local violence?

Before I had time to consider if behavioral science or history held any real answers, I saw an orange light winking on and off in the window of a small house about three hundred meters (a thousand feet) off the starboard side of our chopper. I was puzzled. "Who would display Halloween lights in Iraq, in *February*?" I wondered.

My body sensed the answer before my brain did: my heart pounded and my stomach tightened as the thought popped into my head "It's a muzzle flash from a gun . . . aimed *at us*!" I fumbled with the intercom and keyed the microphone on my headset. "Uh," I said, "contact right. Is that how to say someone's shooting at us over there to starboard?" I cinched the Velcro strap on my body armor and put on my Kevlar helmet as I waited for the answer. It didn't take long.

"Got it, Doctor," came the reply from the cockpit. But our starboard gunner, who had heard the exchange on the intercom, didn't shoot back at the attacker, and the Blackhawk pressed on without changing course or altitude. When the dwelling was out of sight, the copilot came on the intercom: "They take potshots all the time, Doctor." Then he clicked off. His tone indicated that potshots were nothing to worry about, and that I shouldn't distract him if I saw them again. But I kept scanning the countryside for more "Halloween lights" all the way to Hillah. Gone were deep thoughts about Mesopotamian history.

THE HUMAN TERRAIN

Some two years later, in a new job as director of science and technology for the U.S. Intelligence Community, I eventually did find time to think about behavioral science again, and even approved several initiatives that explored the very questions that first occurred to me on the trip to Hillah. We knew that our harsh treatment of prisoners at Abu Ghraib had made it very difficult to win the "hearts and minds" of Iraqis, so I gave the green light to a project called Educing Information, which reviewed decades of experience with military, police, and intelligence interrogations to identify methods of questioning detainees that were both humane and effective. I also appointed a cultural anthropologist and other behavioral scientists to my outside advisory board to develop "soft science" projects that would help intelligence agencies better navigate the human terrain. These initiatives will take years to pay off, if ever, but I was convinced that behavioral science had much more to contribute to the struggle against terrorism than hard science ever would. Hard science could be effective in winning what the military calls *near battles*— such as taking a hill or securing a road—while soft science could win *deep battles*—such as getting an adversary to negotiate peace or to surrender unconditionally.

The so-called soft sciences, including psychology, cultural anthropology, and political science, could explore why disaffected people turn violent in the first place. Do tribal codes of justice compel them to seek revenge? Has their honor—a life-or-death concept in some cultures—been violated? Then soft science can build on answers to such questions to promote nonviolent solutions. In some societies, for example, an outsider who has killed a member of a family can reduce the chance that surviving family members will seek revenge if the transgressor restores the honor and respect of the bereaved family by offering them an apology and financial compensation for the killing. In this example, preemptively addressing the motivations and intentions of a potential enemy can make the capabilities of that potential enemy largely irrelevant.

In contrast, hard sciences, like physics, engineering, and chemistry, cope with terrorism after it has already occurred, treating symptoms of the disease without curing it. Once a group of extremists decides to adopt terror tactics, sophisticated telescopes can sometimes find the extremist's training camps. Or, after radicals have released nerve gas, chemical sensors can pinpoint where the gas has dispersed and what kind of nerve agent it is. In this, hard science can limit damage inflicted by terrorists by helping to neutralize a training camp or identify an antidote to a nerve agent. But hard science only reacts to national security problems that already exist; it can't prevent the problems from happening in the first place. Only the soft sciences can do that.

Others were coming to the same conclusion. The Defense Science Board, a blue ribbon panel of scientists and engineers that advises the U.S. secretary of defense on science policy, in 2006 issued a report that placed study of the "Human Terrain" at the top of the list of Defense Department science priorities. By *Human Terrain* the Defense Science Board meant understanding and dealing with the cultural, psychological, and anthropological underpinnings of conflicts in Iraq, Afghanistan, and elsewhere. Shortly after the report, the Defense Department sharply increased funding for research in social and behavioral science, and the army began to staff human terrain teams with linguists and anthropologists and deploy them downrange to help our forces better interact with local populations.

Most of my colleagues who served in Iraq during the Surge, which produced a drop in IED attacks throughout 2007 and 2008, said that the decreased violence had more to do with Coalition Forces working within the cultural and tribal framework of Iraq, than with an increase in troop strength. General Petraeus, who took command of the Coalition in 2007, encouraged his officers to work alongside historical power brokers such as tribal sheiks. By moving his troops out of a few large bases and dispersing them to local security stations throughout the country, Petraeus ensured that Coalition Forces worked closely with Iraqi government and tribal forces, a move that engendered trust as much as it improved safety. As local security stations improved regional safety, citizens became increasingly willing to turn in insurgents and weapons, creating a virtuous circle that further improved security and Iraqis' willingness to shift their support from insurgents to Coalition Forces.

A sweeping new plan for counterinsurgency that Petraeus coauthored in 2006, based on his experiences in Mosul, argued that putting priority on capturing and killing insurgents often alienated local populations. The report said a better approach was to recognize that civil considerations were the "center of gravity" of counterinsurgency operations, and that victory depended on building trust among local populations. The strategy paid off: Coalition Forces gave traditional Iraqi leaders financial support and other resources to suppress Al Qaeda foreign fighters and Iraqi insurgents, and soon violence against both Iraqis and Coalition Forces diminished. Explaining the effectiveness of empowering local Iraqi authorities to combat violence, Petraeus told Congress, "The most significant development in the past six months likely has been the increasing emergence of tribes and local citizens rejecting Al Qaeda and other extremists."

Looking back on my experiences, and the promising results of soft science in Iraq and Saudi Arabia, I regretted letting two years go by before tackling the questions that arose on the chopper ride to Hillah. As a psychologist, I'd been trained to go after deep, underlying causes of problems, not just their superficial symptoms, but I'd allowed the day-to-day struggle with the symptoms of terrorism—IEDs—to distract me. I had focused on the immediate at the expense of the important.

Behavioral science might take many years to produce a major decrease in terrorism, but it was more likely to have a much deeper, longer lasting impact than the more near-term hard-science solutions I'd been sponsoring back in 2004. In the parlance of roadside bombs, the soft science of counterterrorism had a lot longer fuse than the hard science, but the longer fuse would burn to a *much* bigger bang.

FROM EVOLUTION TO REVOLUTION

The distinction between the relatively small, near-term contributions of hard science in the struggle against terrorism and the much larger, but longer term benefits of soft science illustrates an important dichotomy that arises when confronting any challenge: For most problems, there are quick fixes that temporarily decrease the severity of a problem but do not fundamentally make the problem go away. Conversely, there are often more difficult solutions that take much longer to implement, but that will make a problem disappear.

For instance, you can mask symptoms of a stomach ulcer in a few minutes by swallowing antacids, but you'll have to visit the doctor, undergo tests, and then take antibiotics for many weeks to kill the bacteria that caused the ulcer in the first place. If you can't save enough to put your kids through college, you could switch jobs within a few months, adding 10 percent to your salary, and hope the extra money will be enough. Or you could go to night school, get a college degree yourself, double your salary, and be certain to save enough for your children. Cut back on smoking and you can ease your

smoker's cough; give up cigarettes completely and yo[...]
to your life. Turn a double-digit profit by flipping a prop[...]
digit profits by holding on to a property for many years[...]
examples is the idea that small fixes lead to small wins, wh[...]
forts lead to bigger, longer lasting achievements. And who [...]

These little picture/big picture questions are being asked by organizations everywhere. Consider Honda, which started a modest business in postwar Japan by modifying another manufacturer's electrical generator engines to make powered bicycles. Honda's gradual improvements to the generator engine drove the company's sales up, but not nearly as much as the huge leap in sales Honda achieved by making innovative engines from scratch, and eventually riding that wave of innovative engine design to become the world's fifth largest auto maker. Likewise, Taco Bell tried to turn around a steep decline in sales by incrementally tweaking its business processes, but only when they scrapped their green-eyeshade way of doing business and replaced it with TACO (Total Automation of Company Operations) were they able to add $500 million to their yearly sales.

In these cases the companies took years, not months, to completely overhaul their products and business processes. These overhauls changed the two companies' business not by degree, but by kind. Honda went from modifying small generator engines to being one of the largest car and motorcycle manufacturers in the world. Taco Bell transformed itself from a slow-footed Industrial Age company to an agile Information Age enterprise. These kinds of revolutionary versus evolutionary transformations take time because they require the coordinated efforts of many different people and organizations.

Radical reforms can also require painful, time-consuming changes to an organization's culture. IBM's CEO Lou Gerstner, who saved the stodgy computer monolith from breakup by shifting the company's focus from computer mainframes to more profitable information technology services, said one of his toughest challenges was overcoming IBM's "inbred and ingrown" culture in which engineers "studied things to death" and their bosses "presided rather than acted." It took several years for Gerstner to change IBM's culture through innovations such as a new compensation system that stressed speed over thoughtfulness, customers over internal politics, and cross-divisional cooperation over territoriality.

Visionaries like Gerstner often find that getting people to accept an innovative idea takes much longer than coming up with the innovation itself. After a couple years of research, Australian physicians Barry Marshall and Robin Warren found compelling evidence in 1982 that bacteria—not excess stomach acid—caused stomach ulcers. But it took a decade-long sales campaign by Marshall, including a demonstration where Marshall infected himself with the ulcer-causing bacteria *Helicobact pylori,* to convince conservative doctors that microbes caused ulcers. Marshall and Warren ultimately got the Nobel Prize for their work, which paved the way for doctors to cure ulcers with antibiotics rather than just treating ulcer symptoms with antacids. Fridtjof Nansen, a renowned arctic explorer whose tireless humanitarian work repatriating prisoners and refugees after World War I also earned him a Nobel Prize, summed up the strong connection between long fuses and big bangs: "The difficult is what takes a little time, the impossible takes a little longer."

DISTRACTION AND REACTION

We're surrounded by distractions that prevent us from focusing on all but the most immediate goals. On that helicopter ride to Hillah, for instance, I stopped thinking about the behavioral science of terrorism because I was being shot at and was trying to survive. It may seem that this situation is too extreme to be relevant to your world, but the very extremity of the helicopter experience is what makes it so useful for understanding how the human brain reacts to more routine distractions.

My heart raced and my stomach tensed when I realized that "Halloween lights" were actually muzzle flashes. These physiological reactions started when my brain told my adrenal glands to dump large doses of adrenaline into my bloodstream to prepare me to either fight a mortal threat or run from it. This fight-or-flight response is hardwired into our nervous systems by millions of years of evolution. The distractions that confronted our distant ancestors often were life threatening, so having a low threshold for releasing adrenaline made a lot of sense: better to overreact to a potential threat and waste a little energy, than to underreact and end up a tiger's breakfast.

Put another way, short-term success did lead to long-term success for all but a few thousand years of our evolution. You'd think that in the modern world, where most of us never encounter mortal threats, our brains would be more judicious about triggering the fight-or-flight response. But the human brain hasn't changed much since *Homo sapiens* first appeared in Paleolithic Africa about 200,000 years ago.

To get a gut sense—literally—of how little your brain has changed from that of your distant ancestors, imagine how your body would react during a finance meeting when you learn that your budget will be cut. Your brain sees a threat, causing adrenaline to speed into your bloodstream, tensing your muscles, speeding up your breathing, and quickening your heartbeat. Even though the budget cut is not some predator that you must instantly flee or kill, your paleolithic brain unconsciously assumes it is because 200,000 years ago, when there were no budget meetings, many threats were predators. Spurred on by a healthy jolt of adrenaline, you'll focus a lot of attention and resources on the looming budget cut, even at the expense of less urgent, but more important issues. This shift of attention and resources to cope with immediate threats occurs without your conscious participation. Consciousness involves thought, thought eats up time, and wasting time—so your brain reasons—narrows options for escape.

You don't have one brain, but at least two. The brain you're most aware of is the one that perceives, thinks, plans, decides, and acts. Most of that conscious activity takes place in a recently evolved part of our brain called the neocortex. If you've ever seen a picture of the brain, the neocortex is that mass of twisted, tubular-looking structures folded in on themselves on the surface. Except for a small stem at the base of the brain and a cauliflower-like structure called the cerebellum tucked behind the cerebral hemispheres, what you see in pictures of the brain is *all* neocortex.

But you have a completely separate brain, one that works faster than the speed of thought and tries to keep you out of immediate danger. This second brain consists of neural circuits, including a group of nerve cells and nerve fibers collectively called the limbic system, buried deep below the surface of the neocortex. The limbic system, which includes neural structures you may have heard of, such as the amygdala (which processes fear responses), the nucleus accumbens (associated with pleasure and rewards), and the hippocampus (which helps encode memories), was present in our ancestors tens of millions of years before the emergence of *Homo sapiens*. Older still are clusters of nerve cells located in your brainstem that regulate vital life functions such as breathing, blood pressure, and heart rate. Again, these ancient cells do their job without your awareness. When was the last time you asked your heart to beat faster or commanded your blood pressure to rise?

The fact is that the vast majority of our feelings, behaviors, and perceptions are not of our conscious choosing at all, but the result of the collective actions of many fast, but unconscious, processes operating covertly inside our brains. Understanding this is critical to overcoming the brain's often counterproductive tendency to choose small wins now over big wins later, because choices hidden from the cold light of reason go unquestioned and unchecked, regardless of their accuracy. But once you understand how and why your brain makes choices, you can decide for yourself if the choices are right, and convince your brain, when necessary, that it's not acting in its best interests.

NEUROECONOMICS: THE HOW AND WHY OF NOW OR LATER

A new field of research called neuroeconomics has brought to light the ancient little-now-over-a-lot-later scripts that run automatically in our brains. In a typical neuroeconomics experiment, researchers ask college students to choose one of two cash awards. One award would be paid out quickly, while the second would be paid sometime later. By systematically comparing students' preferences for different cash amounts delivered with different time delays, researchers determine the students' built-in tolerance for delayed gratification. For example, many students choose $10 paid immediately over $11 paid the following day.

At first glance, this choice seems illogical because the rate of inflation and lost investment income from one day's delay in getting $10 (if it were put in a bank account) are not nearly enough to make $11 tomorrow worth less than $10 today. Neither is the risk that the experimenter or the student will die before the $11 payoff can be made.

However, the students' choices are not illogical when viewed from a Paleolithic perspective. In that ancient era, and even a couple million or so years preceding it, humans and protohumans, such as *Homo erectus,* were nomads who hunted game and gathered roots, edible shrubs, fruit, nuts, and insects. Unlike squirrels and birds, humans did not store food for future use, but ate it almost as soon as they found it. This strategy made sense in an uncertain world where rival humans or scavengers could steal your food or even kill you before you could enjoy it. Also, hauling food back to a safe place and storing it consumed energy that humans on a subsistence diet could ill afford to waste. The phrase "eat drink and be merry, for tomorrow you may die" may have modern origins, but it aptly describes the attitudes of our distant ancestors, who often did die "tomorrow."

The dominant factor that governed our ancestors' decision making was extreme uncertainty about what tomorrow would bring. Such high-risk environments favored survival of people who focused all of their energy on living today to fight tomorrow. The odds were stacked against people who were willing to take risks and who delayed a little gratification now in hopes of getting a lot of gratification later. Take the wrong risk and *later* might not come at all.

Evolution has bred patience out of us.

We don't have to look very hard to find modern examples of our impatience. In the latest recession, governments across the globe took on staggering, long-term debt to fund short-term stimulus packages to stop a deep recession from turning into a full-blown depression. This new debt, added to existing deficits, will, at a minimum, create major inflationary pressures that future generations will have to cope with. It's possible that these huge national deficits will cause hyperinflation and currency devaluation that will be far worse than the original economic downturn the stimulus packages sought to avoid. But such long-range economic problems are just that . . . long-range. They are not as immediately troubling—or as politically charged—as here-and-now crises such as high unemployment and skyrocketing gas prices.

The short-term let-tomorrow-take-care-of-itself instincts that lead us to rack up monumental budget deficits also drive us to voraciously consume natural resources with scant regard for future consequences. Arguments over the role of fossil fuels in global warming often ignore the wider implications of our accelerating consumption of oil: a few generations of humans living between 1900 and 2100 will have consumed almost all of the world's oil, depriving later generations of not only fuel, but also a rich source of fertilizers, plastics, and pharmaceuticals. Naturalist Tim Flannery, who studied the tendency of prehistoric humans to hunt food sources to extinction—such as Moa birds in New Zealand and mammoths in North America—aptly labeled humans *future eaters.*

We eat our tomorrows in order to survive our todays.

Neuroeconomic research has quantified just how impatient we are and, by inference, just how risky our ancestors thought their future was. Harvard neuroeconomist David Laibson has calculated the amount that we devalue distant rewards out of an unconscious belief that our near futures are very risky. Shifting his research out of the laboratory Laibson and his colleagues compiled extensive data on choices that real consumers make about financial activities such as credit card borrowing, investing in retirement plans, and saving for the future. Laibson's analysis revealed that consumer behavior—for example, tolerating extremely high interest on credit card loans—is based on the unconscious assumption that the rate at which the value of money decreases one year in the future (due to inflation, risk, and other factors) is 30 percent, but decreases only 5 percent per year two or more years into the future. "In other words," Laibson wrote, "delaying a reward by a year reduces its value by 30 percent, but delaying the same reward an additional year only generates an additional 5 percent devaluation."

Because the true rate at which the value of money decreased over time was about 5 percent per year during the period of Laibson's study, consumers whom he analyzed assumed that the value of a payoff now over a future reward decreased six times (30 percent divided by 5 percent) faster than the actual decrease. Put another way, our ancient scripts—evolved in an eat-or-be-eaten past—make us assume that the near future is six times riskier than it actually is.

Laibson and others who study now-or-later choices call their work neuroeconomics because their experiments study brain activity of test subjects while the subjects are making decisions. Neuroeconomists believe that looking inside the brain while it makes decisions will yield deep insights about why people make "irrational" choices. They typically gather data by placing subjects in a functional magnetic resonance imaging machine. This fMRI—a scary-looking superconductor—takes high-resolution images that reveal which brain regions are most active under different test conditions. For example, when a subject wiggles a finger, the part of the subject's brain that commands the wiggle will light up with neural activity. Laibson and Samuel McClure of Princeton examined fMRI activity in both the limbic system and neocortex of subjects who were making now-or-later choices. The researchers found that the limbic system lit up most when subjects were offered immediate rewards. As the delay in potential rewards increased, this activity decreased, suggesting that powerful responses in our "emotional" limbic brain compel us to choose instant rewards. If you've ever decided to put off a diet for another day when offered a yummy treat, you have firsthand experience of just how compelling your limbic system can be.

The fMRI studies suggested a different function for parts of the more recently evolved neocortex such as the lateral orbitofrontal cortex (LOFC), a structure that neuroscientists believe plays a role in making analytic judgments. The LOFC and other cortical structures responded strongly to *any* offer of cash, whether instant or delayed. McClure and Laibson interpreted these results to mean that more recently evolved parts of our brain activate when called upon to weigh the merits of any proposition, regardless of its time scale. In contrast, the limbic system only turns on when immediate payoffs are to be had. This explains why as the possibility of instant gratification diminishes, our emotional limbic brain quiets down, leaving our cortical brain to make more "rational" decisions. It also explains why I failed for two years to pursue a long fuse, big bang opportunity to counter terrorism. My limbic brain, having been shot at, then confronted with one urgent IED problem after another, never quieted down long enough to give my patient neocortex a chance.

SHORT FUSES TO FIRECRACKERS

Working as a senior executive in fields as diverse as aerospace, entertainment, and intelligence, I've observed that organizations everywhere are so consumed with short-term problems and goals that they have little time to create and nurture long-term opportunities. I'm not alone in this. A great many of my colleagues have also expressed dismay that because near-term problems and opportunities consume so much attention, there's very little time to confront the deep causes of organizational problems or to pursue radically new products or business processes that would transform our business. What little spare time managers do have is spent chasing small, quick wins, instead of long-range big ones, and, of course, putting out the fires that daily threaten their existence. A like-minded friend in the defense industry, prone to thinking in terms of explosions, once confided, "I spend so much time lighting short fuses to firecrackers I never get to light long fuses to dynamite."

By short fuses to firecrackers my friend meant endless meetings, employee problems, irate customers, delinquent vendors, IT outages, reporting deadlines, impatient bosses—all of which conspired day in and day out to get in the way of effective long-term thinking.

The tyranny of the urgent stifles the pursuit of the important.

I've been to dozens of business retreats that tried to escape short fuse problems long enough to find and ignite long fuse, big bang wins for the organization. Without exception, the retreats surfaced terrific ideas that we vigorously pursued . . . for a week or two after the retreat ended. Then, the tyranny of the urgent forced us back into the same pattern of ignoring the important. I remember one executive retreat at Hughes Aircraft shortly after the collapse of the Soviet Union. All the senior leaders who took part in the meeting at a posh golf resort a hundred miles north of Los Angeles understood that the defense industry had just experienced a once-in-a-generation event that would profoundly change our business. We brainstormed different ways to "leverage our core competency" in military simulation and training to penetrate exciting new markets, such as the embryonic virtual reality entertainment business. We retained our enthusiasm for these new ideas for about a month after the retreat ended, but a financial crisis at one of our subsidiaries refocused all of our energies on cost cutting. We never got back on track pursuing lofty ambitions for going after exciting new markets, and within two years our billion-dollar business unit dissolved.

LONG FUSES TO DYNAMITE

Big bangs are revolutionary changes that don't just improve products, processes, or people, but completely transform them. They aren't lit by tweaking or adding features to an existing product, but by creating a breakthrough in a product or service that opens up vast new markets for a company.

When Kimberly-Clark moved from selling paper products to packaged consumer goods—that was a big bang. Another occurred when Procter & Gamble, creating breakthrough after breakthrough, moved from soaps to laundry to skin care to its fast-growing health care initiative. In the 1980s, Citibank changed the banking business forever when they slashed processing times for credit transactions from days to minutes by reorganizing their business into an efficient, computerized transaction processing factory, as opposed to the traditional paper-and-pencil financial services company they had been. Citibank's fundamental reframing of their business illustrates an essential quality of big bangs: they don't incrementally improve our games, they completely *change* them.

If big bangs are game changers, what are long fuses?

In Laibson's neuroeconomic framework, long fuses are projects, initiatives, or investments that arise more from our logical neocortex than from our risk-averse limbic systems. Historically, wealthy organizations, such as the U.S. government, that can tolerate high risk by virtue of guaranteed incomes (taxes and borrowing) are big sponsors of long fuse projects. Unburdened by a need to earn quarterly profits for stockholders, governments of wealthy nations can fund interstate highway systems, universities, and other projects that will pay off in a big way, but not for decades. Government-funded basic research is the most extreme—and compelling—example of "logical" long fuse thinking. Basic science seeks to unravel nature's secrets, not to develop products that can quickly make money. But unraveling nature's secrets can ultimately produce spectacular big bang results. The digital revolution that contributes trillions of dollars to today's economy traces its routes to quantum physics research in the early 1900s. This research led to the discovery of the transistor in the 1940s and rapid improvements of digital computers in the 1950s. By investing in basic sciences such as quantum physics, governments display the cool logic of the neocortex, in which the true math of risk and reward, not the emotional, Paleolithic fear of risk, dominates. In the case of basic research, governments accurately calculate that the very high risk—and long lead times—of scientific research are more than offset by the enormous rewards that flow from fundamental scientific advances. Put another way (except in emergencies such as looming depressions), governments often behave like "rational" subjects in Laibson's experiments, opting for $11 tomorrow versus $10 today.

Private businesses also undertake basic research, but it's no coincidence that most examples of such research take place in monopolies, such as AT&T's Bell Labs, that are not subject to normal market pressures. When the courts broke up AT&T in 1982, basic research at Bell Labs plummeted as their parent company faced intense pressure to generate quarterly profits.

Although most basic research today is funded by governments, profit-oriented companies with dividend-hungry shareholders and strong competitors also pursue long fuse objectives. But these projects usually deliver some kind of short-term payoff well in advance of achieving a distant goal. Pharmaceutical companies, for instance, take five years or more to develop a new drug and bring it to market. But when these companies put a promising new drug into the development pipeline, they can point to the new start as evidence of the company's growth potential. If Wall Street is convinced of the drug's promise, the company's stock price may rise far ahead of any revenue from the new drug, as investors anticipate appreciation of the company's net worth.

This last example illustrates a crucial point about pursuing successful long fuse initiatives: most of us face intense short-term pressures because we *don't* work for wealthy governments or monopolies. Like pharmaceutical companies, we must find near-term benefits from long-term pursuits to sustain the motivation of our organization's stakeholders. Essentially, our logical neocortexes must find creative ways to keep our give-it-to-me-now limbic systems happy.

This task is rarely easy, but it is eminently doable—even straightforward—once a few basics of applied brain science have been mastered.

DOG YEARS

Business settings, where there's usually a clear relationship between the work you do and the rewards you get, provide a good illustration of the temporal distinction between long and short fuses. In the business world, a long fuse is any pursuit that takes longer than one year. In most places that's the longest interval between now and the next time your boss decides what raise to give you. The theory here is that our brains engage in behaviors that get us rewarded and avoid those that either garner no rewards or, worse, elicit punishments. So *long fuse* is not defined by the calendar, but by the longest duration your brain believes is tolerable for gaining rewards or avoiding punishments.

It turns out that the brain gives disproportionate importance to immediate versus distant outcomes on time scales much *less* than one year. In your own work life, most of your day consists of evading torpedoes that will hit days or weeks away. Nevertheless, because most of us spend at least *some* time thinking about our next raise, bonus, or promotion, but almost *no* time planning beyond that, I'll define short fuse as less than one year. The duration of long fuses will soon shrink because the pace of change in virtually every facet of life is accelerating. The biggest culprit is technology, which for the foreseeable future will dramatically increase the speed of computers, networks, communication systems, and all that depends on digital technology— which is to say, practically everything. Digital camera manufacturers, who once launched new models every year, now routinely introduce new cameras every six months. Billionaires once took decades to earn their fortunes, now Internet entrepreneurs get to the billion milestone in little over a year. Wall Street monoliths such as Bear Stearns and Lehman Brothers, and banks such as Washington Mutual, wink out of existence in a few weeks.

Futurist Ray Kurzweil argues that technology will accelerate the pace of change for the foreseeable future because quickening has been gathering momentum for millions of years. By measuring the elapsed time between successive big bang technical innovations, what he calls paradigm shifts, Kurzweil concluded that each new wave of human innovation came on the scene in about one tenth the time of its predecessor. It took humans millions of years to use fire for cooking after the advent of stone tools, but crafted shelters emerged only a few hundred thousand years after fire. The next big innovation, clothing, arrived tens of thousands of years after crafted shelters. This accelerating pace continued into the present era, where the elapsed time between successive innovations, such as gunpowder and the printing press, shrank from hundreds of years, to tens of years. That, by the way, is the gap between the telegraph and the telephone. Today, major innovations, such as new generations of computers, follow one another every few years. Since the 1980s, when PCs first hit the market, the speed and performance of PCs have doubled every eighteen months. Similarly, $200 buys about twice the amount of hard disc storage every twelve months.

An expression popular in Silicon Valley, which is responsible for much of this recent quickening, is that we're now living in dog years, where everything ages seven times faster than it used to. If the dog year concept is valid, then my definition of long fuse is contracting toward one seventh of a year. Whether or not we really are hurtling toward canine time, learning now to light long fuses will soon help you thrive in months rather than years. In the fast-moving digital camera business, designers who had to wait a year to learn whether their new camera increased profits, and earned them a bonus, now only have to wait half that time.

The important is becoming increasingly urgent.

Humans may be driving this acceleration—doubtless out of a desire for ever faster gratification—but the fact is that most human brains are ill-equipped to exploit the big changes that other human brains create. Marshall and Warren's ten-year struggle to gain acceptance for their radical idea about ulcers was typical of the uphill battle innovators face. Galileo spent the last nine years of his life under house arrest for writing that the Earth orbited the sun. Despite winning a Nobel Prize, physicist Luis Alvarez died with a tarnished reputation for suggesting—correctly as it turned out—that an asteroid impact doomed the dinosaurs.

Modern humans evolved from ancestors who routinely faced extreme dangers, so we're risk-averse creatures who prefer not to stray from comfort zones into uncertain futures, even when those futures promise big bang improvements to our lives. One way to overcome our brains' hardwired risk aversion is to break down risky long-term ventures into a long succession of quicker, lower risk steps. But our brains have other scripts, besides those that bias us toward low-risk, high-speed results, that we must also co-opt to lure us out of our comfort zones.

The key is finding the way to work around our hardwired, short–time horizon orientation and discovering ways to light those *long fuses,* to nurture long-term opportunities or to nudge projects along that may someday provide explosive results and huge returns.

LONG FUSE, BIG BANG THINKING

Long fuse, big bang thinking is critical to the sustained success of business. We should all be doing it, but we're not. Look what happens, though, when we do: IBM reviving itself by shifting its internal investments from hardware, where margins were declining, into services, where faster and greater growth and profitability would be possible. Or Southwest Airlines buying fuel at a discount on futures markets well before it was actually needed. This well-run airline's long view enabled it to continue to offer discounted fares in the face of rapidly rising fuel costs and still turn a profit.

All too often, though, we are condemned to thinking like the Polaroid and Kodak executives who failed to recognize the importance of digital imaging and the threat it posed to their traditional film-based businesses. They didn't light the long fuse, didn't grasp the significance of the digital revolution, didn't invest enough in digital technology, and lost their market share to competitors who did.

Or witness the recent debacle on Wall Street, where greed coupled with short–time horizon thinking led investment bank executives to ignore the long-term dangers of the subprime mortgages they were pouring billions of dollars into. The result: the biggest bang financial disaster in history. The lesson: even with our well-being or very survival at stake, we are unequipped to look toward the future and face up to the dangers or opportunities lurking there.

I have spent my career learning how to get around our hardwired, short-term approach to the world, and I have studied individuals and entities who have figured it out, companies like Disney, Apple, and Wal-Mart, and organizations like DARPA (the central R&D organization for the Department of Defense). All of them have learned to work with our short-term hardwiring, getting people to lay down long fuses, tend to them, and keep them smoldering, in time igniting *big bang* successes—products, processes, or results that make history.

We need people and organizations that *pro-act,* that can create big futures while achieving better near-term performance. The irony is that it takes no more resources or energy to be proactive to long-term opportunites than it takes to be reactive to short-term threats and opportunities. The key is in knowing how to apply the right techniques to get the most out of human nature.

The long fuse, big bang way of thinking encourages us all to translate long-term opportunities into short-term projects that work *with* human behavior, rather than *against* it. Moreover, it enables organizations to get to tomorrow's products and services in ways that will improve operating performance today.

While most of us believe that shifting focus from the near horizon to the far horizon will hurt near-term operating results, in fact the opposite is true. Practitioners of long fuse methods will succeed not by changing *what* their organizations do on a day-to-day basis, but by subtly altering *how* they do it.

EXPLOSIVE PHENOMENA, EXPLOSIVE GROWTH

As the pace of change in our world accelerates, hot new phenomena like Facebook seem to come out of nowhere with increasing frequency. But careful study reveals that such big bangs do indeed have long fuses that usually smolder for years before igniting explosive growth. Facebook first garnered major attention in 2007, but it actually started three years earlier. The Internet itself was up and running in the early seventies, *two decades* before it became a household word.

Some things are worth waiting for. Big bang opportunities take time to develop and deliver. They can double profits. They can move a business into hot new growth markets or move it out of dying ones. They are the killer apps, the iPods, Facebooks, Googles, and their equivalents in other industries. Even an industry as "low tech" as home furnishing can produce big bangs, as when Ethan Allen developed its own new killer app by bundling interior design services with product sales, satisfying customers' unmet need for professional help to create aesthetically pleasing interior *solutions* instead of just selling furniture. Other big bangs may consist of developing vital answers to questions such as what new competitors or disruptive technologies must a company contend with and which may be safely ignored.

When we see Google, Apple, or Facebook roll out a killer app, our tendency is to think "Great, but my organization couldn't do that," because we perceive that the Googles of the world are uniquely talented—or uniquely lucky—at spotting big bang opportunities. But spotting big bang opportunities is not just about talent or luck. Like all human endeavors, it's about working with the inherent strengths of human nature while simultaneously working *around* our natural weaknesses. Just as evolution hardwired us to excel at reacting to short fuse threats, and to ignore long fuse opportunities, evolution has also bred into us certain strengths and weaknesses for spotting big wins. For example, the hyper-risky environment of our Paleolithic ancestors not only biased us toward short-term thinking, but also wired our brains to take certain perceptual shortcuts that helped us make quick life-or-death decisions. These shortcuts bought our brains perceptual speed at the price of perceptual completeness: our brains zero in on what they think is important—such as the presence of a prey animal hiding in a bush—by tuning out what they think is *unimportant*—such as the color of the bush. This triage strategy has left modern humans with perceptual blind spots that hide many big bang opportunities among details that our brains tune out as unimportant. Armed with an understanding of where these blind spots are—without relying on unusual talent or unusual luck—we can shed light on them and surface big bang opportunities that we otherwise would miss.

This approach, learning to work with our brains' wiring, is the essence of successful long fuse, big bang thinking and the essence of this book. I will tell the stories of visionary individuals and organizations who found different but highly effective ways to co-opt the brain's hardwiring to attain the uncommon patience and uncommon vision that are hallmarks of long fuse, big bang successes. These stories will show that big bang wins are not the exclusive province of the uniquely talented or uniquely lucky, but are available to anyone willing to look inside themselves for the answers that evolution has wired into their brains.

RECAP

Working Around Our Hardwired, Short–Time Horizon Orientation

All too often the tyranny of the urgent stifles the pursuit of the important. Our day-to-day struggles, pressing though they may be, can defeat our long-term goals and obscure opportunities. Unfortunately, we're surrounded by distractions that prevent us from focusing on all but the most immediate goals. Moreover, we're actually hardwired to react to short-term success and immediate gratification. It seems that we're governed by an ancient script, and that the vast majority of our feelings, behaviors, and perceptions are not of our conscious choosing, but are the collective actions of many fast but unconscious processes. Knowing this, understanding how and why your brain makes choices, you can decide if the choices are right and convince your brain to act in its best interest. It is possible to work around our hardwired, short–time horizon orientation to discover ways to light long fuses, to nurture long-term opportunities, and to nudge projects along that may lead to some new product, process, or breakthrough.

CHAPTER 2

The Brain's Playbook

THE ENERGY IMPERATIVE

The man in the photograph is lean and fit. He wears a modern blue denim shirt but has torn off its sleeves, giving his graceful arms unrestricted range of motion. Strings of traditional beads drape bandoleer-style over his shirt, and a spotted animal pelt hangs off the front of his belt. In the man's left hand are a bow and two arrows.

His name is Gonga. He belongs to the Hadzabe, a nomadic tribe that camps in and around Tanzania's Rift Valley and neighboring Serengeti Plateau. The photograph of Gonga accompanies an article in London's *Daily Mail* by Andrew Malone, one of the only journalists ever to visit the remote East African tribe.

"Only when I am sleeping, I am not a hunter," Gonga tells Malone. "I am a hunter all the time I am awake. That is what I am and who I am. I kill animals for meat."

The Hadzabe are the last known hunter-gatherers in Africa, following a way of life that's changed little since the Stone Age. Their language, related to ancient click dialects of Africa, is like no other in the region. Because he must hunt to eat, Gonga's priorities closely mirror those of our distant ancestors, yielding important clues about the ancient imperatives that drive modern behavior.

Even if you hadn't read how much Gonga hunts, you'd guess he placed a high priority on food just by looking at him. Like others in his tribe, Gonga is well nourished but thin. This isn't surprising; anthropologists estimate that Hadzabe men and women spend up to seven hours a day hunting and gathering food. That's not the sixteen hours a day Gonga claims, but it still exceeds the average physical activity of people in industrialized societies by a wide margin. Energy inflow for the Hadzabe equals energy outflow, but just barely. As of 2009, the Hadzabe people had shrunk to just fifteen hundred, largely due to a shortage of food.

If you were just barely able to consume as many calories as you burned, you'd look for the most calorie-rich food you could. The Hadzabe do this by gathering honey. Gonga's son, Philimon, told Andrew Malone that bee stings are an occupational hazard. "The bees get our blood, but we get their honey."

Even in societies with an abundance of food, we seek out nutrition high in sugar and fat because our Paleolithic brains—which instinctively believe we're constantly on the verge of starvation—are hardwired to prefer things that taste sweet and rich. The current obesity epidemic (more than 1 billion adults worldwide are overweight, according to the World Health Organization) is a compelling illustration of the disconnect between our ancient brains and our modern environment. Our Paleolithic brains think it makes sense to eat as much sugar and fat as quickly as we can, because not only will strenuous hunting and gathering activity soon burn up all those calories, but we can't know where our next meal is coming from. Of course most of us don't exercise vigorously and do know where our next meal is coming from, but we can't seem to convince our brains of that.

Another way our brains unconsciously try to stop us from starving to death is by restricting the number of calories that we burn through unnecessary activity. Our brains understand that we have to expend energy to find food, take care of our young, maintain households, and fight mortal threats, but they consider any activity that doesn't contribute to our survival or that of our kin a luxury. Anthropologists studying primitive societies such as the !Kung people of Southern Africa have found that when hunter-gatherers are not procuring food, they usually take it easy, sitting under trees, telling stories, sleeping, or engaging in low-energy activities such as sewing or tool making.

People in affluent societies similarly value their leisure time, tending to park themselves on a couch when they're not working. Even those of us who exercise regularly can't resist the powerful urge to conserve calories. Anthropologist Don Symons said: "I'm always amused to observe the little thrill I get when I find a parking place right in front of the gym—where I'm about to burn up five hundred or six hundred calories—so I don't have to walk that extra fifty feet. Old psychology, new conditions."

The imperative to conserve energy is so deeply ingrained in our genes that our brains actually alter our perceptions to insure that we don't overexert ourselves. Perceptual psychologist Denny Proffitt of the University of Virginia discovered that people who are tired from exertion perceive hills to be steeper than they actually are, discouraging these tired individuals from climbing. Such perceptual shifts, according to Proffitt, enforce an evolutionary mandate for "economy of action."

Physical exertion such as hill climbing isn't the only way we burn energy. Our brains—even at rest—consume 20 percent of our daily calorie expenditure. This burn rate doubles when we try to solve unfamiliar problems or learn new tasks, upping our bodies' total energy consumption by as much as 10 percent. Although this may not seem like much, on a subsistence diet like the Hadzabe's, a 10 percent calorie deficit continued day after day could be fatal. No wonder we have to coax our Stone Age brains to solve hard problems, take on unfamiliar tasks, or expend energy looking for long fuse, big bang wins. Our brains believe we'll starve to death if we think too much.

ECONOMY OF ACTION

We now have some insight about the origins of the notorious "comfort zone" that weds us to old habits. Change takes mental effort, mental effort takes calories, and calories, if not managed properly, take lives. We also have insights about what we're up against when we try to push ourselves and others out of comfort zones: millions of years of evolution are constantly whispering to our unconscious, *Careful with calories, careful.* No matter how persuasive we might be about the need to change old habits—no matter how hard we try—we are not more persuasive than millions of years of evolution. That's why it's necessary to co-opt, not fight, the brain's ancient logic.

Just as it's important to co-opt our impatient brains by swapping short fuses for long ones, it's also important to provide the brain with quick rewards, especially those that don't require a great expenditure of energy, to steer it gradually toward a big bang.

Fast is good, fast and *easy* is better.

Here's an example of how to co-opt the brain's desire to spend energy in the smallest increments possible. When I ran a Department of Defense research lab in 2003, the biggest drag on my scientists' productivity was the long lead time required to buy technology for experiments. Six months or more would go by from the time we told the Purchasing Department what we wanted until our vendor or contractor got an order. In a world where hot new technologies were coming on the market at an accelerating pace, our long purchasing cycle made it impossible to stay on technology's cutting edge. Worse, because we were trying to keep pace with Iraqi insurgents' rapidly evolving IEDs, we needed to get that new technology quickly. We set for ourselves the big bang goal of cutting our purchasing times in half.

The purchasing department was actually quite efficient by U.S. government standards, but like all federal contracting groups, it had a long series of boxes to check before placing orders. Purchasing had to make sure we had funds to cover the order, then it had to evaluate whether or not to compete the award and to assess whether potential vendors qualified for federal contracts and so on.

To compound the problem, Purchasing did not report to our research lab and had a very heavy workload buying goods and services for other departments in the aftermath of 9/11.

Our challenge in Research was to get busy purchasing managers to work with us on creative but legal ways to cut the box-checking process in half. Perhaps it's more accurate to say that our challenge was to get the brains of purchasing managers, already burning a lot of calories with a heavy workload, to burn even more calories solving a hard problem for us.

As we took on this challenge, I drew on my experience in graduate school getting calorie-conscious brains to make radical changes. In those days, I was working with rabbit brains, but I suspected that what worked for one mammal would very likely work for another.

My goal in graduate school was to train rabbits to perform a complex sensory discrimination. I was investigating how neurons in the rabbit's brain decode visual information to help the rabbit see small details. To understand the visual neurons better, I needed to give the rabbits an eye test to establish just how acute their vision was. But how do you test a rabbit's vision? You can't ask it to read from an eye chart. So I trained rabbits to press a bar whenever a visual stimulus consisting of a series of parallel lines appeared above the bar. After a rabbit learned to do this, I then decreased the spacing between the parallel lines until the rabbit no longer pressed the bar, suggesting that he could no longer make out the narrow spaces between the parallel lines. This was equivalent to determining which line on an eye chart a human can no longer read.

I trained rabbits on this task using a technique called *shaping,* where you start with a natural behavior of an organism and, over many small steps, *shape* the natural behavior into an unnatural one. In my experiments, the rabbits' natural behavior was to sniff around the cage for water or food. I got started by waiting until a rabbit randomly moved toward the response bar, then immediately gave the thirsty animal water from a spout under the bar. Soon, the rabbits learned that just getting close to the bar would earn them a drink. But after several rewards for getting close to the bar, I would only give the animal water when its snout actually touched the bar. After that, rabbits had to press down on the bar to earn a drink. I continued in this step-by-step process until the rabbits learned that they would only get a reward when they pressed the bar after a visual stimulus of parallel lines appeared above the bar. This shaping procedure worked, because each step of the way, the rabbit only had to learn a small change in behavior, expending a small amount of "mental" energy.

The way to get Department of Defense purchasing managers to help us with a difficult problem seemed clear: catch the managers in natural behaviors that crudely approximated what we needed, instantly reward them, then gradually raise the level of help Purchasing had to give us to earn a reward. Over time this process would shape our colleagues' behavior into cutting order times in half. At each step along the way, Purchasing employees would only have to spend a few extra brain calories to change their ways.

Federal purchasing managers may be motivated by beverages, but unlike rabbits, they are not motivated by water, so we had to come up with rewards that our colleagues would find motivating. We decided the best reward would be something very rare and valuable in any large bureaucracy: public praise from another department. Once a week the general who ran the enterprise held a senior staff meeting, where each department reported status. Immediately after our first face-to-face meeting with the Purchasing Department, where they simply agreed to listen to our ambitious goals, we announced in the general's status meeting that Purchasing was doing a great job helping us keep pace with the IED problem and other projects in the War on Terror.

Over the ensuing weeks, we continued to praise Purchasing, but each time we made our praise a little more expensive. Purchasing had to attend meetings with us *and* agree to provide metrics on how long the average purchase order took to process. Then Purchasing had to gather statistics on how much time each individual approval—in a long succession of approvals required to get an order placed—took to obtain. Once we identified the lengthiest approvals, we asked for suggestions about how to shorten them.

Week after week, we kept raising the bar in small increments.

When I left the organization two years later, this gradual shaping process had cut average purchasing times by one third. Not all the way to our big bang goal of 50 percent, but not bad either. I sometimes feel guilty about treating conscientious professionals like lab animals, but the stakes were high and I felt compelled to go with, rather than against, the brain's imperative for economy of action.

THE BRAIN: AN OWNER'S MANUAL

Thinking about this approach of going with the brain's hardwired preference for rewards that come fast and easy, I started to revise my view of the brain. In graduate school and as a postdoctoral fellow in Neuroanatomy, I had been taught that the brain is unimaginably complex and does not give up its mysteries easily. The more I learned about the fiendish intricacies of the three-pound organ, the more I despaired of ever divining anything useful about it in the laboratory. But after thirty years of observing the brain do its thing in the "real" world of the workplace, and serving for seven years as a volunteer psychotherapist in a mental health center, I realized that for all its complexities and subtleties, the brain has a sort of operator's manual that spells out surprisingly simple rules for how it reacts to many situations.

Max Krasnow, an evolutionary psychologist at the University of Santa Barbara who studies how ancient environments shape modern behaviors, has observed that the brain seems to have a "playbook" similar to those used by football teams, who, before a game, write down what they will do if the game unfolds in different directions. A football playbook could contain guidelines such as "If we're behind in the fourth quarter by less than two touchdowns, throw lots of short passes," "If we're behind by more than two touchdowns, throw lots of long passes," and so forth.

Our brain's playbook similarly contains a long list of if-then contingencies that help us act quickly and unconsciously, without wasting precious time—or energy—making decisions. Example plays are "If you have food, eat it all now," "If you don't have food, spend the energy required to get it, but no more," "Don't waste mental energy solving hard problems, unless your survival depends on it."

I like to think of my brain, and the brains around me, as opposing football teams that have to out-coach each other to achieve long fuse, big bang victories. As with football, out-coaching an opponent is a lot easier when you have his playbook. You know what your adversary plans to do before he does it, so you can prepare your team before the game and make crafty play calls during it. For instance, if you know an opposing football team will run instead of pass in a particular situation, you can lull them into a false sense of confidence by making your defense look like it's set up to defend against a passing attack. When the ball is snapped, and it's too late for the opponent to change plays, you immediately rush all your pass defenders forward to stop the run.

Take things fast, and take things easy. Two very important plays in the brain's playbook. A simple way to apply the insights in this book to your world is to look at the plays in the brain's ancient playbook and decide which of them can be best exploited to solve a long fuse, big bang problem confronting you. This is the approach Dr. XX took in her long quest to bring women's health care in America up to par with men's.

MASK BIG IDEAS AS SMALL ONES

Dr. XX, who asked to be identified by her two X chromosomes instead of her name, is very much a product of the sixties. She graduated from UC Berkeley just as the sixties antiwar movement was heating up, and went to graduate school in Cambridge, Massachusetts, another hotbed of dissent. There, she planned and participated in numerous Viet Nam War protests and became a strong advocate of women's rights. When Dr. XX got an MD after earning a PhD in Molecular Biology, she started to focus on women's health, specializing in obstetrics and gynecology and contributing to the Boston Women's Health Book Collective work *Our Bodies, Ourselves*. She also published a successful novel, based on her own internship, that described in detail the sexism of the male-dominated medical establishment. "I only made it a novel and changed a few names to avoid lawsuits," she confided. "All the crap in there actually happened."

Dr. XX's passion for women's rights and women's health made her acutely aware of inequities in America's health care system. As she moved up in the medical profession through the 1970s and 1980s, first as a resident at Harvard, then as a faculty member of another Ivy League medical school, she saw ample evidence that doctors of both sexes did not treat female patients as diligently as their male counterparts. For example, doctors were trained to look for symptoms of heart attack that included pain in the chest, jaw, and arm; shortness of breath; and light-headedness. Whenever emergency room physicians saw these symptoms, they took immediate and aggressive steps, such as ordering angiograms or referring patients for coronary bypass surgery to reduce further damage to the heart. But some women experiencing heart attacks do not have this cluster of symptoms, instead presenting with nausea, vomiting, or indigestion. As a result, many female heart patients died because doctors were much less likely to interpret their symptoms as a heart attack and follow up with aggressive tests and treatments.

Emergency room doctors and cardiologists weren't necessarily discriminating against their female patients. Heart disease had historically been thought of as a man's disease, so when doctors saw female patients experiencing discomfort, heart attack was not at the top of their list of diagnostic possibilities. Also there was no research to suggest that women experienced heart attacks differently from men.

Dr. XX realized that the chief reason medical science knew so little about heart disease in women was that almost all medical research was done on males. "They didn't even use female lab rats in experiments," she told me.

In 1985, after conducting pioneering work improving women's fertility, Dr. XX left Ivy League medicine to take a senior post at the National Institutes of Health in the Washington, DC, area, where she could exert a greater influence on health policy in America. What she saw at NIH appalled her. Out of the thousands of doctors on NIH's payroll, there were only three gynecologists. Congresswoman Pat Schroeder, when informed of the situation, remarked, "There are three gynecologists and thirty-nine veterinarians at NIH." Cats, dogs, and horses were more important than women to the nation's health care agenda.

After surveying the political landscape (it was the height of the Reagan era), Dr. XX decided that launching a frontal assault on gender inequality in health care was unwise. Friends who were savvy about the ways of Washington had counseled her not to "eat the elephant whole" but swallow it in "chewable chunks." A few years later the White House learned the hard way that you can't eat the elephant whole in Washington, when the Clintons failed to get the town to embrace their comprehensive health care reform agenda.

Dr. XX's first "chewable chunk" was to persuade Congress to sharply increase the number of gynecologists at NIH. Given that far fewer than 1 percent of NIH's doctors were focusing on the health needs of more than half the U.S. population (females comprise 50.7 percent), the move was not a hard sell, even in the conservative Reagan years. The nearly tenfold increase in NIH gynecologists was a key first step, though, because it created a critical mass of women's health professionals inside the Washington beltway. Over the next two decades this new group was to prove invaluable for evangelizing women's health.

In 1986, under pressure from Dr. XX and her new allies, NIH adopted a policy encouraging inclusion of women in medical research (and female rats in laboratory experiments). Four years later, she got Congress to pass twenty different bills that improved women's health research, access to health care, and disease prevention services. Shortly after that, Congress formally established the Office of Women's Health Research at NIH to insure inclusion of women in clinical trials and to increase women's access to health care and preventative disease programs. For her groundbreaking work energizing the women's health movement, the most prestigious body of scientists and physicians in the country—the National Academy—elected Dr. XX a member of its Institute of Medicine.

Dr. XX also helped found the Society for Women's Health Research, a Washington, DC, advocacy group that sponsors gender-based medical research and pushes for greater equality of health care. As a result of the society's campaigns, not to mention the atmosphere of awareness that Dr. XX helped create, dozens of research projects were launched that revealed important clinical differences between men and women in almost every field of medicine, including neurology (women often react to strokes differently than men), immunology (women are 2.7 times more likely than men to get autoimmune diseases such as lupus and MS), and mental health (many more women suffer from depression than men). New findings such as these are greatly increasing doctors' understanding of how to diagnose and treat women's illnesses and are gradually elevating the quality of health care for women to be on a par with men's.

EXPLOITING THE BRAIN'S PLAYBOOK

Improving the health of millions of women over a span of twenty years was definitely a big bang achievement.

Which plays in the brain's playbook did Dr. XX exploit to ignite this big bang?

First, there's the concept of the "chewable chunk."

We already know that it's easier to sell things that don't require a lot of time and effort. Dr. XX's gynecologist hiring initiative fit this pattern perfectly. The extra money needed to hire fifteen to twenty new gynecologists was the equivalent of a rounding error in the Department of Health and Human Services' mammoth multihundred-billion-dollar yearly budget, and the hiring could be done fairly quickly. But there was more to the digestability of Dr. XX's first "chewable chunk" than its low cost and speed of implementation. It also had a low-risk profile for all concerned.

In Washington, most decisions are made based on the "optics" of an idea, which is how the idea will look to voters, the press, and influential interest groups, such as political action committees, who make large campaign contributions. After Dr. XX's awareness campaign called attention to the low numbers of gynecologists at NIH, politicians in both Congress and in the Reagan administration found it very low risk to endorse hiring more gynecologists. Indeed these politicians may have seen greater risk in *not* enacting the measure. No president since Jimmy Carter has won an election without capturing a majority of the women's vote. Dr. XX knew this, of course, and used it to maximum effect over her decades-long campaign.

The play that Dr. XX exploited first in her gynecologist hiring campaign, then in later initiatives, went something like this: "When choosing between courses of action, pick the least risky." She exploited this play over and over again in different ways. Her successful lobbying of Congress to change NIH irritated powerful bureaucrats above her in the Department of Health and Human Services who didn't appreciate such "end around" behavior by a subordinate. There are very few things that will get a civil servant fired in Washington, but going around your boss to Congress is one of them. It's not legal (which is why she wants her name concealed), and it's definitely not kosher.

Dr. XX doubtless would have been fired for her unorthodox lobbying efforts but for her skillful use of the "go for lower risk" play in the playbook. She developed such strong relationships with members of both parties in the House of Representatives and the Senate that she quickly became un-fireable. To Dr. XX's bosses, it would have been far riskier to get rid of her and invoke the wrath of Congress than to keep her on the payroll and look the other way when she bent—indeed broke—the rules about proselytizing Congress.

Another way that Dr. XX managed to keep her job was that she understood she wasn't dealing with any single brain to get her way, but the brains of many bureaucrats and politicians striving to form a consensus. Brains that try to reach consensus among themselves in large organizations in effect create a larger organism with its own habits, ways of doing business, and yes, plays in a playbook. Social psychologists have discovered that groups have "plays" that can differ significantly from the plays of individuals that comprise the group. For instance, people acting as a group are much more likely to become violent in a given situation—like a racial confrontation—than individual members of the same group facing the same situation. Of special importance to Dr. XX was the play most used by the group of people collectively known as the federal government. The play is "Do everything slowly." This play is not a purposeful strategy, but an emergent property of all large groups, especially those whose founders designed in checks and balances to prevent any one part (for example the presidency) acting precipitously without consent of the other parts (for example Congress and the judiciary). The glacial slowness of the government worked to Dr. XX's advantage, because she could get into a congressional office, write a new bill, and get back to work long before her masters could learn of her transgression and stop her. Her quick sorties under the noses of sluggish bureaucrats reminded me of the strategy I used in graduate school to give large pythons injections of antibiotics.

After I finished research with rabbits, I studied the brains of large snakes such as boas and pythons. My largest snake, a twelve-foot-long, ten-inch-diameter reticulate python named Asshole (because he was always trying to bite me), frequently came down with an affliction known as mouth rot. This bacterial infection can be fatal if not treated, so about once or twice a month

I had to give Asshole an injection of streptomycin. The trick to doing this without being bitten, or even eaten, was to inject the snake in the end of its tail. The nerve impulses took so long to travel from the animal's tail to its brain, that I had a second or two to deliver the drug and close the cage before the python realized he'd been stuck. Dr. XX knew that the federal government was like Asshole; you could jab it and survive, because by the time it realized what had happened, the damage had been done.

Dr. XX's story surfaces a way to co-opt brains that has wider implications than just selling a proposal or keeping one's job. Embodied in her approach is the notion that sometimes you have to disguise big ideas as small ones if you want to light a long fuse to a big bang. Dr. XX's big idea was to make men's and women's health equal. But in the mid 1980s it would have been extremely risky for politicians to attempt to make health care gender neutral in one giant leap. The powerful, male-dominated medical profession would have lobbied hard against such a sweeping initiative, as it did a few years later against the Clintons. So Dr. XX disguised her politically risky idea as a very low-risk request for more gynecologists. She continued on that path, offering one low-risk initiative after another until the women's health movement had safely gestated.

Dr. XX, the fertility expert, had gotten Washington pregnant with a big idea before they woke up and realized it *was* a big idea.

MORE THAN ONE PLAYBOOK

American football isn't the only sport that uses a playbook to help coaches and athletes make quick decisions in the heat of battle. In judo, for example, the best athletes study a new opponent carefully, weighing the adversary's strengths and weaknesses against their own in order to formulate a strategy for using an opponent's strengths against him. For example, an athlete who knows that his opponent is stronger than he is can anticipate that his opponent *also* knows this and will attempt to overpower him in a match. Therefore the weaker athlete can craft a strategy similar to that described by Judo Tom, a black belt who wrote this about coping with stronger adversaries, in an online judo forum: "My best throw in judo is a shoulder throw . . . where I turn my back and throw the guy over me. One of the best ways for me to set this up is to push on my opponent and try to move him backwards. . . .

As soon as he resists and pushes forward on me I allow him to push and pull him towards me robbing him of his balance. I can then turn and get underneath him and finish the throw much easier then if I simply just tried to pull him onto me."

The judo analogy is helpful for two reasons. For one thing, our opponent, the brain, is much stronger than we are. It got in top shape by going up against one mortal threat after another for millions of years, so we can't hope to match its speed, conditioning, and stamina. As the weaker athlete, we have no choice but to use the brain's great strength against it; study the brain's playbook and figure out in advance how we'll catch the brain off balance and throw it to the mat. Don't ever try a brute force assault.

Secondly, as in judo, it is essential that we keep our own balance. As difficult as it may be, we should try not to get emotional or frustrated when brains around us do what they do naturally.

I learned this the hard way at Hughes Aircraft in the late 1980s. I believed passionately in a radical new kind of visual simulation technology called voxel rendering that my R&D lab was developing. Voxel rendering would, for the first time, let flight simulators generate out-of-cockpit imagery that looked like the real world, instead of the cartoonish representations of terrain and runways that were standard at the time. I viewed the project's many enemies as Luddites who lacked imagination or vision. These Luddites, I told myself, had lost touch with the Hughes Aircraft philosophy (sparked by Howard Hughes himself), to specialize in jaw-dropping advances that left our customers and competitors wondering "How did they *do* that?"

Before World War II, Howard Hughes had invented flush rivets for airplane skins that radically reduced aerodynamic drag, increasing aircraft speed and reducing fuel consumption. After the war, he rolled out long series of groundbreaking innovations in airborne radar, electro-optics, and air-to-air missiles. Hughes Research Labs developed the first laser, and Hughes Space Systems the first spin-stabilized satellite. I thought that opponents of the voxel project were more interested in playing it safe than in going for the big win as Howard would have done, and I let this attitude show in budget meetings and management reviews. I pointed out that most of the voxel project's detractors were executives who'd come to the company through acquisitions and couldn't be expected to "get" the Hughes culture of earth-shaking innovation. For their part, corporate adversaries were able to use these ill-advised personal attacks against me, successfully painting me as a zealot who played dirty in order to advance a wasteful, Quixotic attempt at visual perfection. In contrast to my emotion-laden appeals to keep Howard's dream alive, opponents took pains to appear measured and reasonable, making practical arguments such as "perfection is the enemy of good enough" and asking questions such as "now that the Berlin Wall has fallen, who in the military will want voxel technology?" I came across as emotional and off balance, while my opponents appeared sober and on point. Hughes leadership went for the dispassionate approach and killed the voxel project.

THE POINT OF VIEW OF THE HIGHLY UNCERTAIN

During an introspective postmortem following this defeat, I realized that I should have had more respect for colleagues whose conservative views opposed mine. I believed at the time that rational minds shouldn't be so resistant to change, and I harshly judged cautious coworkers as irrational stick-in-the-muds. Upon reflection, however, I realized that the brains of these colleagues were conservative for very sound evolutionary reasons, and were actually quite rational from the point of view of the highly uncertain, ancient world that shaped modern brains.

Hughes Aircraft in 1990 faced a situation similar to that of a Paleolithic hunter-gatherer at the start of a severe drought: it had to preserve scarce resources in order to survive. Because the fall of the Berlin Wall meant that defense spending was likely to plummet, investing millions in the high-risk voxel project was just too risky. Nineteen ninety was a time of down market in the defense industry, and budgets were lean. Even if I didn't agree with my opponents' conservative thinking, I had to agree that it was actually quite reasonable. Viewed from this perspective, my colleagues' tendency to resist radical change seemed no longer like a character flaw, but like a force of nature that had retained its relevance in modern situations such as looming market downturns. Getting angry when colleagues resisted risky ideas made about as much sense as getting mad at a hurricane in Florida or an earthquake in California. If you live in those places, strong forces of nature just go with the territory. And so it is in corporate America.

Once I was able to reframe stick-in-the-mud behavior as a rational force of nature to be respected, I was able to avoid the anger and frustration that pulled me off balance. This new perspective proved invaluable to my later long fuse, big bang efforts both at Disney and in the government. I continued to push for revolutionary instead of evolutionary innovations, but I no longer got angry at conservative thinkers who opposed my point of view. I refrained from personal attacks, dialed down the passion of my delivery a few notches, and included risk-management concepts in my pitches.

I would point out, for example (in as sober a tone as I could muster), that our corporate investment portfolio needed a certain percentage of high-risk/high-return projects in order to balance our overabundance of low-risk/low-return projects. This new approach worked far better than the tack I had taken at Hughes, for several reasons. First, by letting go of my anger, and the accompanying urge to attack, I less often caused more conservative thinkers to get angry back at me and to invest considerable energy opposing my arguments. As much as we'd like to believe professionals in business settings act in the best interests of their organization, in reality businesspeople spend most of their energy fighting personal battles with coworker rivals. When I stopped attacking people who opposed me, I (usually) avoided getting on that list of rivals. Intellectual adversaries less often became emotional adversaries, and they directed most of their competitive energies elsewhere.

A second reason that my new approach worked better was that it appeared to be much more balanced. At Hughes I had argued for the voxel project by asserting that the company always needed to be at the bleeding edge of technology. Terms like "always" and "bleeding edge" seem extreme. In contrast, when I later pushed for the creation of a high-risk/high-reward research organization (Intelligence Advanced Research Projects Activity—IARPA) as director of science and technology for the intelligence community, I emphasized the portfolio-balance idea, arguing that intelligence R&D investments were far out of balance, heavily focusing on evolutionary versus revolutionary advances. Even though the concept for IARPA was every bit as radical as the earlier voxel project, it *seemed* to promote—as opposed to upset—people's natural desire for balance. Therefore, despite spirited *intellectual* opposition, the IARPA proposal ultimately succeeded.

As is so often the case, I found the most important brain to out-coach was my own.

OUT-COACHING THE BRAIN

Conquering ourselves is a good idea in theory, but how do we do it in practice?

Most of us are acutely aware of one shortcoming or another, but fail repeatedly to change behaviors that we know we need to change. We resolve time after time to stop drinking, eating, smoking, or talking too much at parties, but somehow, we keep doing it. We tell ourselves not to overreact when a business rival baits us, but, in the heat of battle, we go on the attack anyhow. We drive too fast, recycle too little, and spend more time on the couch building up a gut than on the jogging track working up a sweat. At work we tell ourselves to spend more time planning for the future than fighting fires, but we automatically drop everything when the next "emergency" pops up. Somehow, when the emergency is over, we never quite get back to lighting that long fuse.

It's almost as if someone else is in control of our behaviors and we are passive observers—even victims—of their decisions.

The fact is, someone else *is* in charge of our behaviors. What we normally think of as "us" is our conscious mind, the faculty that consciously perceives, feels, remembers, and thinks. But evolution has decided that this conscious faculty reacts far too slowly to be trusted making decisions that must take place in a fraction of a second. So our brains vest most control of our behavior in very fast, unconscious processes. Even behaviors that we normally think of as conscious—such as speech—are largely unconscious.

Consider what happens in a normal conversation. We listen to what another person says and then respond with our own comments. But as we speak, we don't think about how to breathe or how to position our tongue, lips, and teeth for each phrase. And we don't know the exact words that are going to come out until we hear them ourselves. If you don't believe this, chat with any friend and you'll see that it's true! The "someone else" in charge of our behavior is a set of unconscious, automated scripts.

A harrowing experience I had in the Kuwaiti desert at the end of the first Gulf War vividly illustrates this evolution.

While still at Hughes in the spring of 1991, I led a small team of engineers who were developing faster ways to put out the six-hundred-plus oil fires Saddam Hussein had set before leaving Kuwait a few weeks earlier. In order to perfect our technology—thermal imaging sensors that could quickly spot where the well fractures were located—we had to drive out to burning oil wells through the many land mines that the Iraqi Army had buried in the oil fields. Before going out each day, we brushed up on the appearance of the different Russian mines the Iraqis had buried, including how these mines looked when submerged in different kinds of soil. Some buried mines looked like bumps, some like dips, some like abnormally flat patches of earth, and some—scariest of all—like untouched desert terrain.

During one of our excursions to the Ahmadi Fields southwest of Kuwait City, my job was to sit in the passenger seat of our 4X4 pickup with my head out the window and scan the landscape ahead (there were no paved roads) for mines as we inched our way across the desert at five to ten miles an hour. In the late afternoon, when slanting sunlight highlighted bumps in the terrain, I noticed a very shallow mound about ten yards ahead. I thought, "Well, it's about the diameter of a Russian anti-tank mine, but there are tire tracks on it, so someone has already safely driven over it. But wait, Russian anti-tank mines are set to go off only when very heavy vehicles roll over them. A light pickup like ours doesn't normally trigger them, but the mines do get primed a little, so that when a second or third pickup drives over them, they sometimes blow." All during this tortuous line of reasoning, our truck had been advancing toward the bump. I finally shouted, "Oh, my God, I think we might be about to run over an anti-tank mine." The driver slammed on the brakes, but not in time. Somewhere between "Oh my God" and "over an anti-tank mine" our right front tire had rolled onto the bump. For a few tense moments we waited for the explosion that—thankfully— never came. The driver took a deep breath, slowly eased his tight grip off the wheel, and glared at me. "Next time," he said through clenched teeth, "just say STOP." After rolling gently off the bump, we didn't hang around to determine whether it actually was a mine, but I got to drive after that, forever relieved of spotter duty.

CHANGE THE PERCEPTION, CHANGE THE BEHAVIOR

Evolution, like my team in Kuwait, has learned to take control away from thinkers and give it to doers. In our brains, the "doers" are automatic scripts that are very fast because they follow very simple logic such as "If an animal is bigger than you, escape it; if it's smaller, chase it." Understanding how these automated scripts work is the key to out-coaching our brains and doing a better job of lighting long fuses to big bangs. The basic approach—judo style—isn't to fight the scripts, or to try to delete them, but to subtly edit them.

We get clues about how to do this by looking more closely at some scripts we've already talked about. Professor Proffitt's research, showing that our brain gets us to conserve energy by making us perceive hills as steeper when we get tired, reveals how behavior change happens naturally. When our brain senses that we're tired, it doesn't directly change our hill-climbing behavior, but modifies this behavior indirectly by altering our perception of the hill. A big advantage of this approach is simplicity. Our brain doesn't need a long and complicated script that weighs many if-then combinations of our tired-ness, available calories, and hill steepness, it simply has to tweak the input to a very simple if-shallow-climb, if-steep-avoid rule. By shifting our perception of the hill from shallow to steep, our brain swiftly leads us down the "avoid" branch of the unconscious behavioral script. This elegant approach to modi-fying behavior is computationally simple, so our brains don't have to con-sume many calories computing it, and because it's simple, it's fast.

The take-home lesson here is that we can out-coach our brain by stealing a page from its own playbook. In this case the play is: "To change the behav-iors, change the perception."

When I was able to perceive conservative attitudes of business colleagues as inevitable products of evolution instead of small-mindedness, I let go of the anger that pulled me off balance and undermined my big bang aspira-tions. It's easy to imagine other ways the "modify perception to modify be-havior" play can help us focus on big bang results. When an emergency pops up on our radar screen, we can subtly shift our perception of the emergency from being a threat to being an opportunity to pursue a distant win.

At Disney Imagineering R&D, where I worked in the nineties, we actu-ally grew to appreciate got-to-have-it-yesterday emergency requests from corporate headquarters because we saw them as opportunities to educate busy corporate leaders about our vision of the future. For instance, shortly after Michael Ovitz took over as Disney's president in 1997, he asked us to prepare a "big wow, multimedia extravaganza" that would "knock the socks off" the audience at a magazine publishers' convention he planned to address in Ber-muda in a few weeks. After we recovered from our panic—writing a script, then designing, building, and rehearsing an "extravaganza" in a few short weeks seemed impossible—we realized that Ovitz had given us a chance to advance our vision of the mobile multimedia future, in which Disney magazines and books would be distributed wirelessly to thin tablets with "electronic" paper. We went into overdrive, building a mock-up of an "e-magazine" and shooting a futuristic video showing a day in the life of an e-magazine's consumer. The mock-up was a big hit with Ovitz's audience, and our e-magazine video later proved invaluable in sharing our vision with others at Disney and in shaping our thinking about the mobile future. By changing our perception of Ovitz's request from short-term problem into a long-term opportunity, we had effectively out-coached our brains.

RECAP

How to Eat an Elephant

Although the brain is an exotic, mysterious organ that scientists are just beginning to understand, in some respects it's remarkably simple, responding more or less predictably to situations that evoke Paleolithic memories of danger and starvation. One of the most important scripts from the brain's ancient book of rules is "Expend as little energy as possible." This script biases us, when presented with alternative choices, to take the path of least resistance. Knowing this, it is possible to get people and organizations to accomplish ambitious, long-term goals if we divide the pursuit of those goals into many small, easy steps. Paula Goode, a former IBM executive, put it this way: "You can eat an elephant, but you have to do it by biting off a million chewable chunks."

CHAPTER 3

Pursuing the Distant Win

LONG RANGE VISIONARIES

What differentiates visionary leaders from the rest of us? What made Peter the Great, Gandhi, and Martin Luther King so effective? How did Mustafa Atatürk manage to modernize Turkey? As he was building a financial empire, what did Warren Buffett see when he closed his eyes at night and waited for sleep to overtake him?

As the title *visionary* implies, one thing all of these great men shared was a compelling vision of a future that wasn't just incrementally better than the present, but fundamentally and radically better. Visionary leaders think big.

But thinking big can't be the only secret ingredient to visionary leadership or we'd have a huge surplus of visionary leaders. Most of the kids I grew up with fantasized about being President one day. A few of them had even wider aspirations. A high school buddy named Lee thought he had a serious chance of ruling the world, maybe the solar system. Under Lee's dynamic leadership, Earth would build a better tomorrow by conquering our neighboring planets. But the last time I checked, none of my childhood friends were in any danger of being elected President, and Lee was far behind schedule. So thinking big is necessary to become a visionary leader, but far from sufficient. What's missing? Although it would be convenient if there were a single answer, history teaches us that there isn't. Peter the Great was a military commander who employed very different methods to expand Russia's culture and influence than the pacifist Gandhi used to free India. Newton revolutionized the world of physics through meticulous experiments, such as plotting the path of light rays through a glass prism, while Einstein revolutionized physics again centuries later, not by tracing light rays in the laboratory, but by simply imagining what light rays saw as they raced through the universe. Warren Buffett is a keen judge of management talent, possessing an uncanny ability to identify—and to invest in—entrepreneurs capable of building big futures for their companies.

Despite such stylistic differences, we know that all visionaries who bring about radical change must share at least one quality that goes beyond having clear visions of big futures: they must also be skilled at connecting the future they see back to the present the rest of us see. Even Isaac Newton, who worked mostly alone and didn't need to persuade anyone else to pursue his vision, still had to translate his groundbreaking discoveries into language that mere mortals could understand, then apply those discoveries to solving practical here-and-now problems. Humans don't individually build big futures in the future, we do it collectively, one step at a time, in a series of slowly advancing "presents."

WHAT DO I DO DIFFERENTLY TODAY?

Imagine that you wanted to improve your current organization by a factor of a hundred along one dimension or another; a hundred times more sales, more profits, more productivity, or more products. What would you do today to start down that path? What about tomorrow and the day after that? Sooner or later, all effective visionaries must have good answers to those questions, otherwise their visions remain stuck in their heads. Having a good answer to "What do I do different *today?*" is especially important because, as we now know from studying the brain, most of us live in today and let tomorrow take care of itself. Without here-and-now incentives to move forward, we'll never get to the there-and-then. Visionaries who don't find ways to make the future pay off today remain visionaries; visionaries who do find ways to make the future pay off evolve into visionary leaders.

I've been fortunate to have had a ringside seat while a biomedical visionary pulled this off: my brother Bill, whose research throughout the 1980s at Harvard Medical School uncovered much of what we know today about how the HIV (AIDS) virus works and how to treat HIV infections. The story of how Bill effectively connected his vision of a big future back to a pedestrian present begins when Bill was a teenager in 1960. From an early age, he was curious about biology, with a special interest in viruses and bacteria. His fascination with microbes stemmed from a belief that the bugs were sophisticated, ultra-miniature machines that sensed and reacted intelligently to their environments, moved toward food, ate the food, secreted waste, and ultimately reproduced. How did they pack so much sophistication and capability into such small spaces? Bill wanted to know. (*Needed* to know was more like it.) Unwilling to wait a few years to pursue his passion for biology in college—long-range visionaries, by the way, do not achieve success by delaying gratification—Bill created a simple laboratory in our house and began his research there.

Bill was particularly interested in a class of bugs called *hemolytic bacteria*. These bugs, which include streptococcus, are called hemolytic (literally, "blood cutter") because they break down blood cells. Living on a naval base in China Lake, California, where our father was a rocket scientist, Bill couldn't order the dangerous microbes through the mail. So he took swabs from his own throat, cultured them in petri dishes, then grew and multiplied the small number of streptococcus microbes that lived in his throat (as indeed, they live in *all* of our throats).

Bill wrapped his bacteria-laden petri dishes in aluminum foil and hid them in the family refrigerator, behind cartons of milk and jars of ricotta cheese that my mother ate for lunch. Miraculously, Bill's bugs never infected my mother, but my father, and Bill himself, weren't so lucky. Bill's research put my dad in the hospital and kept Bill in bed with a sore throat for much of the summer. But this setback did not stop him from investigating how microorganisms accomplish so much with so little. Bill went on to get a bachelor's in Chemistry and a PhD in Microbiology before setting up his own laboratory as a faculty member at Harvard Medical School.

By 1980, his interest in microorganisms had shifted to viruses. He was curious about a class of exotic pathogens, called retroviruses, that "crossed over" from animals, such as chimps and monkeys, to infect humans. Most viruses invade the outer compartment, called cytoplasm, of a victim's cells and remain there, taking over the cell's factory for making proteins and commanding that factory to manufacture new viruses. But retroviruses dive deep into the cell's inner compartment—the nucleus—and splice themselves directly into nuclear genes, which then issue instructions to the protein factories outside the nucleus to make copies of the virus.

As evidence accumulated in 1980 and 1981 that an array of new and unusual maladies, such as Kaposi's sarcoma, pneumocystis pneumonia, and lymphatic disease were afflicting large numbers of gay men, the first mystery to unravel was "What kinds of infectious agents—bacteria, fungi, or viruses—caused the cluster of symptoms?" When he first heard about the disease, Bill suspected the culprit was a retrovirus, like HTLV or hepatitis B, because the mode of transmission of the new pathogen—exchange of bodily fluids—closely resembled that of known retroviruses. Intrigued, my brother quickly shifted the focus of his virology lab to study the mysterious new killer. He said that going into the lab during the first years of the AIDS epidemic was a thrilling adventure, like being a detective in a murder mystery. He knew it would take hundreds of scientists decades to unravel the secrets of the killer virus and to defeat it, but each day brought fresh excitement when small clues surfaced in his lab or those of close colleagues, like Bob Gallo or Max Essex.

My brother and his coworkers gathered a series of clues that helped prove AIDS was caused by one or more retroviruses. By 1984, Bob Gallo, Luc Montagnier, and colleagues had determined that a single culprit, a retrovirus now called human immunodeficiency virus (HIV), was responsible for the diverse symptoms of the infected patients. Over the next five years, the detective work focused on sequencing the virus's genetic code and assembling an inventory of the virus's molecular toolbox.

The first part of this research laid out the exact sequence of molecules that comprised all the genes in the virus, and gave a full description of the killer, analogous to facial features, height, weight, hair color, blood type, and fingerprints of a human killer. The second area of focus sought to identify the different tools, special molecules called *enzymes,* that speed up chemical reactions, help the virus break into a victim's cells, then hijack the genes and the nano-factories found there to make more deadly viruses. This focus on enzymes was especially important, because it could lead directly to new treatments that would make one or more of the lethal enzymes useless. By analogy, if you know a killer opens a deadbolt with picklocks, you can squirt glue into the lock to keep the killer out.

My brother's lab painstakingly assembled the first complete genetic sequence of HIV, which provided important clues about the tools the killer used, because genetic codes describe how to make different enzymes, or tools, out of proteins. This tight relationship between genetic code and enzyme tools is equivalent to police detectives knowing that a murderer prefers lockpicks simply because he wears a mustache, is more than six feet tall, and has

O-positive blood. The Harvard team exploited their knowledge of HIV's genetic code to discover different tools that HIV uses to latch onto cells' outer membranes, enter their outer and inner compartments (cytoplasm and nuclei), chop itself into smaller pieces that are easy to replicate, convert viral genetic code (RNA) into DNA, splice that DNA into cells' healthy DNA, then make protein building blocks for a completely new copy of killer tools.

The most prevalent types of HIV therapies today, reverse transcriptase inhibitors and protease inhibitors, disable two tools: those that convert viral RNA into DNA (reverse transcriptase) and those that chop up viral segments into manageable pieces (protease). Drug companies are working hard on ways to disable HIV's other tools as well.

As you can appreciate from the complicated way the virus works, virologists got the opportunity to match wits with an incredibly nuanced and sophisticated killer. My brother grew especially excited when his team uncovered clues—like puzzling sequences in middle regions of HIV's genetic code—that had never been seen before anywhere in biology. HIV, it seemed, was the most inventive and resourceful pathogen biologists had ever encountered.

The daily thrill of the chase wasn't the only motivation that kept Bill and others going. Long before they had any hope of curing the disease, they could still take satisfaction in smaller, quicker victories that prevented infection or prolonged the lives of AIDS sufferers. The first such triumph was a test that detected HIV in the blood, cutting down spread of the disease through transfusions or risky sex. Then, reverse transcriptase inhibitors, such as AZT, began to prolong lives. Next, protease inhibitors, like Nelfinavir, and potent combinations of reverse transcriptase inhibitors and protease inhibitors extended longevity of HIV victims still further.

Bill's efforts to fight AIDS were not confined to the laboratory. A close colleague, retrovirus research pioneer Dr. Joe Sodroski of Cambridge University, said:

Bill Haseltine recognized the impact that HIV-1 would have on global health long before the devastating nature of the AIDS pandemic became apparent. So in those early days, Bill and Bob Gallo and their colleagues, myself included, shared a real sense of making an impact on the history of the world with our work.

This sense that HIV would have a catastrophic, historical impact led Bill in 1985 to partner with Elizabeth Taylor to testify before the U.S. Senate that the trickle of AIDS cases in the early 1980s would inexorably turn into a flood. Describing Bill's efforts before Congress, *New England Monthly* journalist Barry Werth wrote in 1988:

> "We see a wave of devastating disease approaching . . ." The prognosis—careful, measured, authoritative—filled the crowded Senate hearing room as it was meant to, as a clarion call. "The magnitude and nature of the problem is crystal clear."
>
> Bill Haseltine had not been a national figure before and was hardly known outside the relatively small community of microbiologists who normally would be the only ones to care about or understand what he had to say. But his speech to the Senate Appropriations Subcommittee in September 1985 urging dramatically increased federal support for the fight against AIDS was as much a breakthrough as Essex's discovery of gpl20. Haseltine, it turned out, had a gift for talking about AIDS in a manner at once both relentlessly dire and upbeat. He could explain the disease in its most depressing details, yet convey such confidence about biomedicine's ability to fight it that he left one feeling exhilarated, even hopeful. He was the ideal spokesman. The media, ever eager for a simple take-home message in the mountains of data and counterdata they were being asked to comprehend, sought him out. Presidential campaign staffs asked his advice. Lay funding agencies coveted his counsel.

Bill's persuasive scientific logic and Elizabeth Taylor's passion for the problem proved a potent combination; Congress agreed that AIDS was indeed a long fuse, big bang phenomenon that must be tackled aggressively, and they increased funding for AIDS research by over a factor of ten. Bill, working with Taylor, Gallo, and others, had succeeded in connecting his vision of the future back to the present, where it could be acted upon. One essential strategy for making this connection was to persuade Congress, the media, and the public that AIDS was a dire future threat, but one that could ultimately be controlled if significant and sustained research were begun *to-*

day. Another essential strategy was to keep himself and his research team motivated as they pursued the daily struggle to understand the virus.

THE LONG-TERM BENEFITS OF INSTANT GRATIFICATION

Throughout Bill's ten-year journey of discovery in the laboratory, there was a long series of new clues, new mysteries, and new clinical benefits for AIDS sufferers to reward his efforts. He did not have to delay gratification very long, because he had chosen a path that supplied an almost endless string of daily gratifications. Each morning, Bill asked himself, "What can we do *today* to advance the lab's work and keep the AIDS research team motivated?" He made sure that everyone who worked for him immediately knew when new clues about the virus surfaced, and he constantly looked for excuses to celebrate. Even when there were no new discoveries to trumpet, he would pass out champagne to celebrate other victories, like the acceptance for publication of a scientific paper from the lab.

Bill kept himself, and his team of scientists, motivated by *catering to* their brains' craving for instant gratification, rather than denying it. The irony here is that I was a brain scientist who couldn't initially figure out how to co-opt my own brain in the war on terror, while my brother, who studied organisms with *no* brains, did figure it out in the war on AIDS.

As we saw from Barry Werth's description of Bill's successful campaign with the media and with Congress, from the long-range pursuit of AIDS, Bill managed to reap near-term rewards that went well beyond the daily thrill of unraveling scientific mysteries. He garnered global recognition for his Harvard team and the satisfaction of energizing Congress to act aggressively. He also got to hang out with glamorous movie stars like Elizabeth Taylor.

Other visionaries have also learned how to co-opt the brain's short-term wiring in order to overcome difficult challenges. In each case they stuck with long, arduous pursuits by picking many small, quick accomplishments that led, one after another, toward big bang futures. The road to hell may be paved with good intentions, but these leaders showed that the road to success can be paved with instant gratification.

Ellen Sabin, who for seven years was president of the African Medical Research Foundation, a nonprofit organization that is patiently transforming health care in Africa, said that she kept at the long struggle to improve the health of Africans by finding intense satisfaction in very small things. She would make long lists each morning and take great pleasure each time she crossed off a "to do." Ellen routinely rewarded herself twenty to thirty times a day this way. And each night, just before falling asleep at the end of a grueling eighteen-hour day, she would remind herself that she had inched the cause forward.

Ronald Reagan also was big on getting instant gratification from lists. He liked to line through each appointment on his calendar right after the meeting finished and at the end of a busy day enjoy the long column of line-outs.

Perhaps the most inspirational example of a leader who understood how to harness instant gratification was William Griffith Wilson. An alcoholic who got sober in 1934 and stayed sober until his death in 1971, Wilson and another recovering alcoholic, Dr. Bob Smith, developed the twelve-step program that endures today as one of the most effective programs for treating drug and alcohol addiction: Alcoholics Anonymous.

"Bill W" and "Dr. Bob's" twelve-step program acknowledges that distant, ambitious goals are very hard to achieve in one leap. A more practical approach is to break the pursuit down into many smaller steps, each of which is far easier than the ultimate goal. Even after alcoholics complete their twelve steps and get sober, AA counsels them not to try to stay sober forever, but just *one day at a time.* This incremental approach to initiating and preserving a fundamental change in behavior captures a deep insight about how to get our brains to light long fuses to big bangs: *don't try* to get them to light long fuses. Focus instead on persuading the brain to light short fuses that connect, one day at a time, into much longer fuses.

CO-OPTING THE BRAIN'S SHORT-TERM WIRING

My failure with the voxel project at Hughes Aircraft taught me that when it comes to pursuing a distant win, the most important brain to co-opt is my own. Although I had learned this in the early 1990s, I had to learn it over and over again before it finally sunk in. After taking my last job in the government in 2005, I managed to sponsor several long fuse soft-science initiatives that addressed the root causes of terrorism, but I still couldn't resist the daily urge to help out with urgent hard-science problems surrounding wars in Iraq and Afghanistan. I spent so much time downrange immersed in these problems that I lost sight of the reason Congress created my position after 9/11: to move our science and technology to the cutting edge for future generations of intelligence officers.

In early 2006, a day or two after I returned from a long trip to Iraq, my deputy, Steve Nixon, came into my office and conducted what AA'ers call an intervention. He confronted me with my addiction to here-and-now problems and listed all the difficulties my behavior was creating. He reminded me that we'd made scant progress fostering revolutionary new ideas, and said I should stay home and do the job I was supposed to do—not the one I wanted to do. That confrontation wasn't exactly the rock-bottom experience that finally motivates addicts to get sober, but it was enough to change my behavior. I sat down with Steve, and we kicked around ideas for creating an intelligence version of DARPA (Defense Advanced Research Projects Agency) to focus exclusively on big, over-the-horizon advances in technology. As with AA, we knew we couldn't get all the way to our goal in one leap—especially in Washington, where new ideas have to be patiently socialized—so we laid out a detailed step-by-step plan that would let us not only achieve, but celebrate, small victories along the way. Two years later the Intelligence Advanced Research Projects Activity (IARPA) opened for business. Its exclusive charter? Long fuse, big bang.

The daily routine of each of the long fuse, big bang visionaries profiled here varied little from that of most of us: the leaders spent their time producing small, quick results. But these near-term pursuits connected one to another like many short-fuse firecrackers strung end to end. Each firecracker explosion was small but kept a longer burn going toward a stack of dynamite at the end. To set off big bangs, you don't have to change *what* you do every day, just the *way* that you do it. Daily distractions should not be ends in themselves, but lead step-by-step to something big.

CHANGING *HOW*, NOT *WHAT*

The core observation from our discussion about the brain and behavior up to this point can be summed up with one word: *inertia.* Human behavior is like a giant boulder with massive inertia that resists change. Isaac Newton described inertia this way. "A body at rest stays at rest, a body in motion stays in motion." Our brain's desire to stay inside a comfort zone and exert as little energy as possible makes Newton's law of inertia as applicable to human bodies as to mechanical bodies. Our daily work routines can be characterized as the forward motion of a boulder in a constant direction. We arrive in the morning, go through our email, sit in meetings, write reports, make phone calls, try to put out fires, and go home, all the while fretting that we've only partially succeeded with the firefighting. We come to work the next day, repeat the cycle, and continue in the same direction. A few times a year we participate in looks at the future—typically five-year plans for budgets, new products, new services, investments, staffing, capital expenditure, and so forth—but if things start to go wrong, as in a recession, attempts to radically change our trajectory—such as business process re-engineering campaigns—almost inevitably fail because they push against the inertia of corporate habits, culture, and lack of motivation to change. We can nudge large boulders an inch or so, but we can't easily jar them into hard right turns. GM's and Chrysler's bankruptcies in the last recession—where the auto giants found it impossible to shift production to more fuel-efficient cars or to cut costs fast enough to keep them solvent—underscored the difficulty of getting inertia-bound bureaucracies to change course at the last minute.

The boulder analogy offers a simple framework for thinking about practical ways to prepare today for big tomorrows. Imagine that we are back in the Middle Ages trying to defend a castle on a hill from a besieging army. The enemy has spent months building a massive, fortified siege machine that they will roll up to our parapet, climb over, and use to storm our fortress. Further suppose that we have spies who tell us that, having invested heavily in the siege machine, the enemy will cut their losses and go home if we somehow manage to demolish their colossal contraption. Our whole future depends on destroying one siege machine.

We decide that the only way to take out the siege machine is to dig up an enormous boulder in our courtyard, open the gate as the enemy starts to push their machine toward us, aim the boulder toward the machine, and push hard. Our engineers tell us that with gravity assisting, the boulder will start rolling on its own and carry sufficient momentum to do the job, *if* it strikes the siege machine head-on. We only have one boulder, so a miss, or even a glancing blow, means that we lose our castle.

When the fateful day comes, all of our tomorrows ride on a single boulder, or to be more precise, the *aim* of the boulder. Realizing the importance of aim, and intuitively understanding inertia (even though Newton hasn't been born yet), we have our bravest knight ride our swiftest horse alongside the boulder as it rolls downhill. The knight, skilled at jousting, will jab the rolling boulder with a stout pole, nudging it to correct course as it accelerates toward its target. Each jab will only deflect the massive boulder a small fraction of an inch, but cumulatively, a long series of jabs will do the trick if the boulder's original aim was approximately correct.

Putting aside what happens to the brave knight as he nears thousands of angry enemies, this story illustrates how to move behavioral boulders in directions that will secure big futures.

The first insight is that we often need outside help to get new things rolling. In the fortress example, gravity was required both to get the boulder moving and to accelerate it up to a speed where it could destroy the siege machine. The second insight is that it's a good idea to assume our initial aim will be wrong and to plan on delivering a long series of corrective nudges all along the way, so that we aren't faced with the impossible task of moving a large inertia a large distance at the last minute.

I'll illustrate how to apply these two insights for coping with organizational inertia by describing a recent experience I had with a large consulting client. After leaving the government in 2007, I opened a boutique management consulting business specializing in helping large organizations innovate with new technology. Usually I focus less on specific technologies themselves than on the processes that enterprises use to develop or apply innovative technologies. The reason is that the big challenge for increasing profits with new technology is seldom overcoming technical problems, but *aiming* new technology in the right direction. Large organizations that develop or adapt new technologies have massive inertia that limits how much they can change their new product offerings each year. Some may have large factories optimized for producing a narrow range of widgets; others have customers, who also are large bureaucracies, that are slow to adopt new products and new ways of doing things. And almost all large organizations have lugubrious new business processes that favor incremental change over fundamental change.

For instance, I once became intimately involved in crafting the Congressional Budget Justification Book (CBJB) for a large government R&D lab.

Every year the lab had to submit a new CBJB to Congress outlining in great detail what every project, sub-project, and sub-sub-project was going to try to accomplish over the next five years, along with background information, schedule, budget, staffing, and a long list of other project data. The CBJB required so much work that each year the R&D organization had gotten into the habit of using the previous year's CBJB as a foundation, making only minor edits and tweaks to create next year's document. This approach allowed R&D scientists to spend more time on research than with paperwork, but it also insured that their research varied only slightly year after year. All big organizations, public or private, have a process like the CBJB cycle that develops five-year plans, and the temptation for new product and R&D groups in these organizations to simply "tweak" last year's plan is overpowering. Tweaks are quick, tweaks are easy for senior executives to understand. Above all, tweaking existing products is far safer than inventing new ones from scratch.

In 2008 I consulted for a client whose operations included placing small telemetry (remote sensing) devices on products that it shipped around the globe. The telemetry devices relayed environmental conditions, maintenance status of remote sensors, and other real-time data back to regional operations centers on different continents. The client used many different kinds of telemetry radios, depending on local conditions. In urban environments they used cell phones or Wi-Fi systems to take advantage of the local wireless infrastructure. In very remote areas they deployed commercial satellite radios or custom long-range transmitters. In all, the client developed or adapted at least ten different radios to perform the same task.

The client had succumbed to the temptation to tweak the performance of their telemetry radios and therefore was struggling to expand isolated pockets of coverage to encompass the entire globe. Each year, by slightly improving their telemetry sensors, they reached a few percent more of the globe but saw no straightforward way to track all of their products everywhere the products might travel. My recommendation for addressing the problem surprised the client: they expected me to suggest a slash-and-burn approach, including lots of "re's": re-organization, re-engineering, and re-staffing to shake up their R&D organization. But such "re's" usually fail because they try to move an organization's behavioral boulder too far, too fast. Instead, I recommended that the client retain their current organization, business process, and staff—even its time-honored tradition of tweaking. What should change, I suggested, was the *direction* that they tweaked new technology each year. I gave them the following example to drive the point home.

In each year's financial plan, the client's new product group proposed incremental improvements to their different telemetry systems—slightly increasing their data capacity, transmission range, or battery life, and so forth. These yearly technology plans anticipated where technology was going over the next twelve months and described ways to harness those advancements—such as a doubling of memory capacity—to increase the performance of remote monitoring systems. But the plans did not anticipate where relevant technologies were headed in five years or beyond, due to the dog year phenomenon: five years in technology is really like thirty-five years, so who can plan *that* far out? As a consequence, when five years in the future eventually arrived—as it inevitably did at the end of each five-year planning cycle—the client found that they were underutilizing current radio technology and were therefore unable to expand their reach of operations nearly as much as they might have. By picking only "low hanging fruit" in previous years, they hadn't undertaken the long-range efforts needed to fully exploit "today's" technology.

The solution to this problem, I advised, was to create a vision of the distant future, and to connect it back to product development plans in the present, tweaking existing plans to aim them toward the envisioned state of technology in five years. I suggested that, like most technologies, telemetry radios were slowly evolving into computers, where specialized analog components were giving way to specialized digital components, which in turn were giving way to general purpose computers (such as those that power laptops) that executed special purpose software. By 2008, the guts of the two-way radios in cell phones resembled the innards of a PC as much as they did a walkie-talkie's.

This inexorable replacement of specialized radio hardware with general purpose computers running specialized radio software meant that five years hence, the client could replace ten different radios with a single radio that ran ten different software programs. This strategy would dramatically slash the cost of maintaining ten different platforms, allowing the customer to deploy many more radios worldwide and to quickly adapt to changing local conditions. If a hurricane knocked out the local cellular system, the radios could immediately load in satellite radio software to "phone home" through a backup channel. It would also "future proof" the client's radios, such that when a new standard like 4G cell phones rolled out (wireless service as fast as today's wired broadband), the client could change software running in installed radios without changing out the radios themselves.

I had chosen the software radio example not only as a long fuse, big bang win for the client, but also as an example of a project that didn't have to push hard against the considerable inertia of the client's new product development process. A software radio project would be a new start for the client, but it wouldn't require much effort for two reasons.

First, as part of the open source software movement, academics and radio enthusiasts had—for free—written very sophisticated software that decoded and encoded radio signals on general purpose computers instead of special purpose chips. The open source movement has brought us the free operating system Linux that's giving Microsoft Windows a run for its money, as well as the Apache Web server and dozens of other free programs, such as Firefox, that are coming to dominate the Web. Open source software has become so important that it's acting like a force of gravity that greatly accelerates technology projects nudged "downhill." My client wouldn't need to invest heavily in software radio technology, but could simply download free radio software, buy some general purpose hardware, and be up and running with working software radios within a few weeks.

The second, and perhaps more important, reason I suggested the client pursue software radios was that they could do so without fundamentally changing their business processes. As they strove each year to incrementally improve the performance of their radios, they could simply use software radios, instead of special purpose devices to upgrade one of their existing systems. I suggested they start with satellite radios deployed in remote areas, because of the high cost and difficulty of re-provisioning remote radios when, inevitably, frequencies and communication protocols changed. Also, by using today's satellite frequencies and communication protocols, the new radios could be deployed within months, rather than years. Each year, the client could replace a few more hardware radios with more flexible software versions, until they eventually arrived at an all-software radio future.

To the client's development engineers, a software radio project would look like a subtle change to *how* they developed new radios, not a fundamental change to *what* they did each year. The engineers would participate in the yearly new product planning cycle as always, but this time the plans would include a way of connecting a five-year vision—all software radios—to a one-year action plan to develop and deploy *one* version of a software radio for remote satellite relay operations. Moreover, the engineers would get a lot of assistance from the "gravity" of the open source movement as they traveled down this new path. Finally, open source radio software was free, so the cost of a new project start would not tax the client's R&D budget.

The client accepted my recommendation to pursue software radio technology, but I suspect their biggest benefit from the project won't be increasing their global reach, but learning how to connect the distant future back to the pedestrian present. Their leadership may not have the extraordinary talent of a Gandhi or a Churchill, but they could end up *looking* like visionary leaders to grateful stakeholders.

RECAP

Pursuing the Distant Win

The daily routine of spending our time producing small, quick results can pay off, but only if those near-term pursuits are connected one to another. Think of a string of short-fuse firecrackers strung end to end. Small though each firecracker explosion may be, it can keep a longer burn going toward a stick of dynamite at the end. To set off big bangs, you don't have to change *what* you do every day, just the *way* that you do it. Most organizations have evolved tried and true ways of advancing their business year after year and are very slow to change those methods. Strong leaders like G.E.'s Jack Welch or IBM's Lou Gerstner can sometimes completely re-engineer an enterprise's processes, but those of us who are *not* CEOs have to finesse long-range change by carefully altering the *direction* of existing business processes without changing the processes themselves. The secret to changing an organization's behavior turns out to be the same as changing an individual's behavior: co-opt and work *with* natural tendencies instead of *fighting* those tendencies.

CHAPTER 4

Blinkers and Blind Spots

THE BUSINESS OF FUN

Tessa was nervous. She'd wandered into a dangerous neighborhood where locals would almost always attack if they spotted you. Tessa was especially fearful for her older sister, Sydney, whom she'd persuaded to come with her. Even though Sydney had taken the lead navigating their way through the unfamiliar neighborhood—and had gotten the two of them out of one scrape after another—Tessa worried that she'd get Sydney killed by doing something wrong.

Tessa interrupts herself at this point of her story, looks up at me with sparkling blue eyes, and giggles. "Sydney wouldn't actually die, but she'd get really really sad. Her laugh meter would run out and she'd have to go back to the playground to get more laugh points." Tessa, five, and Sydney, nine, are sitting with me at a restaurant near Washington, DC, having breakfast with their parents, Steve and Nancy. The girls are explaining what it feels like to play Disney's Toontown Online. Having been head of Disney's Virtual Reality Studio when it started developing the online experience a decade earlier, I'm anxious to see how kids like the game.

Toontown is a virtual world where PC users create their own toon characters and guide them through a series of battles with "Cogs," evil business-minded robots who try to leach all the fun out of Toontown by turning it into a business park. If frequent battles with Cogs wear toon characters down (depleting their laugh meter), they have to retreat to special playgrounds to replenish their laugh points by playing games, like shooting themselves out of cannons at large targets, swimming through underwater obstacle courses, and playing guessing games with friends.

Sydney and Tessa enjoyed this experience so much that at one point their parents had to forbid them from using it. Nancy said, "Toontown is one

Internet game I'm comfortable with because it's Disney. But it got to the point where begging for Toontown was a 24/7 proposition. It was getting way out of hand. We only allow one hour of TV or computer time a day."

A sly smile appears on Tessa's face. When I ask what she's thinking, she replies, "Sometimes I get up early and sneak on to Toontown when everyone's sleeping."

None of the rest of us at the breakfast table is surprised. Tessa is a perpetual motion machine. She didn't get much out of playing team soccer because she liked rolling in the grass more than running on it. Constantly shifting in her chair at the restaurant, Tessa reminds me of a cartoon teapot, boiling and rocking on the stove. Tessa wants to channel all that energy into being a singer when she grows up. "Or maybe a librarian," she laughs. "That would be fun too."

Sydney takes all this in with quiet amusement. The older sister is shy and reserved, content to let Tessa have the spotlight. Unlike Tessa, Sydney does like team sports, especially volleyball, and wants to be a baker someday. But she shares a passion for Toontown with her younger sister. "I'm curious," Sydney explains. "In the game they don't tell you how to beat the Cogs, so I like to figure it out."

Curious to learn more about the underlying psychological appeal of the game, I ask Sydney what started the two sisters playing Toontown. Sydney doesn't answer, but looks to her parents. Steve takes the cue. "Tessa and I actually started it a couple years ago as part of Camp Daddy. That's when Nancy and Sydney are off doing something else and Tessa and I do fun stuff we don't normally get to do, like eating ice cream." After a Camp Daddy Toontown session, Tessa lured Sydney into the game, and the two regularly started playing together. Steve only occasionally plays along, but a big reason the girls keep returning to Toontown is that they know *Daddy* likes it. Daddy is a technology executive who spends hours every day in regions of cyberspace on the computer—such as technology Web sites—that are mysterious and inaccessible to the girls. But Toontown is a corner of cyberspace that the girls get to share with Daddy. "If I worked all day in a wood shop," Steve said, "Toontown is the equivalent of the girls having their own little wood shop where they can do what Daddy does."

The game also gives the girls a sense of accomplishment: they earn money (jelly beans) to spend on funny gags in toon stores, grow toon gardens, and earn toon trophies that they display in toon rooms of their own design. Finally, the girls make new friends and get to be heroes when they use up their own "laugh points" to help these friends defeat humorless Cogs.

The sisters aren't alone in their passion for the game. There are roughly 1.2 million other users worldwide in the United States, UK, Southeast Asia, Spain, Japan, and France. Many of the users are adults, and—very rare for a massively multiplayer online role-playing game (MMORPG)—half are female. For its broad appeal and novel game play, Toontown has won both a Webby (an online Oscar) and the prestigious MMORPG of the Year from *Computer Gaming World*.

Toontown had grown from a small-scale virtual reality experiment in the late 1990s into a big bang success. But the long fuse that eventually burned to the big bang almost never got lit, because of plays in the brain's playbook.

THE PARABLE OF THE PANDA AND THE RAT

Disney Imagineering started experimenting with virtual reality (VR) in 1990. An eclectic team of show designers, artists, animators, audio specialists, mechanical engineers, and computer scientists built a prototype of a RocketMan experience themed on the Disney film of the same name that had just been released. Users would don a special RocketMan helmet that displayed a 3D computer graphic world that you could fly through in real time. Imagineering had been trying for decades—with mixed success—to give theme park guests a realistic experience of flying. We experimented with wind tunnels and wire suspension. Even magnetic levitation. But none of these approaches were practical for entertaining thousands of guests at a time. Virtual reality held a lot of promise for helping the Glendale, California, design studio finally realize their ambition.

By 1991, the RocketMan prototype was ready to go, and Michael Eisner, along with other top Disney executives, traveled to Salt Lake City, where Imagineering had set up a demonstration in the lab of the 3D computer graphics company Evans and Sutherland. The demonstration, which used Evans and Sutherland graphics supercomputers designed for military and commercial flight simulators, was a resounding success. Eisner gave the go-ahead for the effort to ramp up, setting a goal of putting a virtual reality ride in Walt Disney World Florida as soon as possible.

Under the joint leadership of Jon Snoddy, from Imagineering's Creative Division, and Dave Fink, vice president of R&D, Imagineering established a Virtual Reality Studio to design, build, and install Disney's first VR ride. Eisner liked the idea of a flying ride, but he directed Imagineering to scrap the RocketMan concept in favor of a magic carpet ride planned to coincide with the upcoming release of the animated feature *Aladdin*.

Looking for a job outside the defense industry after the Berlin Wall fell, I joined Imagineering R&D just after the VR Studio's creation in 1992. At Hughes, I had specialized in developing 3D computer image generators, projection optics, and wide-field-of-view displays, so my first job at Disney was to design the head mounted display for the Aladdin ride. For two years the team worked at a feverish pace. Show designers tried and rejected dozens of different ways to tell the Aladdin story interactively. Computer artists and animators recreated Aladdin's Baghdad along with colorful, artificially intelligent characters, such as Aladdin's pesky monkey, that interacted with guests. Our mechanical engineers experimented with alternate ways to control and move flying carpets, while audio engineers and sound designers tinkered with new 3D acoustic effects that immersed users in virtual environments that were as rich acoustically as they were visually. I designed half a dozen different head mounted displays before finding one that a four-year-old child or eighty-year-old grandmother could put on and take off in seconds. By July 2004, we had opened four "seats"—individual guest stations—of Disney's first virtual reality attraction, as part of the new Innoventions Pavilion at Epcot. The attraction only had four seats because Fink and Snoddy didn't want a full-scale opening until we had learned how guests would respond to the novel ride.

Randy Pausch, a VR expert from the University of Virginia (and later Carnegie Mellon, where he delivered his famous *Last Lecture*), joined us for a one-year academic sabbatical to help out with the Aladdin ride. Randy was an energetic, charismatic Disneyphile—basically a kid in a grown-up's body—who had long dreamed of working as an Imagineer. He saw his chance when we ventured into VR, a technology he'd advanced through pioneering work on the Alice authoring system. Alice was one of the first tools that allowed what Randy called "mere mortals"—as opposed to computer programmers—to create virtual reality experiences. Alice is still available for download at www.alice.org, for anyone wishing to see firsthand just how successful Randy was at allowing "normal humans" access to VR authoring tools.

Randy's job on Aladdin was to assess whether we had done an adequate job of designing the guest's flight controls and preventing the vertigo and motion sickness that traditionally plagued military VR flight simulators. We also asked Randy to critique how well we told the Aladdin story and how easy it was for our guests to navigate through the story environment. Eventually, Randy gathered detailed data on tens of thousands of guests and published his findings (mostly positive) in a 1996 article titled "Disney's Aladdin: First Steps Toward Storytelling in Virtual Reality." Randy included me as an author on the paper, not because I had contributed more than a few ideas to it, but because his kid-at-heart playfulness didn't get in the way of shrewd street smarts. By the time the paper was ready for Disney's approval, I'd moved up to be one of the Disney vice presidents whose approval was required, and Randy had calculated—correctly as it turned out—that I'd be more likely to sign off on the paper if my name was on it.

What I remember most about Randy was standing with him on Aladdin's opening day, watching guests take their first rides. We had designed one of the four stations to allow wheelchair access, and a boy of about eight or nine, who'd never walked before, rolled into the special station. We helped him on with the HMD, showed him how to steer the flying carpet, then stood back and watched carefully as the show began.

The neuroscientist in me was anxious. I didn't know exactly what had confined the boy to the chair, but I was concerned it was a serious central nervous system disorder that might cause him to react with nausea, vomiting, headache, or vertigo. My worst fears seemed to be confirmed when the boy started crying after flying the ride for less than a minute. I rushed toward him to take off the HMD, but his mother, who stood nearby, stopped me. "Those are tears of joy," she said. "He's free of his chair for the first time in his life."

The Imagineers who heard the mother started crying too. I think every one of us who witnessed that event remembers it as the most gratifying experience of our Disney career. We didn't know yet whether the ride would be a winner, but there could be no doubt it was a big bang for at least one guest.

One year of rigorous guest testing demonstrated that VR was a hit with other guests as well. But a major obstacle stood in the way of full-scale deployment of VR as a theme park attraction: the technology was simply too expensive. The head mounted displays and graphics supercomputers made each "seat" over ten times more expensive than even the most costly Disney ride. Costs of VR computers were coming down by a factor of two every eighteen to twenty-four months, but we still didn't see a way to economically scale up the technology to serve one thousand to two thousand guests at a time. We scratched our heads and went back to the drawing board.

In 1995 I took over as the head of the VR Studio and worked with the team on turning VR into a money-making business. Disney was experimenting with location based entertainment (LBE)—basically mini interactive theme parks to be located throughout the country—which held promise as a growing new market for us. The relatively low guest traffic of LBEs was a better fit for our expensive Aladdin ride than a full-scale theme park. With under one tenth the traffic of a theme park and higher per-hour revenues (LBEs charged lower admission than theme parks, but shorter guest stays made revenue per hour, per guest higher), a location center such as the DisneyQuest Interactive Theme Park could—in theory—turn a profit with just a few Aladdin seats. By 1998 we had delivered several seats of an upgraded Aladdin ride to the DisneyQuests in Orlando and Chicago, as well as a *Hercules in the Underworld*–themed VR experience.

But virtual reality was still too expensive to deploy broadly. To make matters worse, early results from our most promising customer, Disney Location Based Entertainment, were not encouraging. The Orlando DisneyQuest was doing well, but the Chicago site was struggling and eventually shut down in 2001.

By late 1998, some six years after I had started with Disney, I had grown concerned that we were spending more on R&D than we would ever recoup from a theme park deployment. I'd joined Disney because I was passionate about the potential of virtual reality, but the businessman in me began to suspect we'd have to get out of the VR business unless we could find a way to make money. If I was having those thoughts, I was certain it wouldn't be long before executives at corporate would start having them too.

I called together the creative and technical leaders of the VR Studio for a series of meetings to explore different business models for VR. One approach was to find applications that were steadily becoming less expensive to replace those that were not.

We knew that virtual reality had gotten its commercial start this way two decades earlier, when the decreasing costs of flight simulator graphics computers made it cheaper to train airline pilots in flight simulators than in fuel-guzzling airplanes. Flight simulators that generate out-of-cockpit imagery for pilots had become so sophisticated and inexpensive that the first time many pilots actually flew a commercial airliner was with paying passengers aboard. Hoping to find the entertainment equivalent of flight training, we searched every corner of Disney's vast media empire for expensive processes that were growing *more* expensive each year, and that we could replace with relatively inexpensive VR technology. After a few weeks of digging, we found our first candidate in the Disney-owned broadcast network.

There was an interest in Disney-ABC's Daytime Division, which produced soap operas such as *General Hospital,* to save money by replacing physical sets with virtual ones. With virtual sets, actors could perform in front of blue screens while high-performance 3D graphics computers filled in all of the backdrops and props, thereby eliminating costs for buying, staging, and storing physical sets. Those costs were climbing fast, especially in New York City, where studio space was at such a premium that sets had to be struck, stored, unpacked, and set up every day to enable multiple shows to be shot in one studio. Virtual set technology was an attractive alternative to physical sets because—like all computer technology—its cost would continue to decrease by a factor of two every eighteen to twenty-four months for the foreseeable future, while the cost of both studio space and labor in Manhattan would continue to rise for the foreseeable future. We offered to build and test virtual sets for *One Life to Live* and *General Hospital,* but after expressing some enthusiasm for the concept, ABC Daytime decided that taking a headlong leap into the virtual world was too risky. Undeterred, we found another potential customer for VR technology in Disney's TV animation group. TV animation always lags big screen theatrical animation in production values (slickness of artwork, sound, and editing) because TV cartoons are released in far greater quantity than animated cinema features and thus have to be produced quickly and cheaply. When Pixar's smash hit *Toy Story* generated audience demand for computer-generated graphics, Disney's TV animation group struggled to meet that demand with its meager production budgets. Unlike the inexpensive, hand-drawn "2D" products that had dominated TV animation from the beginning, 3D computer graphics required big investments in special image-rendering software, graphics hardware, and highly paid computer artists and programmers. The process of creating 3D computer graphics was also much slower than 2D hand-drawn animation, because 3D characters, backgrounds, and effects had to be meticulously modeled on the computer, then rendered in a time-consuming process that could take several hours per frame, even with clusters of high-performance computers.

Animated shows appear to move smoothly, but they're actually a series of still images that vary slightly from frame to frame, creating the illusion of motion. A minimum of twelve new frames per second are required to smooth out jerkiness and to create movements that look natural. A twenty-minute animated TV show with more than ten thousand unique frames of 3D computer graphics could not be made fast enough for TV animators developing more than twenty new shows a year, and still allow them to check the computer's output for each frame, correct errors, and move on to the next frame.

Our VR technology offered a much faster way to create 3D computer animation at a much lower cost. Because we used supercomputers that took a sixtieth of a second rather than hours to render each new image frame, animators could run through the trial-and-error process of trying different ideas much faster. The production values of our technology did not compare with slower frame-by-frame rendering, but we were able to create a genuine 3D look that might satisfy the audience appetite for high-tech graphics. When TV Animation decided that our sixtieth-of-a-second images didn't measure up to Disney quality standards, we developed technical shortcuts to high-quality, frame-by-frame rendering that significantly speeded up the production process while preserving a look that approximated "big screen" quality.

As with our offer to build virtual sets for ABC Daytime Television, our proposal to create 3D graphics for Disney TV Animation met with early enthusiasm, but was ultimately rejected as too risky. Our low-cost "flight training" strategy had crashed and burned.

Combing through the wreckage of our strategy for clues to our failure, we concluded that it was nearly impossible to replace a historically successful, deeply entrenched way of doing business in a large, profitable company such as Disney. It occurred to us that our situation was similar to that of a novice politician seeking election for the first time: beating an "incumbent" (in this case, businesses processes and employees who had a stake in those processes) is a lot harder than beating another first-time politician. Clayton Christensen's new book *The Innovator's Dilemma* reinforced our conclusions.

Well-run enterprises, according to Christensen, feel compelled to satisfy their customers by continually improving conventional or "sustaining" technologies that keep the business running smoothly and that are known to work. Investing in "disruptive" technologies—such as VR—that customers have never seen before invites disaster by moving an enterprise away from its customers. In Disney's case, there was a very real possibility that customers would not like the look and feel of virtual sets or virtual animated characters, and the company would find itself in the same—intensely uncomfortable— situation that Coca-Cola faced after it replaced Classic Coke with New Coke. Soft drink consumers disapproved of the switch and the company's sales plummeted. It was ironic that Disney, with billions in yearly profits and more than 100,000 employees, was in much less of a position to take risks with new technology than it was when the company started in the 1920s and had only a handful of employees and almost *no* profits to help it recover from bad decisions: in the twenties, there was very little to lose, but in the mid- nineties there were millions of stockholders and more than 100,000 em- ployees to think about, not to mention the equity of one of the world's most valuable brands.

After concluding that there were sound reasons Disney's businesses were reluctant to adopt VR technology, and after reading Christensen's new book, we decided to change tack and look for applications of VR where there was no incumbent process to displace. I thought the most promising business area was Disney's fledgling online group, which had not had time to develop entrenched ways of doing business. I was especially encouraged by rapid improvements in the quality of PC graphics and the speed of Internet connections that would, within a few years, allow us to create VR experiences that we could deliver to home computers over broadband (high-speed Internet) connections.

Downloading software to consumers would eliminate the costs of pro- ducing, boxing, shipping, and marketing software CDs and would let users interact with one another and share experiences in VR social networks.

Although online experiences seemed to me to be our best option for help- ing Disney turn a profit with VR, the VR team had mixed feelings about this new application. Most had joined Imagineering to design and build the first-ever virtual reality theme park experiences, not PC games. The majority of the team wanted to continue development of theme park and location- based experiences until the cost of high-performance VR made that initial goal feasible. They weren't really interested in considering this change of focus. Tension between us on the team mounted as I continued to push online ideas. I wasn't ready to give up.

Captivated by the early success of online virtual worlds such as Ever-Quest and Ultima Online (online games where hundreds of thousands of enthusiasts explored exotic locations, hunted for clues, accumulated magical capabilities, and battled one another for supremacy), I suggested that the studio programmers convert our VR game engine to Java, a programming language that would work with any Internet browser or PC. The VR team pushed back. Java wasn't the right technology for our engine, they said, and Disney would be ill-served by moving to the lower end of performance, because we'd lose the magic that made us different. Families expected more from The Mouse, they argued. We'd destroy our product differentiation and hurt our brand by using the same programming technology that everyone else used. I agreed with them . . . up to a point, but a viable VR theme park business was many years away, and I didn't know how long we could continue to justify our large R&D budget, especially since I was getting a lot of heat from other executives in Imagineering to either make something of the studio or shut it down. I decided to step up the pressure.

I wanted my team to understand that our survival depended on changing our focus to new markets like the Internet, and I knew the perfect way to get my argument across. But first I warned them that I was about to give them an analogy from the animal world. My staff always groaned and rolled their eyes when I bolstered my arguments with examples from neuroscience or animal behavior, and this time was no exception. They crossed their arms, doodled, and exchanged here-he-goes-again glances as I launched into the parable of the panda and the rat.

The panda, I explained, is an exotic, beautiful creature that everyone loves. But the panda only eats bamboo leaves. When bamboo dies out, so do pandas. That's why the cuddly black-and-white marsupials are nearly extinct. Rats, on the other hand, will eat anything. The rodents might not be as cuddly and lovable as pandas, but they'll be around long after humans are extinct. The lesson of nature was clear, I said. The Virtual Reality Studio was a panda that had to morph into a rat.

The next week when I entered the VR conference room for our weekly staff meeting, I noticed a new storyboard pinned to the wall. Walt Disney himself had invented the storyboard method whereby scene-by-scene pencil sketches and dialogue laid out the way an animated film would unfold. Our unit had adapted the storyboard to plan different segments of our VR rides. These sketches covered most every wall in the studio. This new storyboard, however, had a distinctly non-Disney theme.

The first panel showed me, dressed in a white lab coat and holding a clipboard while kicking a hapless panda into the funnel of an elaborate, mad-scientist contraption, complete with convoluted plumbing. I looked a lot like the evil Mr. Burns, owner of the nuclear plant in *The Simpsons.*

In the next panel the panda was being sucked into the maw of the strange machine. "Bad panda," I scolded.

The last frame showed a series of scruffy rats on a conveyor belt emerging from the other end of the panda-to-rat machine. I looked approvingly at the rodents. "Good rats!" I said. "Good rats!"

I got the point.

My team was telling me they'd never turn into rats. I decided to stop harassing them until I could come up with an approach they would embrace. For the next week or two I thought about why my team was pushing back so hard. The most obvious reason was that they were passionate about advancing the state of the art in VR for families and kids and weren't interested in creating second-rate experiences. But that wasn't all.

FUNCTIONAL FIXITY

It had taken us more than five years to figure out how to squeeze every ounce of performance out of the fastest graphics computers in the world to create compelling VR worlds. Therefore, the studio didn't expect VR to be appealing unless it used expensive computers that could generate very high-quality graphics and special effects. Home computers back in the 1990s could only draw very crude 3D computer graphics. Worse, because VR applications would have to be designed to play smoothly on the lowest performance PCs, in order to work on the largest number of home computers possible, we'd have to make VR characters, environments, and special effects incredibly simple. Too simple. How could any experience so crude deliver Disney magic?

The problem reminded me of a demonstration that psychology professors sometimes perform in their classes. The professors ask college students how they would get a rope hanging from the ceiling to touch opposite walls of a large room. Rules of the experiment forbid grabbing the rope and walking it from one wall to the other. Aside from the rope, the only other object in the room is an ordinary pair of pliers. Most students don't solve the problem, but a few tie the pliers to the end of the rope then swing the rope toward one wall. With the added heft of the pliers, the rope hits the wall then rebounds—pendulum-style—to strike the opposite wall. The rare students who succeed find the truth by seeing an unlikely use for pliers: dead weight.

The pliers-and-rope experiment is an example of a phenomenon called *functional fixity,* where our brains lock onto the functions that familiar objects are *supposed* to do, blinding us to the full potential of what these objects *could* do. When we overcome functional fixity, a rock serves as a hammer, a pencil becomes a weapon, a cardboard box turns into table, and an acetylene torch lights up a room. Wherever you find big bang innovation, chances are you'll see an example of someone overcoming functional fixity.

Cell phone text messaging accounts for a sizable portion of cell phone operators' profits, because cellular subscribers pay a lot of money for a service that takes up a small fraction of a cellular network's capacity and costs the operators very little. This big bang win for cell operators had humble beginnings in 1991, when Europeans rolled out a digital voice network that included a digital text messaging system for operators to alert subscribers about maintenance problems and changes to their service. Designers of the text system, called, you guessed it, SMS or Short Message Service, never intended that cell subscribers use SMS to communicate with one another.

But CMG, a European cellular technology company, realized in 1992 that SMS could be modified to give subscribers the mobile equivalent of Internet instant messaging. CMG then helped cell operator Vodaphone introduce the first subscriber-to-subscriber text service in 1993. Until 1999 cell subscribers could only text other subscribers on their own cell network, so revenues from SMS were modest. But once operators let customers text subscribers on other operators' networks, SMS traffic exploded and, along with it, profits from text messaging.

The concept of functional fixity highlights an important challenge for finding long fuses to big bangs. Big bangs, by definition, take us into unfamiliar territory, where the unlikely becomes a reality. Thus our brains are apt to overlook potential big bangs, like SMS, that haven't happened yet, just as most students are blind to the opportunities in a pair of pliers.

It seemed to me that some of my colleagues in the VR Studio were experiencing a kind of functional fixity that made them overlook the possibilities of VR experience on home computers. Home computers were meant to be used for spreadsheets, email, and solitaire games, not virtual reality. I had no idea what compelling VR experiences on low-end PCs might look like, or indeed whether it was even possible to create such experiences. But I knew that if we didn't find a solution, virtualty reality was likely to go out of business at Disney Imagineering.

I was stuck firmly inside a discomfort zone. However, except for my incessant harping about the need to diversify, the VR team was not particularly uncomfortable. They enjoyed their work, and most of them clung to the belief that the studio had a future in very high-end VR applications, confident that Disney would not abandon its culture of innovating with cutting edge entertainment technology. Also, the others on the team weren't exposed to the criticism I received from other executives—on almost a daily basis— for advocating continued investments in VR. Each week I was experiencing greater pain from *not* changing our focus, than I would from changing it, but my team wasn't feeling the same pain. I needed a new play.

MATCHING TALENT TO TASK

The panda-to-rat storyboard had stayed up on the wall for weeks. Looking at that panda made me think of China, and thinking of China made me think of Buddhism and a clinical supervisor I'd had while volunteering as a psychotherapist at a community mental health center in Manhattan Beach. The supervisor was a big believer in Eastern philosophy, especially the Buddhist idea that unhappiness comes from resisting one's true inner nature. He advised us not to push our patients to change who they were in order to relieve psychic suffering, but to learn to accept themselves with all of their flaws. A shy patient who was unhappy in a job that required him to interact a lot with people would be counseled, for instance, not to get more extroverted, but to find a new job where shyness wasn't a liability.

Such insights are not limited to Buddhism. The Gallup Organization, which has a large human resource management consulting practice, calls such career moves "matching talent to task." From a broad range of work settings they have gathered statistics suggesting that managers get much better results from their workforces by reinforcing the strengths of individual workers, than by trying to correct their weaknesses. If an employee is a world-class circuit designer but has terrible writing skills, the employee and his company will benefit much more from classes that make him an even better circuit designer, than they will from classes that attempt to shore up his poor writing skills.

If Buddha and Gallup are right, then the brain has a play that essentially says: "Stick to what you do best." Looking at the panda storyboard, I got an idea about how to exploit this play for the VR Studio. At the next staff meeting, I didn't launch into a harangue about what dire straits we were in, nor did I push my ideas about low-end PC VR applications. Instead, I simply challenged the team to find a way to remain a panda without being a Theme Park Panda or a Location Based Entertainment Panda.

After a few weeks, the team came back to me with a theme park VR concept. Only this theme park would not be in the physical world, but in cyberspace. We'd get around the problem of expensive equipment by using our guests' own PCs and Internet connections, creating all of our experiences out of inexpensive bits (software) instead of expensive atoms (specialized VR hardware). Even though the graphics and special effects would be simple, the overall experience would be rich because users could create their own characters, play a wide variety of unusual games, meet thousands of other users, constantly learn new tricks and explore new places. The team also made a major breakthrough in figuring out how to let strangers who met for the first time in our VR world communicate with one another without compromising privacy or child safety. The proposed new experience would be state-of-the-art VR in all facets but one: the graphics would be simple. It wasn't an exotic Theme Park Panda, but it looked much more like a panda than a rat. Users would interact with virtual Disney characters, enjoy virtual rides, and play virtual games, but would spend *real* dollars on monthly subscriptions and online purchases.

I was thrilled. The team had looked into their functional fixity blind spot and discovered an exciting opportunity. A virtual theme park would not only give us a foothold in the fast-growing Internet market (this was in the middle of the nineties dot.com bubble), but would also help our traditional theme park business expand into cyberspace. I gave the green light, and development of Toontown Online got under way. The studio's creative team scoped out a game that thousands of kids could play together online, and the software team designed and built a special VR game engine that accommodated millions of players. The VR Studio called this new engine Panda 3D.

I took away an important lesson from the Toontown experience. Don't use brain science as a motivation for your actions unless you enjoy being met by eye rolls and grimaces. If you keep your reasons to yourself and simply put artificial blinders on your team that stop them from looking in the usual places, your team will have no choice but to probe the unexplored reaches of their vision. Most importantly, when the team eventually spots big bang opportunities, the ideas for exploiting them will be the *team's* ideas, not yours, so they'll be much more likely to embrace them.

Overcoming functional fixity to create an online virtual experience was essential to Toontown's ultimate success, but far from sufficient. We still had to work around an entirely different blind spot to persuade the rest of Disney to embrace the new idea.

BLINDED BY DESIRE

Stop reading for a moment and look up. As you gaze ahead, your brain gives you the comforting illusion that you see everything there is to be seen in your field of view. But in fact there are two respectably large blind spots that mask potentially important details in front of you. If you don't believe it, check out this graphic.

   **X**

Close your right eye, fix your gaze on the X while holding the book at arm's length. Then, very slowly bring the book toward you as you continue to fixate on the X. When the book is about a foot from your face, the "big bang" stack of dynamite will disappear into a blind spot in your left eye. This defect in your vision corresponds to the part of your retina (the region at the back of your eye that has light-sensitive receptors) where your optic nerve creates a receptor-free "dead zone" as the nerve penetrates your retina on its path to connect with your brain. You can uncover the blind spot in your right eye by closing your left eye as you fix your gaze on the stack of dynamite while repeating the experiment. About a foot in front of your face the X will disappear.

Functional fixity works much the same way, creating blind spots out of expectation: our brains see what they expect to see and don't see what they don't expect to see. But our brains also blind us to big bang opportunities by making us see what we *want* to see and not see what we *don't* want to see.

At Disney in the nineties, one of the new developments that some executives (who have long since left the firm) did not want to see was that the fast-growing Internet was about to jar some of the company's businesses out of their comfort zones.

Disney Interactive, which developed and marketed computer games for PCs and game consoles, was an example of such a business. In the late nineties, most game software was sold in shrink-wrapped compact disc packages through retail stores, because most consumers' Internet connections were too slow for downloading complete games. But the rapid spread of high-speed broadband connections was about to change that. Within a few years, the majority of game buyers in the United States would be able to download large games in just a few minutes. Some Disney Interactive executives were excited at the prospect of selling directly to consumers through the Internet, but I believe others worried—consciously or unconsciously—that a move to Internet sales would shift the balance of power in Disney from the bricks-and-mortar interactive group to the rival online group. A more subtle, but equally serious challenge for Disney Interactive was that high-speed Internet connections threatened to change not only their sales model, but the very nature of video games themselves. High-speed connections would make it easy for players to connect with other players, transforming games from solitary experiences to shared ones, and Disney Interactive had less experience with social networking and multiplayer games than Disney Online, an additional factor that could shift the balance of power away from the interactive group.

Although I never heard anyone at Disney Interactive say so, Toontown represented a double threat. The new game would be sold exclusively over broadband connections by the online group *and* was specially designed to promote social networking. As a result, a few key executives in the Disney Interactive group mounted a campaign to kill the project.

One of the more fascinating dimensions of this campaign was that I believe the anxieties that drove it were largely unconscious. In friendly conversations with Disney Interactive executives before the smoldering Toontown dispute erupted into open warfare, I never heard them fret about broadband game distribution disrupting their sales model, nor did I see them worry over the prospect of a shift in games from single user to multi-user experiences. Both of these possibilities were distant and theoretical. In the meantime, they had a business to run! But the psychotherapist in me (you can never resist playing shrink once you've actually been one) suspected that some of the executives actually *did* worry unconsciously about the implications of these trends for their group's standing in the company. One reason for this being unconscious was that fretting about the future is painful, so we all minimize, or even completely tune out, bad news. Another reason was that we don't like to view ourselves as turf fighters who place personal ambitions above the greater good. All of us have territorial instincts, but such impulses aren't *nice,* so we push awareness of them below the surface. Instead of experiencing painful anxieties over threats to our ambitions, we shift the perceived locus of the problem from inside ourselves—e.g., Internet distribution could be a problem for *me* personally—to outside ourselves—e.g., Toontown is a lousy game that will be a problem for *Disney.*

Our tendency to translate unconscious resistance to change into conscious thoughts such as "That proposal is flawed" leads us to kill many big bang ideas before they can ignite. "I'm all for progressive change," we think, "just not with *this* particular bad idea." We aren't aware that our brains routinely supply us with plausible-sounding reasons to reject new ideas, so we don't critically examine our own reactions and therefore let big opportunities get away from us. This is another example of our brain influencing our behavior by influencing our perceptions: our brain steers us away from painful decisions by making them appear to be *bad* decisions. A crucial first step to long fuse, big bang thinking is to acknowledge that we all can be overly critical of disruptive changes. The same clinical supervisor who taught me about Eastern philosophy suggested how we can escape this mental trap: "In order to let something go, we first have to admit we have it."

I believe in their heart of hearts the Disney Interactive executives who fought us truly thought Toontown would damage Disney's brand. They argued, with genuine conviction, that the game's computer graphics lacked the polish of Disney's meticulously rendered games. They also pointed out that Toontown didn't have enough content to keep individual gamers occupied for more than a few hours and relied on the unproven appeal of online conversations and social interactions to keep users playing the game.

Disney Interactive proved to be a formidable opponent because Michael Eisner, who ran Disney, knew a lot about TV, movies, and theme parks, but acknowledged that he didn't have an intuitive feel for the game business. After seeing a Toonown demonstration, Michael turned to me and shrugged. "Well," he said, "it could be great or it could suck; I'm not the guy to say." As a result Michael deferred to Disney Interactive, and our efforts to launch the new experience foundered. The Disney online group was on our side, but they were investing heavily in other ventures and couldn't take on the risk of an unproven VR business model.

Disney Interactive's opposition stalled us until we found a way to shed light into what I perceived to be their don't-want-to-see blind spot and demonstrated that the risks of Toontown were manageable. We gave away thousands of free copies of Toontown at gaming conventions, Disneyana gatherings, and through other grassroots distribution channels, quickly gathering thousands of users who loved Toontown and who generated positive buzz in chat forums, blogs, and game magazines. This buzz led a top Japanese game company to offer to buy the rights to Toontown for the Asian market.

Disney never accepted the Japanese company's offer, but the fact that a major actor in the game business wanted Toontown made the game look a lot less risky. Disney Interactive's objections lost their impact, and Disney Online soon launched a market trial of the game. The trial ran for over a year, proving that the company could indeed make a profit with online VR, so Toontown was ultimately launched as a full-blown business.

WHY OUR BRAINS IGNORE BAD NEWS

I feel guilty about singling out a few Disney executives to illustrate the don't-see-what-we-don't-want-to-blind spot, because we all have this defect, and it hides big bang opportunities—and threats—from everyone. If we have lots of money invested in stocks when the market dives, we're prone to see the downturn as a temporary "correction." Early in romantic relationships, we don't notice flaws in a lover that are obvious to our friends. Love is blind, and so is its opposite; when we dislike someone, we are oblivious to their positive traits because we don't want the object of our loathing to be *good* any more than we want objects of our love to be *bad*. Perhaps I didn't initially see the muzzle flashes in Iraq for what they really were, in part because I didn't *want* to be shot at.

It's easy to understand why our brains should save energy by telling us what we already expect. Our brain is most efficient when it focuses only on the small fraction of available information that's likely to matter. But what's the evolutionary payoff of filtering out information we don't *want*? After all, some of the most important details to notice back in the Stone Age were inconvenient truths, such as game becoming scarce or watering holes drying up. Indeed, as we've seen with the fight-or-flight response, the brain sometimes does pass along bad news, when there's overwhelming evidence that we're in immediate danger.

The key to resolving this paradox lies in understanding just how overwhelming our brain thinks evidence of a looming danger is. The brain will expend considerable energy dealing with immediate and unambiguous threats, such as a bear who's decided to share a cave with us. But the brain doesn't see the odds in investing energy in potential threats that might never materialize.

Let's assume for the moment that we all were like Cassandra, the character from Greek mythology who constantly foresaw disaster. As imaginative as humans are, we'd waste emotional energy obsessing about possible future tragedies that would never happen. Worse, we'd waste physical energy running away from imagined threats, building fortifications or preparing for battle. So our brains automatically blind us to possible bad news, so that we'll conserve energy to deal with actual bad news.

Unfortunately, the bad news our brains filter out almost always carries with it potentially good news about big bang opportunities. For example, Ken Olson, CEO of computer giant Digital Equipment Corporation (DEC), observed in 1977, "There is no reason for any individual to have a computer in his home." DEC is now defunct, largely because they neither expected nor wanted PCs to compete with their extensive line of time-shared minicom-puters, such as the VAX. By the time DEC finally realized that personal computing represented a huge opportunity, they entered the exploding PC market too late to overcome IBM and Microsoft's lead.

Rare leaders do let bad news filter in and are able to take advantage of the good news that accompanies it. By 1995, the rapid rise of the Web threat-ened Microsoft's dominance of the PC market that DEC had missed. Before the Web, Microsoft's Windows operating system and associated "killer apps," such as Word, Excel, and Outlook, were the chief reasons that people bought PCs. But e-commerce; Web news, entertainment, and information sites; not to mention chat rooms, instant messaging, and Web mail, were fast becom-ing *better* reasons to own PCs. The center of gravity of personal computing was about to shift from an area where Microsoft was strong to one where they weren't. Rather than ignore the threat, Bill Gates embraced it, embed-ding Web features into all of Microsoft's Office applications and investing heavily in a Microsoft Web portal (MSN), Web browser (Internet Explorer), and Web server.

Microsoft's rapid adjustment to looming bad news helped them thrive and grow. What began as a threat in 1995, by 2008 was adding $3.2 billion to Microsoft's revenues through online services. Although a few billion dol-lars aren't a big bang when compared to Microsoft's total revenue of $66B in 2008, Bill Gates's Web strategy did help his company avoid the type of big bang that demolished DEC.

RECAP

Uncovering Big Bang Opportunities Hiding in Plain Sight

The problem isn't so much that we have blind spots, but that our brains blind us to the existence of these blind spots. So not only are we blind to unexpected and unwanted possibilities, but we are *unaware* of this blindness. Therefore, we go through each day confident that we'll spot new opportunities and threats as they pop up, when, in reality, we are oblivious to many big opportunities and threats staring us right in the face. This means that we don't actually have to look very hard for big new opportunities. All we have to do is accept that we have perceptual and emotional blind spots, then force ourselves to look into them. When we force ourselves to go through this uncomfortable process, we'll usually discover new long fuses *and* big bangs.

CHAPTER 5

Turning Others' Failures into Your Successes

BLINDED BY DESIRE

The series of volcanic eruptions in the spring of 2009 was spectacular, jetting steam and ash twenty thousand feet into the air. Gargantuan explosions are noteworthy anywhere, but these events in the South Pacific, six miles off the main island of Tonga, Tongatapu, were special. The erupting volcanoes were underwater, so their ejecta shot from directly under the ocean's surface, rising fast into crenelated, dark clouds that hunched over the water like monsters in a 1950s Japanese science-fiction movie.

Roughly half of the islands that make up the Tongan archipelago of 167 islands midway between New Zealand and Hawaii were formed from volcanoes similar to those that erupted in 2009. Because it is situated at the boundary of two tectonic plates (separate pieces of the Earth's crust that float on the planet's molten core) where molten magma wells up, volcanoes and volcanic islands are common in the region. Millions of years after the Tongan islands rose from the sea, seafarers from other inhabited islands colonized them. *Tonga* means "south" in Polynesian, and anthropologists believe that islanders from Fiji and other regions north of Tonga migrated to the archipelago about three thousand years ago.

The Dutch explorers Willem Schouten and Jacob Lemair were the first Europeans to visit Tonga, in 1616, but regular visits from Europeans didn't start until Captain Cook stopped there in 1773 and 1777. Cook, observing the mellow behavior of the islanders, named the archipelago "The Friendly Islands," unaware that the only reason he left the islands alive was that feuding island nobles couldn't agree on which of them should kill him. Captain Cook gave King Fatafehi Paulaho a Galapagos tortoise that roamed the grounds of the royal compound until the reptile died almost two hundred years later.

The modern nation of Tonga has a population of 103,000, living on 48 of the country's 171 islands. It is a constitutional monarchy, ruled by the Tu'i Kanokupolu Dynasty, which stretches back to 1610. Tonga's economy is based on fishing, coconuts, bananas, vanilla, and coffee beans.

In 1987, Matt Nilson, a naturalized American citizen from Sweden who'd moved to Tonga after his retirement, met with Tonga's Crown Princess Salote Pilolevu Tuita to ask her to arrange a meeting with her father, King Taufa'ahau Tupou IV. Nilson, a PhD engineer and former executive of Intelsat, the international consortium of satellite operators, had a business proposition for the king. How would Tonga like to go into outer space?

Nilson had made a profit some years earlier through buying then reselling cellular phone spectrum (akin to frequency channels for TV and radio) in the United States. This maneuver—buying cellular spectrum before there is a strong market for it—is like land speculation, where you buy property adjacent to a planned housing complex, hoping that its value for a shopping mall will rise sharply someday.

Nilson had a novel idea for how the kingdom could benefit from getting in early on what promised to be a large market for satellite telecommunications services in the Pacific. Tonga should apply for unused licenses to operate communication satellites orbiting the equator above and to either side of the island nation. Tonga could use one of the new satellites to help the widely separated islands of the kingdom communicate with one another, and lease the remaining licenses to other satellite operators. Tupou found Nilson's arguments persuasive and told Nilson to pursue the idea further.

With Nilson's help, in 1988 Tonga applied to the International Frequency Registration Board in Geneva for licenses to operate twenty-seven unclaimed geostationary telecommunications satellites in the Asia Pacific region. A geostationary satellite orbits the Earth at an altitude of 22,500 miles, where the movement of the satellite exactly matches the rotational speed of the Earth. As a result, such satellites appear from the ground to be permanently fixed at one spot in the sky. This orbital stability is highly attractive for relaying communications from one point on the Earth to another, because only one satellite is needed to move signals over twelve thousand miles (the half circumference of the Earth each geostationary satellite can "see"). Satellites in lower orbits move across the sky and "see" less of the Earth's surface at any given time, so many more of them are needed to relay signals over long distances. However, in order to prevent mutual interference from radio transmissions to and from adjacent orbital slots, geostationary satellites must be separated from one another by two degrees, allowing for only 180 different slots around the 360-degree perimeter of the Earth. Geostationary slots are just like desirable beachfront property, there's only a limited supply. Tonga, representing just .000016 of the Earth's population, had applied for a whopping 15 percent of the entire world's supply of this scarce property. The application immediately raised the ire of the telecommunications industry. By gentleman's agreement, nations were only supposed to apply for slots that they could use. There was no way, so prevailing wisdom went, that a nation of 103,000 needed more than one satellite. And where was Tonga going to get the billions of dollars needed to buy, launch, and operate so many "geo birds"? The consensus in the satellite industry was that Tonga's application was a cynical violation of the loose rules that governed award of satellite slots—a kind of space grab. Dean Burch, director general of Intelsat, said, "The country's real motivation was to sell [slots] to the highest bidder," not to use the slots for their own telecommunications needs.

The same year Tonga filed its application, King Taufa'ahau Tupou authorized Nilson to set up a commercial venture that would act on behalf of the kingdom, leasing orbital slots and operating satellites. The company was named Friendly Islands Satellite Communications Ltd., but it is more commonly called Tongasat. Nilson, who provided seed funding for the new venture, owned 20 percent of the company, while Princess Salote Pilolevu Tuita owned 40 percent. The remaining shares were divided between two of Nilson's business partners. The Tongan government and royal family paid nothing for the princess's 40 percent stake.

Throughout the three-year campaign to secure the satellite licenses, both Nilson and the Tongan government denied they had exploited a loophole in licensing rules merely for profit. The International Frequency Registration Board agreed with them. In 1991, after Tongasat scaled back its application, the company was awarded six slots. The following year, Tongasat got a seventh slot. However, controversy continued to swirl around the Tongan venture. In 1993 Tongasat leased one of its slots, "134 East," to a Hong Kong operator who moved a satellite into the slot, only to discover that it was not possible to get clean signals to and from the spacecraft. Tonga suspected foul play. The lease to the Hong Kong firm had irritated Indonesia, which, by virtue of a murky handshake agreement, also operated a satellite at 134 East. Tonga alleged that Indonesia was jamming the Hong Kong satellite with high-power signals. An Indonesian satellite executive, when pressed, didn't deny the allegation, and the two nations eventually reached an agreement that allowed the Hong Kong satellite to operate unmolested.

A year later, Tongasat's board of directors dismissed Nilson as managing director following irregularities that surfaced in a PriceWaterhouse audit and allegations of conflict of interest. Nilson countered with a suit against Tongasat to secure his share of revenue and equity. The dispute was resolved with an out-of-court settlement, but the attorney general of Tonga tried to have the settlement nullified, on the grounds that Nilson had gotten far more value out of Tongasat than the Tongan people had. Pro-democracy advocates in the kingdom also argued that the royal family earned money from Tongasat that should have gone to the Tongan people. Tongasat became a rallying point for populist factions seeking to weaken the monarchy. Princess Pilolevu, a Christian, deflected all of the negative press around Tongasat, asserting that the company had a divine purpose: "I believe that God intended us to do this work otherwise we could have become just another foreigner knocking on doors in Beijing for years without having a chance to meet the leaders of China."

Tongasat, according to the princess, would help her kingdom convert Communist China to Christianity by leasing the Asian giant much needed communications channels and by establishing a Hong Kong office that would serve as a base for Tongan missionaries to evangelize Chinese on the mainland.

The princess's missionary ambitions with China did not bear fruit, but by 2008, Tongasat had made enough profit from leasing orbital slots to pay back a loan made to it by the government. Princess Pilolevu's share of the company, now 60 percent owing to a gift of one of the Tongasat owners at his death, was estimated to be worth about $25 million. That was one tenth of Tonga's entire 2008 gross national product (GNP). A solid big bang win for the Tongan royal family.

The blind spot in Intelsat's perception that allowed Nilson and Tonga to score this win was not just a failure of expectation. Intelesat also didn't *want* any nation to violate the gentleman's agreement that kept geostationary satellite applicants from getting greedy. Our brains not only tune out information we don't expect, but also information we don't want.

PUTTING BLIND SPOTS TO WORK FOR YOU WITH THE MAGIC MATRIX

On trips "downrange" to Iraq and Afghanistan, I frequently got drawn into brainstorming sessions with other intelligence and military officers about our terrorist adversaries. The conversations were always the same: how do we do a better job of finding "the bad guys"? Top-ranking insurgents and terrorists in particular had gotten very skilled at escaping detection, and the perpetual question before us was "How do they do it?" I can't describe the answers we came up with, but I can shed light on how we used awareness of the brain's blind spots to ask *questions* that sometimes led us to useful answers.

At one of the brainstorming sessions in Iraq, I explained that I was a neuroscientist and told the group about brain evolution and the blind spots we all have. I suggested that we might surface new ideas for finding terrorists by systematically looking for bad guys in our blind spots, while paying close attention to potential blind spots our adversaries might have. The group in Iraq hadn't known me long enough to roll their eyes at the prospect of yet another brain story, so they perked up. "Cool," they said, not fully realizing what they were in for. "Tell us more." So I went to a whiteboard and wrote:

Finished files are the result of years of scientific study
combined with the experience of years

I asked the group to count the number of Fs in the sentence. Most of them came back with "three." I smiled. "Look again." In about a minute, one of the officers said triumphantly, "Five!" "Keep looking," I urged. Finally, everyone said they saw all six Fs, three of which were lurking in the "of's" that we've learned to ignore as unimportant. Terrorists, I suggested, are like the Fs in the "of's": they hide where we won't look. Encouraged by nods and smiles around the table, I pressed on, drawing an eight-cell matrix:

	US	THEM
Expect		
Don't Expect		
Want		
Don't Want		

I explained again that our brains (and terrorist brains) see only what they expect and want, and that we might surface new clues by looking into both our blind spots and those of our enemies. We then filled in each cell of the matrix by asking, "Where do we expect bad guys to hide and *not* expect them to hide, and where do bad guys expect us to look and *not* to look?" Similarly, "Where do we want to find bad guys and *not* to find them, and where do they want to hide and *not* want to hide?" After about an hour we had filled in all eight cells and surfaced some promising ideas that hadn't previously occurred to us. Although I can't describe what these ideas were, I will say that the discussion was highly productive and that I use what I now call the "magic matrix" heavily in my management consulting practice. The matrix is especially helpful for clients who are engaged in a pitched battle with tough competitors. By far the most useful results come from clients adopting the point of view of their adversaries and imagining how the world looks, and more importantly *doesn't* look, to them. Most executives I know are so absorbed with internal problems that they rarely spend much time seeing the world through their competitors' eyes, and so they miss both big threats and big opportunities.

Winston Churchill was a big believer in doing this. After World War II he observed, "No matter how enmeshed a commander becomes in the elaboration of his own thoughts, it is sometimes necessary to take the enemy into account."

RECAP

Playing to Win

The Tony Award–winning producer David Merrick observed, "It's not enough that I should succeed—others should fail." If we're brutally honest with ourselves, we'll admit that our achievements are more satisfying when they stand out against a lack of accomplishment by our colleagues. But sometimes our accomplishments aren't just heightened by others' failures, they depend on those failures. This is the case in all competitive situations, such as football games, that pit one party against another.

The business world is also very competitive, where one organization often only wins if another loses. Bids for government contracts and licenses, and competitions for skilled workers, are just a few examples. Love can sometimes be win-lose, and war almost always is.

In each of these examples, it's important to look not only into our own blind spots for threats and opportunities, but to pay close attention to our *adversary's* blind spots as well. What we find there will be pure opportunity.

CHAPTER 6

Secret Weapons

POPULATION GENETICS AND BIG BANGS

Homo sapiens are a herd species. We depend on one another both for emotional support and for survival. We share useful information. We divide up labor on projects, assigning talent to task where possible, and we cooperate to get jobs done. In many ways we act not as individual organisms, but as parts of much larger composite organisms, such as families, tribes, companies, or nations.

We are hardwired to cooperate with one another because natural selection favored survival of our ancestors who banded together for common good. As part of the genetic programming that makes us cooperate, our brains evolved language and an exquisite ability to read not just facial expressions, but other nonverbal signals, such as gestures and posture, that tell us what others are thinking and feeling.

Given that we have evolved into a kind of collective organism comprised of different parts, it's natural to wonder whether evolution wanted those different parts to have the same skills, personalities, and temperaments. On the one hand, it would seem that groups made up of members who all had the same interests, personalities, and values would have been the most harmonious and effective. For example, if all members of a group had risk-averse temperaments, there would have been very few arguments about whether a group should pursue high-risk activities, like migrating to a distant land where game was rumored to be bountiful. Time and energy would not have been wasted fighting over such issues, and the group could have reached consensus and taken action quickly.

On the other hand, there is peril in "groupthink." The hypothetical ancestral group whose members all had low-risk temperaments might not have engaged in squabbles, but it might also have starved to death when local food supplies dried up and high-risk migration to unknown lands proved necessary.

Biologists who study sexual reproduction provide clues about whether wide differences in temperament, outlook, and personality might have a positive or negative net effect. The whole point of sex, these scientists believe, is to reshuffle and mix up genes to increase genetic diversity of the species as a whole. Organisms such as bacteria, which do not have sex but simply divide and pass on exact copies of their genes from one generation to another, are apt to go extinct when their environments change in ways that do not favor their genes. But organisms who do have sex, like humans, have offspring that are not only different from each parent, but different from their siblings because sexual reproduction randomly shuffles and recombines the genes of the two parents. These differences among individual humans come in very handy. For example, immune systems of individual humans genetically differ from one another, so pathogens, such as the plague bacteria, that kill one sibling may leave another unscathed. If all siblings had identical genes that were susceptible to the plague, then the entire family would die out.

So what do population genetics and resistance to plague have to do with the success of opportunities and organizations?

In any population, the mixing of two different sets of genes through sexual reproduction insures that there will be considerable variation among the genes of members of that population, and some of those varied genes will code for intelligence and personality traits. There is now very compelling evidence that personality traits such as agreeableness and introversion and cognitive abilities such as math and language prowess are heritable, and therefore subject to evolution through natural selection. Research also shows that like many heritable traits that are shuffled with sexual reproduction, personality and cognitive attributes vary significantly within and across families.

It's important to emphasize here that evolution does not favor variation in heritable traits simply for the sake of diversity. Rather, diversity in a population—be it a species, a family, or an organization—is only preserved when the net effect of that diversity, such as resistance to disease, helps the species as a whole survive. In many respects humans are astonishingly similar to one another in traits where diversity conveys no advantage. Almost all of us have the same vision, hearing, and predilection for language. We all walk upright and digest meat and plants with equal ease. Our genes only differ from one another by .1 percent, much less than comparable variation within other species such as apes and dogs.

When trait diversity persists from one generation to the next, there are usually sound evolutionary reasons for it. Evolutionary psychologists now believe that difference in temperament and personality within a group help that group survive in a number of ways. Everyone in a group can't be a leader, so groups are more cohesive and effective when some of their members are content with following while others want to lead. Also, the group as a whole benefits when some, but not all, of its members are risk takers. The risk takers will travel long distances into unexplored territory to find new resources for the group, while the more risk-averse will preserve and protect the resources the group already has.

Other dimensions of diversity also help groups maintain a wide mix of abilities that let them adapt and respond to uncertain, changing environments. We now know that human intelligence is not a unitary construct as was once believed—you're either smart or you're not—but has many distinct varieties. People with equal IQs for general intelligence differ widely in spatial abilities (such as drawing and sculpting), verbal skills, math skills, social skills, motor coordination, and musical skills. When individuals excel at one of these abilities, they tend not to be as good at the others. Thus, within any group, there will always be specialists who do what they do best as artisans and craftsmen, accountants, communicators, or athletes.

Evolution has decided that groups do better when they're comprised of specialists instead of generalists. The imperative to preserve cognitive and personality diversity has written a play in the brain's playbook that optimizes the mix of talents within groups. The play says to each individual brain, "Pick an important skill to excel at."

This means that even in enormous government bureaucracies there will always be visionary mavericks with unique personalities and skills to light long fuses to big bangs. Consider the case of China Lake and the Sidewinder missile.

A BANG SO BIG IT HAD TO BE STOLEN

The Chinese MiG-17 pilot was doomed. Even though his Russian fighter jet could fly higher than his opponent's F86, the Taiwanese F86 had managed to get behind him and launch a missile. The missile was some sort of secret weapon that the Americans had just given their anti-Communist allies, and it had proven incredibly effective in recent weeks, letting Taiwanese pilots shoot down over ten MiGs for every F86 they lost. The anxious MiG-17 pilot now understood why so many of his comrades had fallen victim to the American missile. No matter how hard he turned, he couldn't shake the fast-closing threat. The missile seemed to read his mind, anticipating and countering every move he made. Impact was only seconds away. This mystery weapon wasn't just a little better than those Taiwan had previously deployed against him and his brother pilots, it was a *lot* better. Like all fighter aircraft since World War I, to kill their opponents Taiwanese jets had been relying on machine guns that had a range of a few thousand feet. But this new American missile was lethal when fired from *miles* away. In a single leap, the Americans had made machine guns virtually obsolete in air-to-air combat.

It was the fall of 1958, at the height of the latest conflict between Taiwan and Mainland China. After the Communists had deposed the nationalist Chinese government of Chiang Kai-shek in 1947, the nationalists had retreated to the island of Taiwan, and skirmishes between the two powers continued. The current conflict had begun when the People's Republic attacked two nationalist islands in the Taiwan strait with artillery barrages. The confrontation had escalated into an air war between Communist MiGs and Taiwanese F86s.

The Chinese MiG pilot with the missile hot on his tail didn't eject before the weapon struck his jet. He may have thought he still had a chance to outmaneuver the missile, or he could have decided that ejecting from his plane was riskier than sticking with it. Many pilots died or were maimed while ejecting from fast-moving jets, as ejection seat technology was relatively new and unreliable. Whatever the pilot's reasons, his decision to stick with his plane proved to be a good one. Although the missile hit him, it failed to explode, leaving his jet damaged, but flyable. The pilot limped back to an air base and landed safely. As he inspected his plane for damage, the pilot was astonished to find that he'd returned to base with more weaponry than he'd left with. The enemy's mysterious new missile was lodged firmly in his fuselage. The pilot must have smiled as he realized he'd just become a hero. His masters and their allies in Moscow had been desperate to get their hands on this devastating new weapon, code-named Sidewinder, in order to reverse engineer it, build their own version, and restore parity to Russian and American air-to-air weapons. The sense of urgency was heightened by the fact that the new missile not only had much longer range than machine guns, but also possessed "fire and forget" capability. With guns, pilots had to constantly maneuver their jets to lock their sights on an enemy. But with the new missiles, pilots simply had to line up the shot, "pickle off" the long-range missile, and let the missile's brain do the rest while the pilots searched for new kills.

The new weapon was literally a long fuse, big bang.

Although the Russians eventually did reverse engineer the Sidewinder, naming their own version the K-13/R3-S, they only partially closed the gap in air-to-air capabilities. The first R3 S1 was inferior to the American version, and to make matters worse, the Americans kept improving Sidewinder, faster than the Russians could copy it. How did the Americans pull off the Sidewinder miracle, and how did they keep adding to it with one innovation after another?

DON'T CALL IT A MISSILE

The Sidewinder missile and its Russian clone traced their roots to a small research project begun twelve years before that fateful dogfight over the Taiwan Strait. Bill McLean, a physicist at the Naval Ordnance Test Station at China Lake, California, was exploring new ways to guide air-to-air weapons to their targets. Recently appointed head of a division that designed weapon guidance systems, Dr. McLean was concerned that the traditional way navy fighters had shot down opposing aircraft—with machine guns—wouldn't work against fast-moving jet fighters. The Germans had actually deployed jet fighters late in World War II, and it was only a matter of time before the Russians would field them too. What was needed, McLean believed, was a seeker that could automatically track the rapid movements of an enemy jet and guide a weapon all the way from launch to impact.

McLean had experience with guided weapons, having worked at the National Bureau of Standards in Washington pioneering the development of the first fully autonomous self-guided weapon, the BAT. This weapon, which was basically a large model airplane with radar in its nose and a warhead in its belly, saw action in the Pacific in the closing days of World War II. After launch, the BAT's radar would look for reflections from a metallic target, lock on to the target, and guide the small aircraft all the way to impact. The BAT was crude by modern standards, but it destroyed enough Japanese ground targets to prove that smart weapons could work.

Despite his success with radar guidance against ground targets in the BAT, McLean didn't think radar was the right choice for tracking aircraft. Radars were bulky, expensive, complex, and finicky, and would require pilots who launched radar-guided weapons to lock their radars on the target all the way to missile impact to guide their weapon home. The naval aviators at China Lake didn't want to babysit a weapon after launch, preferring instead to "fire and forget." But there were two major obstacles to developing fire-and-forget weapons that didn't use radar. First, the only alternative at the time, heat seeking, had never worked. Although all aircraft engines emitted strong heat signatures, no one had ever managed to track them with the rudimentary infrared (thermal) imagers available in the 1940s. Second, the Pentagon had decided that radars *were* viable for air combat and had thrown not just its weight, but its funding, behind radar-guided missiles.

In theory, radar seekers—unlike thermal trackers—could track enemy aircraft through clouds and thus provide an "all weather" attack capability. McLean and many of his colleagues at China Lake argued that tracking air targets through clouds had little value, because the majority of dogfights occurred above the clouds, where the complexity, cost, and low reliability of radar trackers made them much less desirable than far simpler, cheaper infrared trackers. But the Pentagon had turned a deaf ear to such arguments and officially endorsed radar missile seekers. To make matters worse for McLean, most of the brass in the Pentagon didn't want China Lake developing any new weapons at all. The remote navy station in the Mojave Desert was ideal for testing weapons, not designing them. "It's not your job," one irritated Washington official told McLean's boss when informed China Lake wanted to invent air-to-air missiles. This official had succumbed to a type of functional fixity common in large bureaucracies, where managers can't imagine uses for an organization beyond its stated purpose. Just as most college students in the pliers-rope experiment struggle to see a tool as more than a tool, most of the Pentagon failed to see China Lake, with all its world-class scientists and engineers, as more than a place to test weapons designed by others.

But Bill McLean was not burdened by such functional fixity. He kept his unorthodox activity going with discretionary funds that Washington didn't audit, advancing the state of the art of thermal imaging and tracking technology. This was decades before procurement scandals eliminated such "slush funds," so McLean had much more latitude than his modern counterparts would have in performing research without obtaining prior approval.

Having worked in Washington, McLean understood the perils of doing research in areas that senior officials didn't favor. Bureaucrats were capable of sniffing out and killing competing projects that weren't strictly in their jurisdiction by bad-mouthing the projects to Congress, who would then slash funds for the project. Thus, even though he didn't need approval from official Washington for his infrared seeker project, McLean hid it from them. Instead of calling the project "Infrared Missile Seeker," he labeled it "Special Fuse Project 602." If he were ever audited, he could argue that he was indirectly doing missile fuse research, since all missile warheads needed fuses, and all fuses needed guidance on when and where to ignite. With all of this obfuscation and misdirection, China Lake was taking care to hide their secret weapon from prying eyes in both Moscow *and* Washington.

For the next five years Bill McLean and his team of navy scientists and engineers worked discreetly on infrared missile technology. When the China Lake group improved infrared sensors to the point where they accurately tracked aircraft from the ground, McLean needed much more money than he had in his discretionary account to incorporate an infrared seeker into a prototype missile. China Lake did have a few influential allies in Washington, including the navy's Bureau of Ordnance, who found money to keep McLean's project going. But the funding from the bureau came with strong advice: "Don't call it a missile." As McLean's project slowly grew, its name kept changing. At one point it was Local Project 612, then Feasibility Study 567. By 1951 work on the project—now named Sidewinder after a local pit viper that used infrared pits to track warm-blooded prey—had progressed so well that China Lake's allies in Washington felt they could bring Sidewinder out of hiding and make it an official missile program.

McLean and China Lake were given sufficient funds to design, build, and test a complete infrared missile. However, they were still cautioned to keep a low profile because the Pentagon had approved full production of two radar-guided air-to-air missiles: the Falcon and the Sparrow. As long as Sidewinder remained an obscure project, it wouldn't threaten the funding for these big-ticket missile projects. But if Sidewinder successes ever prompted Congress to challenge funding for Falcon and Sparrow, it was a sure bet that powerful proponents of the radar missiles would mount an all-out effort to shoot down China Lake's heat-seeking weapon.

Over the next two years, the Sidewinder team designed, tested, redesigned, and retested the missile twelve times. Lieutenant Wally Schirra, who would ultimately become one of America's first astronauts, fired the first test shot. That shot, and eleven others that followed, all missed their radio-controlled air targets over China Lake's test ranges. There were vibration problems, there was interference from electrical noise, there were difficulties with power sources, and so forth. When the team fixed one of these glitches, another new one would crop up. Acutely aware that their failures were being noted by radar missile advocates, the Sidewinder team began to experience flagging morale. Then, on September 11, 1953, Sidewinder scored its first success. Although it did not actually strike the unmanned drone aircraft, painstaking analysis of film from cameras that tracked the missile showed that Sidewinder had flown so close to its unmanned aircraft target that it would have destroyed the target if the missile had been armed with a proximity-fused warhead that exploded when it sensed that a target was within lethal range. The success was no accident; later tests also succeeded, showing that the navy had at last developed a workable fire-and-forget weapon capable of destroying fast-moving jet aircraft.

A FLASHLIGHT AND STEPLADDER

After the Sidewinder's success on the test range, navy leadership in the Pentagon could no longer ignore the promise of thermally guided missiles. The navy officially adopted the Sidewinder for use on its aircraft carrier fighters and designated it for production as the AIM-9 (Air Intercept Missile 9). The navy's decision was made easier by continuing difficulties with the Sparrow and Falcon radar-guided missiles. As McLean had predicted, radar seekers were proving too complex and unreliable for the rigors of air-to-air combat. The vast array of electronics needed to generate and process radar signals, and receive radio guidance from pilots to control the missile's flight path, made radar missiles as complicated as the fighter jets that carried them.

The Sidewinder, in contrast, was incredibly simple. Dr. Howie Wilcox, a lead engineer on Sidewinder, said the inexpensive missile had "the electronic complexity of a table top radio and the mechanical complexity of a washing machine." As a result, the Sidewinder was smaller, lighter, and far cheaper than either the Sparrow or the Falcon.

But the air force, who operated far more fighters than the navy, was not sold on Sidewinder. Air force leaders continued to succumb to the lure of the all-weather capability of radar technology, even though their own radar seeker projects were floundering. Bill McLean and Howie Wilcox had tried several times to sell Sidewinder to the air force. Dr. Wilcox took the lead in many of the sales pitches, bringing with him the perfect salesman's personality. Where McLean was reserved and cerebral, Wilcox was affable and accessible. He had a million-volt smile, drew amusing stick figure cartoons, and exuded natural charm. When Wilcox got down to business, he showed the air force films of one Sidewinder kill after another. Then, in easy-to-understand language, he described Sidewinder's projected manufacturing costs (low) and ease of operation and maintenance (high). But Wilcox's charisma and impressive data ultimately failed to persuade the air force to drop its all-radar missile posture. The China Lakers, whose motto was "Perfect is the enemy of good enough," were frustrated by this intransigence. By pursuing a "perfect" all-weather missile, the air force was overlooking a missile that was good enough for most air combat situations.

Growing up at China Lake, I often heard the "perfect is the enemy of good enough" credo along with another one that characterized Bill McLeans's next move: "A no is just a slow yes." Through influential contacts at Caltech, where he had gotten his PhD, McLean arranged to meet a special assistant to the secretary of the air force, Trevor Gardner, and offer him a challenge. The air force should sponsor a "shoot-off" between Sidewinder and Falcon. If Sidewinder won, the air force would incorporate the infrared missile into its arsenal. Gardner accepted the challenge, and a shoot-off was arranged at New Mexico's Holloman Air Force Base in June of 1955.

The contest soon turned into a Rocky Balboa–meets–Apollo Creed encounter. The air force gave its Falcon every advantage, including the latest fighter jets to launch the missiles, hundreds of technicians, and rooms full of sophisticated support and test equipment. The navy underdogs were given an aging fighter to launch their Sidewinders, one corner of an old hangar, and no technicians or test equipment. Incensed by the unfairness of this arrangement, McLean went to the Falcon team leader and demanded some added equipment. When asked what he required, McLean said, "How about a flashlight and a stepladder?"

McLean, of course, was rubbing it in. Sidewinder was so simple, it didn't need armies of technicians or rooms of equipment. The night before the first test, while the air force literally cradled the Falcon in cotton to protect its delicate electronics, McLean ordered that the Sidewinder be mounted on the aging fighter that would launch it the next day. A night out in the open would "do it good," McLean explained.

The next day, after winning a coin toss to go first, the Sidewinder flew flawlessly, destroying its radio-controlled target drone with a direct hit. The Falcon went next, but was unable to launch when air force engineers couldn't release the complex interlocks that prevented the missile from firing accidentally. Sidewinder went again, this time flying up the tailpipe of its target. Falcon failed to launch, let alone hit any targets, for all of its remaining tests. Sidewinder had decisively won the shoot-off . . . or so China Lake thought.

In the weeks that followed the Holloman test, air force officials argued that Sidewinder had still not proven itself, because none of the tests were against high-altitude targets, such as bombers capable of delivering nuclear weapons. A thermally guided missile, they argued, could easily be "blinded by the sun" when looking up at high-altitude bombers. Radar-guided missiles could not be blinded in this way.

At first, this new obstacle seemed insurmountable. Sidewinder was capable of climbing to well over forty thousand feet, but neither the air force nor the navy had any test drones that could fly that high. China Lake thought about the challenge and came back to the air force with a highly unorthodox proposal. What if a fighter took off with two weapons, an unguided rocket that would launch first and climb to a high altitude and a Sidewinder that would launch second, catching up to and shooting down the first rocket.

The air force was skeptical. China Lake was essentially proposing to shoot down one bullet with another, something that had never been done before. However, believing they had nothing to lose by letting China Lake attempt the bizarre experiment, the air force consented and set up a second test at Holloman in August 1955. During this test, pilots launched six unguided rockets, each followed by a Sidewinder to track it down. Based on visual sightings, the pilots reported that all six Sidewinders flew to within "lethal distances," where a proximity fuse (which ignited when a missile's warhead was close enough to a target to destroy it) would have destroyed real targets. Word of the success spread rapidly through the close-knit community of air force fighter pilots, and a groundswell of support for Sidewinder mounted.

Later analysis of test footage of the six Sidewinder shots showed that the Holloman test pilots' visual reports were wrong. Most of the Sidewinders had not passed within lethal distance of their targets. But the negative reports came too late to derail the Sidewinder. Rank-and-file air force pilots were by now so firmly behind the thermally guided missile that its inclusion in the air force inventory became inevitable. The air force formally welcomed Sidewinder into its service in 1956. Ten years after it had begun in secrecy, Special Fuse Project 602 had hit the big time.

The most important part of the Sidewinder story is not what Bill McLean managed to do, but what his protectors in Washington did. The Navy Bureau of Weapons, to which China Lake reported in the 1940s, preserved much needed diversity within the missile development program by funding McLean and helping him hide his novel approach to tracking enemy jets until it was mature enough to withstand the inevitable attacks from powerful Washington insiders.

In every organization, there are almost always people like McLean who are pursuing long fuse, big bang visions in secret. Just as trait diversity insures that any group will have mavericks, it also insures that there will be a healthy number of conservative, orthodox thinkers, many of them in leadership positions, who are uncomfortable with the mavericks' risky ideas. Mavericks everywhere understand this and take pains to hide their work from "the powers that be" until the work is so far along that it can stand on its own.

I have seen this phenomenon repeat itself over and over again. At Disney Imagineering R&D, we even called some of our secret work "Sidewinder projects" in honor of the master of obfuscation, Bill McLean. The head mounted display now used in Disney VR attractions at Epcot was just such a project. We had to keep the design a secret from my immediate superior, who insisted on a much more complex, "perfect is the enemy of good enough" approach.

To be a radical change agent, you don't necessarily have to come up with the radical ideas yourself; someone else in your enterprise will already be thinking outside the box. If you're a leader or wield influence in your group, your job is to find these mavericks, feed them resources under the table, and help them stay in your organization's blind spot until their work is far enough along to withstand attacks from conservative adversaries.

The Navy Bureau of Weapons succeeded with this strategy because they had executive authority and money that they could bootleg to China Lake. But what if you want to foster a "Sidewinder project" of your own and don't have authority or money; can you still ignite a long fuse, big bang project?

The remarkable stories of CIA officers Don Burke and Sean Dennehy—who played major roles in reforming America's Intelligence Community—suggest that you can.

THE OUTSIDER

When I first met Don Burke in 2006, I noticed something different about him. Thin and just over six feet, with sandy hair and lively blue eyes, Don looked like someone had taken him apart and put his parts back together slightly off kilter. His movements were stiff and a little awkward. When he smiled, it was only with his eyes, as if his mouth wanted to smile too but couldn't keep up with the rest of his face.

I later learned that Don suffered from a form of muscular dystrophy called FSHD that did make it hard for him to smile. Born and raised in Garrison Keillor's hometown, Anoka, Minnesota, Don first learned that he had the hereditary disease when he couldn't do a single sit-up, pull-up, or push-up in the President's Physical Fitness Program in middle school. Trips to the doctor revealed that he had developed the same disease that had stricken his grandmother.

Because Don didn't show any other evidence of his disease, his classmates assumed he was healthy, but wimpy. "Other kids ridiculed and taunted me for my skinny arms and clumsiness," Don said. Healthy up until the age of thirteen, Don now felt like an outsider. "You have two choices when you get that kind of scorn," he told me. "You can either go inside yourself into a protective shell, or learn to value yourself despite the criticism."

Don chose the second approach. A gifted student, he graduated from Embry Riddle Aeronautical University and eventually joined the CIA, where he developed new technology for collecting and analyzing intelligence. In a roundabout way Don's disease helped him quickly advance through the ranks of CIA officers. Never knowing when he might lose the ability to get around on his own, Don didn't wait to pursue promising new technologies. He cut through red tape whenever possible, earning a reputation for getting a lot done in a short amount of time. By 2005 Don had moved up into a middle management position in CIA's Science and Technology Directorate, where he led a team of engineers and technology analysts helping officers collect and analyze intelligence. "The job was sort of like Q in the James Bond movies," Don explained. His group didn't engage in day-to-day operations, but supported those at CIA who did.

As with Q, most of Don's work aided in outfitting officers with high-tech gadgets. A large component of the work required developing knowledge management tools that helped find and distill information from the agency's, and the broader Intelligence Community's, vast and bewilderingly complex data warehouse to facilitate a particular mission—a task that was increasingly similar to traditional intelligence analysis.

Intelligence analysts are basically detectives who sift through mounds of raw intelligence and write reports on the capabilities and intentions of foreign powers and terrorists. Analysts try to gather as much information as they can about their foreign targets, whether those targets are individuals or organizations. The best analysts immerse themselves in every detail of the targets' environment in order to "get inside their heads" and learn to think like their targets, so that they can better understand previous target actions and predict future actions. This task has grown steadily more difficult over the past twenty years, as the information revolution created an explosion of data that qualified as intelligence. Some analysts, for instance, are technologists who study foreign technology such as communications equipment. In the 1960s, a country like the Soviet Union would have designed, built, and operated its own communications technology, with the result that an analyst looking for information on that technology was confined to a fairly limited search space. But today, some of the most sophisticated communications technology that an adversary might use, such as an iPhone, is available to everyone. Thus, an analyst investigating communications technology has to study not just specially designed foreign technology, but a much larger, fast-growing inventory of commercial and consumer technology. Now traditional intelligence analysts and technology analysts are being swamped by a tsunami of information.

After 9/11, the CIA hired more analysts to help cope with this information overload, but the volume of relevant information has been growing much
faster than the intelligence workforce. Part of Don's job was to help analysts
use new information technology to bridge the growing gap between the number of analysts and the amount of information to be analyzed. In contrast to
the Cold War era, when the CIA and other national security agencies spent
hundreds of millions of dollars to develop their own special technologies, much
of Don's effort focused on adapting tools developed by commercial companies such as Google, Oracle, and Microsoft. Although intelligence information remains supersecret, increasingly the tools that Don and other officers
use to store, organize, retrieve, and analyze massive amounts of intelligence
are the same as those used by knowledge workers everywhere.

By 2005, Don had caught the attention of a senior manager in the CIA's
Directorate of Science and Technology (DS&T) who had been keeping a close
eye on the information revolution and its growing impact on the DS&T's
mission. The senior manager wondered how the rapid advances in technology
might force the DS&T to reevaluate its traditional structure and whether, in
fact, it had already reshaped work roles. For example, most DS&T officers
were trained to manage technology development projects or to operate intelligence technology in the field, not to analyze technologies of foreign powers.

So this senior manager wanted Don Burke, who'd shown a capacity for
out-of-the-box thinking, to find an answer to a question that had perplexed the
leaders of the Directorate of Science and Technology: "In today's fast changing world, what exactly is an analyst?" If the answer came back "a lot of technologists working in the DS&T," the organization would have to chart a
new course. Their hiring, training, and promotion strategies would have to
change to reflect an added mission to help analyze other people's technology
as well as inventing CIA technology. For example, engineers who invent new
gadgets are often not content to study other inventors' work. The DS&T had
traditionally hired doers instead of analyzers, and might not have the right
mix of temperaments for the growing analytic workload. Moreover, intelligence analysis requires lengthy, specialized training in investigatory technique, writing, and objective assessment, training that DS&T technologists
rarely got.

The DS&T also needed to know if the definition of "intelligence analyst"
had changed because the charter to perform intelligence analysis belonged

to a completely separate organization, the CIA's Directorate of Intelligence (DI). The DI's job was to hire analysts, train them, and focus them on writing intelligence reports and assessments on every conceivable topic from crop failures in Central Asia to terrorist threats to America's homeland. The DI was also home to several scientists and engineers who reported on developments in foreign weapons and technology. The DS&T's increasing involvement in technology analysis had blurred the traditional division of labor between it and the DI, raising potentially thorny issues of bureaucratic responsibility and "turf." If the DS&T's work was going to increasingly encroach on the DI's charter, then DS&T leadership needed to anticipate and figure out how to cope with the problem.

Don spent four months exploring "What is an analyst?" as "Study #1." He interviewed a wide variety of DS&T officers and gained deep insights into the way CIA really ran, as opposed to the way it was *supposed* to run. For example, as in most enterprises, the official CIA organization chart, which defined who reported to whom, often had less impact on the day-to-day activities of employees than the unofficial, unstructured web of informal relationships that defined who knew and *liked* whom. Don discovered that officers whose formal job description was "doer" were acting more and more like "analyzers," helping DI officers that they knew and respected understand foreign technologies. DS&T scientists and engineers were answering a long list of questions about how different technologies worked, what their strengths and weaknesses were, and so forth. These technical insights helped the DI make crucial assessments. Was new foreign technology ready for operation? Was it better or worse than our own technology? How could it be defeated?

During his "out brief" on Study #1 to the director of the DS&T, Stephanie O'Sullivan, Don observed that the DS&T's ability to analyze technology was hampered by the lack of a single repository for relevant technical information. A great deal of useful technical data was effectively lost because it was stored in people's heads, on individual PCs, or sequestered on segregated data networks where very few people could access it. Also, barriers to sharing classified information prevented technologists from talking to one another about their work, so there was considerable duplication of effort when the same information was dug up, communicated to a niche customer, and salted away in some private cache. Finally, as many baby boomers retired from the agency, useful technical information was "walking out the door" as senior officers took their knowledge with them.

Stephanie thanked Don for his work, and asked him if he would explore ways to help the DS&T officers improve their ability to "capture what we know." Don considered Stephanie's question carefully. He knew that such requests had been made many times before, and the initiatives always withered because concentrating so much technical information in one easy-to-access archive would run against the grain of the CIA's culture. The agency relied heavily on human "assets" (foreigners who gather intelligence on our behalf), who would be killed if their identities or the way they used technology were leaked. CIA officer Aldrich Ames, for example, had given the names of several assets to the KGB, who subsequently arrested, tortured, and executed the Russian nationals. Everyone at the CIA knew that when you shared information, you put lives at risk.

Technical information was rarely as sensitive as assets' identities, but CIA officers had formed the habit of protecting *all* of the agency's secrets as if people's lives depended on it. Classified documents were therefore stored in hundreds of tightly controlled "compartments" that could only be accessed by a few officers with "need to know." Persuading these officers to share knowledge about classified technology was going to be monumentally difficult. Although sharing technical information could increase the CIA's effectiveness and save more lives than it threatened, agency veterans would view anyone who tried to pry secrets out of their heads as dangerous to the CIA's sacred mission. Don realized that accepting Stephanie's challenge could make him more of an outsider than muscular dystrophy ever had.

The decision wasn't difficult. He told Stephanie that he'd see what could be done to tear down barriers to sharing that had been in place for sixty years. If Don could survive the scorn of teenagers who thought he was a wimp, he could certainly survive the scorn of CIA officers who thought he was dangerous.

For the next few months Don worked on "Study #2," sniffing around the agency to learn if anyone else was attempting to consolidate technical information. One way for the DS&T to "capture what we know" in a single place would be to piggyback onto a unified archive that others at the CIA had already started. Despite the CIA's deeply ingrained need-to-know culture, Don thought it likely that some of the younger, tech-savvy officers who'd joined the CIA since 9/11 would try to create at work the same social networking and collaboration tools, such as Wikipedia, that they used at home.

Don's intuition turned out to be correct. The CIA's IT department had deployed a small-scale trial of a wiki where their computer scientists and technicians could share knowledge about networks, computers, and communications systems. As with Wikipedia, any registered user could write articles or edit other people's articles.

After getting a user account and trying out IT's wiki, Don decided that it wouldn't meet the DS&T's needs. The pilot project had a cumbersome interface that was hard for anyone but computer programmers to use. Also, the wiki was confined to the CIA's private internal network, which would make it inaccessible to CIA officers deployed at other agencies or intelligence technologists at agencies such as the NSA.

Don thought that this last restriction would be particularly problematic because the digital revolution had blurred the lines between technology that was useful for the CIA's missions and technology that was useful to missions of other agencies. For example, the CIA had historically focused heavily on technology to support collection of "HUMINT" (intelligence from human assets), such as miniature cameras and clandestine communication devices, while other agencies concentrated on large radio antennas for SIGINT (signals intelligence), large telescopes for IMINT (image intelligence), and custom sensors for MASINT (chemical, biological, and radiation signals intelligence). But by 2005 all of the agencies were using the same technology—especially computers—for much of their work.

For instance, the CIA used computers to store and analyze HUMINT, the NSA to analyze SIGINT, and the National Geospatial-Intelligence Agency (NGA) to analyze IMINT. The CIA could clearly benefit from learning about advances in computer science at different agencies, just as other agencies would benefit from computer advances at the CIA. Therefore, the ideal information sharing system for the DS&T to "piggyback" onto would be one that was open to the CIA's sister agencies. Don kept looking.

Eventually, Don stumbled upon an obscure wiki. You had to know the exact Web address to find it, and only a handful of people in the sprawling Intelligence Community knew of its existence. Unlike the CIA's IT wiki, this new wiki, called Intellipedia, ran on a network called Intelink that was available to the entire Intelligence Community and military. Intelink was a government-only Web for intelligence and military users to communicate with one another and to publish reports that could have wide distribution, such as long-range assessments, reference information, and other data that was not ultrasensitive. After making a few dozen contributions to Intellipedia, Don crossed paths with another CIA officer participating in the information sharing experiment, DI analyst Sean Dennehy. Sean, who managed a group of analysts reporting on Iraq, was spearheading an effort to use Intellipedia as a kind of "Iraqipedia" where civilian and military intelligence officers could share useful information that wouldn't otherwise be available to them.

The war in Iraq had created an insatiable appetite for this kind of information, as intelligence analysts and battlefield commanders looked for clues about how to counter the growing insurgency and sectarian violence in Iraq. As with Wikipedia, Sean's goal for Intellipedia was for the new wiki to have no single editor who determined what material got published; all registered users could post and edit articles from other contributors. This democratic approach to content creation and editing would be a radical departure from the way intelligence agencies had operated for sixty years. Traditionally, managers of different "offices" such as Iraq had edited reports written by analysts working for them and decided who could receive the reports. The reports then went out to a restricted mailing list and were only updated by the organization that had authored them. Intellipedia could transform this one-to-many paradigm into a many-to-many paradigm.

For the first time, many different points of view on a particular intelligence question could be aired in a single article. An original posting of an intelligence report to Intellipedia might assert, for example, that the majority of foreign fighters in Iraq came from country X, with funding from jihadist organization Y. As analysts who had conflicting information read this report, they could edit it, adding alternate interpretations to the original conclusions, along with references backing up their claims. All versions of the original report and subsequent edits were saved, so that users could track the history of the discussion that produced the current edition of the report and form their own conclusions about which of the conflicting assertions were accurate. The net result of this democratic, give-and-take process was intelligence reporting that was both comprehensive and balanced.

Formal intelligence reports are like motion pictures; lots of content ends up on the cutting room floor, where audiences never see it. Unlike the movies, however, intelligence that's edited out can be incredibly valuable to some members of its audience. For example, some reports are written for very high-level "customers," such as the President, who don't want all the details of a particular issue, just the highlights. But other consumers of intelligence, such as military and law enforcement officers, might be intensely interested in the very details that would bore a President. Which dock in a large port did a particular ship leave from? Who are the captain's brothers, cousins, and classmates from school? What ports did the ship visit before it departed from its last one? This kind of detail can be crucial to officers trying to trace movements of people and material, or to flesh out complex relationships among key actors. Intellipedia let anyone in the military or the Intelligence Community with a clearance author and edit articles, providing a single place to store and retrieve such information on Iraq.

During the course of their month-long correspondence inside the wiki, Sean and Don realized that they shared a passion for improving information sharing at the agency. In March 2006, they decided to meet face-to-face for lunch, to get to know each other better and decide what, if anything, they should do about this realization.

At lunch, Don learned that Sean's journey into the community wiki bore striking similarities to his own. Just as the DS&T struggled to "capture what we know" in a single place, the DI's knowledge was scattered across many different databases, desktop files, and the memories of DI officers. As with the DS&T, DI officers followed the principle of "need to know" as opposed to "need to share," further limiting analysts' access to useful information. Sean had been keenly aware of this problem since leaving his job as an air force military intelligence officer in 1998 and joining DI as a foreign military analyst. Assigned to Iraq for the past five years, Sean had studied the country's air defenses before the war, then hunted Saddam Hussein from a base in Iraq in late 2003. Throughout his five years working Iraq, Sean and his fellow DI analysts had been severely hampered by lack of access to "unfinished intelligence" such as working notes, background material, and unpublished ideas and hypotheses that DI analysts developed while working on formally published intelligence reports. Such unfinished material was often much more valuable to analysts than finished reports, because it contained leads, clues, details, and speculations that provided rich context lacking in formal publications.

The Office of Iraq Analysis where Sean worked had archived some of this informal data into an "Iraq Papers Database," but only analysts in the Iraq office had access to it. Hence, officers who might benefit from the Iraq Papers Database, such as DI analysts working Iran, Syria, or Al Qaeda, had to get by without it. To make matters worse, even Iraq analysts with full access to the papers database struggled to find what they needed because the database's clumsy search tool returned either too many or too few relevant hits.

Concerned that this problem was severely limiting the DI's ability to analyze targets in Iraq, Sean volunteered to find a way to expand the DI's access to its own Iraq data and make searching the data much easier. As part of this effort, Sean attended a talk in early 2005 by a CIA IT officer named D. Calvin Andrus, who had just won the Intelligence Community's Galileo Competition for writing up innovative ideas. Andrus's idea, expressed in his winning paper *The Wiki and the Blog: Towards a Complex Adaptive Intelligence Community,* was audacious and controversial. He proposed that intelligence analysts shift to a Web 2.0 mind-set and do their thinking and note taking in public as they prepared finished intelligence reports. Instead of writing Word files that they stored locally on their own PCs, or ultimately in niche archives such as the Iraq Papers Database, Andrus argued that analysts should capture their thoughts in blogs and wikis so that many different people could see them and improve upon them—even before they were published. "Everyone at the briefing laughed at this suggestion," Sean said, "including me. Like everybody else I thought it was wildly impractical, given CIA's culture."

Nevertheless, Andrus's talk prompted Sean to check out Wikipedia for the first time to see what all the fuss over Web 2.0 was about. As he surfed through the open source encyclopedia, Sean had an epiphany. Wikipedia was organized in a manner that not only let everyone see works in progress, background material, and hyperlinked references (footnotes you could click on to get to an article), but that also kept meticulous track of versions. Wikipedia's hyperlinked footnoting and comprehensive version history were precisely what the DI's Iraq office needed to answer the barrage of questions it had been receiving from Congress and the WMD Commission about Iraq's WMD program: "What did you know and when did you know it?" "What were your sources and references for reaching those conclusions?" "Who authored which part of a particular report?" The DI's knowledge management system had not been equal to this task, requiring tens of thousands of labor hours for analysts to manually sort through archives and reconstruct each document's provenance.

As he dug deeper into Wikipedia, Sean realized that he had found not only a way to solve the unfinished intelligence problem, but also a much better way for the DI to answer the inevitable questions that would arise whenever they reported on controversial subjects such as Iraq WMD.

Just as Don Burke did, Sean cast about the agency looking for embryonic wikis, stumbling upon the same IT wiki that Don later found. Sean didn't think the internal wiki would solve the DI's problem for the same reason Don ultimately rejected it: the IT wiki didn't connect outside the CIA. From his experience in air force intelligence, Sean knew that officers outside of the CIA could help the agency and themselves if they had access to the CIA's unfinished intelligence and could contribute material of their own. Sean kept looking.

In the summer of 2005, Sean and Cal Andrus met with the Intelink Management Office, whose main job was to foster better cooperation and information sharing across the community. Encouraged by the prospect of working with an organization whose job was to foster sharing of information, not hoard it, Sean sought out the leader of the Intelink office, an officer we'll call Randy. Randy shared Sean's new enthusiasm for Web 2.0 and the potential it held for the community, but he knew that the wiki he planned to deploy wouldn't flourish without an operational customer who needed it to accomplish their mission. At their first meeting in May, Sean and Randy realized each offered a solution to the other's problem. Randy offered Sean a community-wide wiki, while Sean offered Randy a bona fide customer.

Sean went back to the DI and pitched the idea of putting the Iraq Papers Database on the new Intelink wiki. Realizing that CIA officers were instinctively nervous about disseminating intelligence outside of the Agency, Sean didn't try to sell his concept as a post-9/11 improvement to cross-agency information sharing. Rather he emphasized the speed (immediate), very low cost (zero), and ease of access for DI analysts inside and outside of the Iraq office. His bosses gave him a cautious "go ahead," and Sean worked with Randy and his team to beta test the wiki. The wiki, now called Intellipedia, officially went online in November 2005. Three months later, Don bumped into Sean in the wiki, and a month after that they met for lunch to plot their next moves.

At lunch that day in March 2006, Don and Sean agreed that Intellipedia could evolve into something far more than a repository for unfinished DI intelligence on Iraq or technical information for the DS&T. The new wiki had brought strangers from different organizations—Sean and Don—together for the first time, suggesting exciting possibilities for the rest of the Intelligence Community. Even though the DI and the DS&T belonged to the same agency, they often struggled to communicate with each other or cooperate on joint projects. But now, thanks to the wiki, two officers from different directorates were having lunch, exploring ways to cooperate. Don and Sean imagined the possibilities if tens of thousands of intelligence officers in sixteen different agencies participated in Intellipedia. Many different analysts who worked in separate agencies across the sprawling community studied the same intelligence targets—such as Al Qaeda—but never spoke to one another or compared notes. Given these overlapping interests, how many cross-agency friendships would form in Intellipedia? How many follow-up lunches—like the one they were having—would there be in "real space" to discuss common problems and common solutions? In an era where agencies were hiring tens of thousands of young officers from the Facebook generation, the answer seemed obvious: Intellipedia didn't just have the potential to improve the Intelligence Community, it could completely transform it.

A few weeks later Don met with Stephanie to present a proposal that he and Sean had agreed to. The DS&T should help transform Intellipedia into a community-wide platform for sharing information on all subjects relevant to the Intelligence Community's mission, including technical data, as well as intelligence on Iraq *and* on all other countries. Stephanie immediately liked the idea. Intellipedia would be a major first step in implementing the nation's new intelligence strategy, which called for increased information sharing to prevent another 9/11 and reduced groupthink to avoid another Iraq WMD fiasco. She told Don to "keep going."

Don was excited about expanding Study #2 to encompass sharing of intelligence across the Intelligence Community and the military, not just technical information within the CIA. But he was concerned about the formidable obstacles that lay ahead. He and Sean had no budget or staff and would almost certainly experience "blowback" from veteran officers for trying to put compartmented intelligence at risk. To CIA traditionalists, widening the dissemination of technical information within the DS&T would be bad enough, but exposing actual CIA intelligence reports to other agencies would be catastrophic. Don also worried that, except for a handful of officers like Sean and Stephanie, very few people at the CIA saw a need to improve information sharing or to make the reporting process more democratic.

Henry Ford once observed, "If I had asked my customers what they wanted, they would have said a faster horse." Thus, Ford built his first cars hoping that customers who didn't think they needed them would actually buy them. Don and Sean were in the same position as Ford. Most CIA officers only wanted the equivalent of a faster horse that would improve the efficiency of the work they already did, not a completely new technology that would revolutionize their jobs.

Weighing all of these factors, the prospects for Intellipedia looked grim; Don and Sean had a lot of forces lined up against them, with very few lining up for them. How could they possibly revolutionize the intelligence reporting process with no money, no staff, and no customers? How would they survive attacks from "antibodies" who believed increased sharing would place the CIA's mission in mortal danger?

Sean's success selling Intellipedia to security-conscious bosses in the DI suggested a way to get started. Each step of the way, as they evangelized Intellipedia, Don and Sean wouldn't bring up the broader possibilities of the wiki. Instead, they'd find out what immediate problems different organizations had and offer Intellipedia as a free, fast, easy-to-use solution to those problems. Bootstrapping their way up one problem at a time, they could eventually grow Intellipedia into a major information sharing resource for the entire Intelligence Community.

The first challenge in implementing this strategy was to surmount a chicken-and-egg problem: how did you persuade intelligence analysts who were *not* working Iraq to create and edit articles for Intellipedia? If the new wiki failed to collect a critical mass of useful information on a broad range of topics, it would have very few readers; if it had very few readers, no one would waste their time writing articles.

Don and Sean approached this problem one CIA worker at a time. Instead of trying to sell them on Intellipedia, they'd first ask them what kind of problems they had in undertaking their mission, without using the term *knowledge management*. Knowledge management is a term of art that includes a range of problems such as storage, protection, retrieval, validation, and updating of information. Because the CIA is in the information business, Don and Sean knew that most managers there had one kind of serious challenge or another in managing information, but the term *knowledge management* was a sure way to shut down the conversation immediately, as no one saw his or her job as being a manager of information. Some, like Stephanie, had no easy way to capture the deep knowledge stored in individual employees' heads. Others needed to disseminate updates to a workforce scattered across the globe. Still other managers were finding it difficult to keep track of what their officers were writing and doing. The trick in gaining adoption was to illustrate how Intellipedia could help them do their job more effectively, without focusing on collaboration or knowledge management. Because Intellipedia was a platform that allowed for information to be easily interconnected, knowledge management and information sharing were a natural by-product of individuals using the tool selfishly. In short, Don and Sean marketed a faster horse while actually selling an automobile.

Across the CIA, the tide of information overload had risen above the level of rank-and-file officers and was now swamping officers and managers alike. Don said that there was usually a moment when he was sitting in an officer's office, when they would have an "aha experience" and realize that an intelligence wiki could be a straightforward solution to their problems. Most people at the CIA already used Wikipedia at home, so the interface was familiar to them. Don would quickly demonstrate how easy it was to make contributions and offer to train others if needed. Also, an ODNI (Office of the Director of National Intelligence)–hosted wiki would cost nothing and would use a simple Web browser that CIA users already had. When this "aha" moment occurred, Don didn't need to sell anything. All he had to do was ask a few questions, say a few words about wiki technology, and let the managers connect the dots for themselves.

Although a fair number of managers liked the idea of a wiki, there was still a cultural hurdle against information sharing to overcome. From past experience, Don knew that orders from the top to increase dissemination of information were rarely followed. As in any organization, knowledge was power, and who wanted to give away power? More important, the CIA's *business* was secrets, so to most CIA officers the phrase *shared secret* was an oxymoron. The same reluctance to follow direction from the top applied to adoption of new desktop tools. The agency had rolled out many expensive new knowledge management tools and mandated their adoption, only to find that officers refused to use them. Some of the tools were too complicated, others failed to perform as advertised, none allowed knowledge to be managed as part of an officer's actual work practice.

For these reasons, Don counseled managers who liked the idea of a wiki *not* to force their employees to use Intellipedia, but to make participation voluntary. Don gambled that the CIA would, by 2005, have recruited a critical mass of young officers who were comfortable with social networking and collaboration tools at home and would respond better to polite requests than direct orders. Don also gambled that a voluntary program would lessen the inevitable "blowback" from older officers who viewed information sharing as foolhardy and dangerous.

For the next six months Don and Sean became traveling salesmen for Intellipedia. "We got out of our cubicles, walked the halls, and used every tool at our disposal," Don explained. Innumerable hallway conversations, lunchtime chats, and email postings "evangelized" Intellipedia. Both Don and Sean were what author Malcolm Gladwell called "connectors," with hundreds of contacts in the CIA and the Intelligence Community; the two "Intellipedians" (as they came to call users of the wiki) called, emailed, or met with almost all of these contacts, building grassroots support for their project.

By the fall of 2006, when Don and Sean first came to my office at ODNI headquarters to brief me on Intellipedia, it was clear that their voluntary, grassroots campaign was working. Intellipedia had attracted thousands of authors throughout the Intelligence Community and military, who had contributed tens of thousands of new articles. Intellipedia's page "hit rate" was climbing exponentially month after month.

Encouraged that Don and Sean had accomplished so much, so quickly, with so few resources, I asked if I could help them with extra funding. Without hesitation, they said no. They'd seen many earlier programs fail when "a lot of bodies and dollars were thrown at them." Well-funded programs inevitably suffered from "requirements creep" that piled on too many features that got in one another's way. Also, officially funded programs were all burdened with multilayered bureaucracies that were slow to make decisions and wasted money creating mountains of paperwork. Finally, Don pointed out that when agencies spent money on new systems, they expected to get a return on their investment and therefore tried to force employees to use the new technology. Usually such mandates failed for one of two reasons. Either employees simply refused to do as ordered, or they followed orders but used the new technology exactly as if it were the older technology it replaced, and never changed their work habits or business processes.

The bottom line, according to Don, was that Intellipedia would succeed *because* of a lack of funding, not in spite of it.

LAGRANGE POINTS

Over the next three years, Intellipedia continued to thrive without funding. Don and Sean believed that the wiki needed to grow naturally, as the World Wide Web had, in a grassroots, bottom-up fashion. Part of Intellipedia's great appeal was its countercultural flavor. As long as it was an unofficial, underground operation, Intellipedia was like alcohol to teenagers: exciting because you weren't supposed to do it. Don said, "Sean and I get all the credit for Intellipedia, but the very nature of the wiki tells you the real credit belongs to all of those young kids—and not so young kids my age and older—who had the courage to post the first articles. In those early days, before Intellipedia reached critical mass, contributing to the wiki invited career suicide."

By 2009 there were tens of thousands of users and hundreds of thousands of articles on Intellipedia. And Intellipedia's wide base of contributors and lack of "groupthink" were improving the quality and timeliness of intelligence reporting. For example, when a plane flew into a high-rise in Manhattan in October 2006, officials were immediately concerned about a terrorist attack. Recognizing a need to resolve this dilemma swiftly, Intellipedians immediately wrote a short article on the crash and updated it as fragmentary new information flowed in from diverse sources. With Intellipedia as a central clearinghouse for information, the analysts used instant messaging chat rooms to collect time-sensitive information on the crash and quickly concluded that the incident was not a terrorist attack: Yankee pitcher Cory Lidle had made a tragic piloting error and flown his private plane into an apartment complex.

While the incident ended up not being terrorist-related, the actions of the dozens of analysts updating the incident page more than eighty times in two hours served as a "proof of concept" for how the wiki could change the day-to-day work of community members. Senior leaders began to take notice. Intellipedia was a high-tech re-creation of the blind men and the elephant parable where different blind men each touch a different part of an object so they can pool their knowledge to determine what it is. To a man holding the tail, the beast feels like a vine; to one touching the leg, a tree trunk. By comparing fragmentary experiences, the blind men conclude that they've gotten hold of an elephant. Some Intellipedians contributed information from the police, others from aviation officials, still others from the news media.

Intellipedia was also proving invaluable for the war in Iraq. When evidence surfaced that insurgents might have used chlorine gas in an IED attack, forensics experts there had little technical expertise on how to prove or disprove presence of the chemical weapon. So Intellipedians with deep knowledge of the subject quickly posted an article to help the specialists in the field with instructions on how to find evidence of chlorine. Tom Fingar, the Intelligence Community's top analyst, said: "Twenty-three people at eighteen or nineteen locations around the world chimed in on this thing, and we got a perfectly serviceable set of instructions in two days. Nobody called a meeting, there was no elaborate 'Gotta go back and check with Mom to see if this is the view of my organization.' "

In November 2008, when Islamic terrorists attacked Mumbai, twenty intelligence analysts stationed around the globe quickly convened in Intellipedia to compare notes. Some analysts posted satellite images, others news photos of the terrorists, along with commentary on the attackers' dress and weapons. The analysts, many of whom had been strangers before the attack, swiftly concluded that a claim of responsibility by the unknown group Deccan Mujahideen was a ruse, and that the true source of the attack was Pakistani Al Qaeda affiliate Lashkar-e-Taiba.

Intellipedia's informal, grassroots approach proved in these instances to be much more powerful than the hierarchical way intelligence reports had traditionally been produced. Lacking any bureaucratic oversight, new information shows up in Intellipedia very quickly. Such speed is essential when countering agile threats such as Al Qaeda. Also, Intellipedia articles have an improved chance of being accurate, balanced, comprehensive, and free of the kinds of bias that produced erroneous conclusions about Iraq WMD, because any IC officer can see and contribute what he or she knows. Finally, Intellipedia has another key feature that the 9/11 and WMD Commissions insisted upon: accountability. Unlike Wikipedia, where contributors are anonymous, Intellipedia authors have to reveal their identities. Thus, when Intellipedians make a wrong call, everyone will know it and their reputations will suffer, just as their reputations prosper when they make the right calls. Such openness encourages thorough research and accuracy.

Admiral Mike McConnell, who headed ODNI from 2007 to 2009, agreed that Intellipedia had a major positive impact. He told Congress that the new wiki "enable[d] experts from different disciplines to pool their knowledge, form virtual teams, and quickly make complete intelligence assessments."

As the Intelligence Community's chief technology officer (CTO) from 2005 through 2007, I also saw Intellipedia quickly address longstanding problems that contributed to critical intelligence failures, such as the wrong call on Iraq WMD. I'd witnessed half a dozen large, well-funded "knowledge management" projects fail spectacularly. In just a few months, with no money, no staff, and no formal authority, Don and Sean had accomplished something that armies of contractors spending billions of dollars on abortive knowledge management efforts had failed to do: make America safer. This transformation was all the more remarkable because the predicted "blowback" from traditionalists opposing wider information sharing was severe. Don, Sean, and other Intellipedians were intimidated by some officials, ridiculed, and subjected to hallway "whispering campaigns" to erode their credibility. Tom Fingar, who had actively supported the ODNI's hosting of Intellipedia, said: "There are people who describe [the Intellipedia] project as one of the scariest innovations that I have launched."

When I asked Don how he was able to overcome such opposition with very little management "air cover" and no budget or staff, he gave me two answers that are both highly instructive for anyone wishing to light their own long fuses to big bangs.

First, Intellipedia was impervious to bureaucratic sniping, because it consumed no resources. The normal way that bureaucrats kill projects, cutting the projects' budgets and staffs, simply didn't work against Intellipedia. How could you kill something that wasn't officially alive? It was like trying to slay a vampire.

The lesson for reformers everywhere is that, in an era where many powerful tools, like MediaWiki, are free and young workforces like to use these tools, major transformations in information technology don't have to cost much. When risk-averse managers inevitably try to stop these transformations, there will be no "there there" to attack.

Virtual fuses to big bangs are much harder to stomp out than real ones.

Don said the second reason that Intellipedia succeeded so swiftly was that it occupied the "Lagrange points" of the Intelligence Community. When Don saw the puzzled look on my face, he apologized for the obscure reference to celestial mechanics, a field he had studied at Embry-Riddle Aeronautical University. "A Lagrange point," Don explained, "is that point in space between two bodies, such as the Earth and Sun, where the gravitational pull from the two or more bodies is exactly equal. Thus, if you park a spacecraft exactly at a Lagrange point, it will experience equal pull from each body and stay put. But the balance is very precarious; if you give the spacecraft the slightest nudge towards one body or the other, it will be rapidly pulled towards that body and fall towards it." Don went on, "The cool thing about moving something off of a Lagrange point is that you can produce enormous movements with virtually no effort. Sean and I simply looked for the Lagrange points at CIA and the IC. For example after 9/11 and Iraq WMD, Congress was exerting tremendous gravitational pull for wider sharing of information. Opposing that pull was the Intelligence Community's traditional need-to-know culture. All we had to do was give our wiki a slight nudge in the right direction."

Here was another lesson for achieving big bang results: just as any enterprise will have mavericks like Bill McLean and Don Burke, it will also have Lagrange points where those mavericks can do a lot with a little. Looking back on Sidewinder's history, for example, Bill McLean had a powerful force working in his favor: the military desperately needed a reliable way to shoot down enemy jets. McLean and his China Lakers didn't need a lot of money to nudge America's air-to-air missile program away from the gravitational pull of ineffective radar-seeking missiles; the pull of urgent need supplied most of the momentum.

Taken together, Don's two insights about the reasons for Intellipedia's success suggest an elegant way to get the most bang for your transformational buck: find the mavericks in your organization and move them to the Lagrange points. The results of this exercise in celestial mechanics will be heavenly.

RECAP

Hitting Your Target by
Flying Under the Radar

Humans survive and thrive as a species in part because each new generation produces individuals who differ significantly from one another in skills and temperaments. For instance, in any group, some people will be good at math, others at communicating, while still others will have artistic or musical skills. Groups that nurture and exploit this diversity, matching "talent to task," will produce big bang results, while those that suppress diversity will struggle. Organizations can make revolutionary versus evolutionary advances when they give mavericks such as Bill McLean and Don Burke the freedom to experiment with radically different ways of doing things. Because population genetics insures that all organizations will have (at least) as many risk-averse individuals as mavericks, mavericks need to operate in stealth mode to avoid having high-flying ideas shot down before reaching their targets.

CHAPTER 7

Bringing Big Bangs
Back from the Future

THE PREGNANT BUICK

The disaster wasn't the big man's fault, but most of the blame for the sharp downturn in Buick sales landed in Harley Earl's lap anyway. After all, the six-foot-three former track and field standout from Stanford University *was* the head of GM's Art and Color Section that had styled the 1929 Buick, and everyone in Detroit knew the car's sales had plunged a staggering fifty-six thousand units for just one reason: it looked pregnant.

The new Buick appeared swollen because it had an unusual "belt line," the contour that circles the car below its windows. The 1929 model's belt line had a slight convexity that, viewed head-on, gave the body a subtle bulge. This widening was so slight that if you looked at the boxy, nearly rectangular car today you'd barely notice it. But in 1929, when car bodies were flat planes, the novel design really stood out. Walter Chrysler, head of rival Chrysler Corporation, sealed the Buick's fate when he told the press it looked "pregnant." The comment made great copy and was widely reprinted. In those days, "pregnant" was a scandalous word, so very few consumers would risk the ridicule.

Harley told GM's president, Alfred P. Sloan, that Art and Color had designed a much sleeker look for the 1929 model year, but Engineering and Manufacturing had altered the design to make it easier to produce. It was the factory that had gotten the Buick pregnant, not Art and Color. Either Sloan knew that Earl was telling the truth, or he didn't begrudge his new designer the error, because he kept the Stanford man on the payroll and continued to give him wide latitude styling new cars.

Sloan had been instrumental in hiring the talented car designer; he'd seen the pleasing appearance of Earl's custom car bodies at a New York auto show in 1926. The designs, which were lower, longer, and wider than contemporary designs, had given Sloan an idea about how GM might catch up to market leader Ford in sales: GM cars might sell better than Ford's if they *looked* flashier. Up until the late 1920s automobiles broke down so frequently that a car's reliability was much more important than its looks. But reliability was improving to the point where other factors might dictate which cars sold and which ones didn't. Ironically, the pregnant Buick incident proved that Sloan was right.

Harley Earl was born in Los Angeles in 1893. His father had started a horse-drawn coach business after moving to California in 1889 from Cadillac, Michigan, but in 1903 switched over to building automobiles, changing the name of his company from Earl Coachworks to Earl Automobile Works.

After graduating from Hollywood High, Harley went to Stanford at his father's insistence, but in 1916, after a serious rugby injury, he quit college and went to work for his father styling custom auto bodies for Hollywood stars and studio executives. Earl Automobile Works had been doing a brisk business building custom cars, chariots, and stagecoaches for motion pictures, and the work introduced the Earls to top names, such as box office leader Fatty Arbuckle and director Cecil B. DeMille.

From the very beginning, Earl's designs were more streamlined and much less boxy than contemporary cars. In 1919, reviewing his design of a custom town car displayed at an auto show, the *Los Angeles Times* wrote:

The Chandler town car, in blue, is the classiest thing of its kind ever shown on the Coast or any place else. It is surely distinctive, being a low hung creation; so low that a good-sized man can stand alongside and look right over the top, yet there is sufficient room inside to keep one from being cramped.

As is often the case with the discovery of revolutionary ideas, from penicillin to Teflon, Harley stumbled on a novel way to design new cars by accident. His new technique, which would eventually transform car design worldwide, was literally groundbreaking. In 1910, while camping in a canyon with his younger brother Art, Harley was caught in one of Los Angeles's rare rainstorms. The heavy rains filled hollows in the canyons with a sticky clay that the imaginative teenager scooped up to fashion twenty to thirty different roadsters, town cars, and coupes. Six years later, when Harley went to work for his father, he remembered how useful clay was for modeling and used it as the cornerstone of his design approach. Clay afforded a flexibility that wood and other materials lacked, because it could be instantly remolded to correct design problems.

Don Lee, who owned a Cadillac dealership down the street from Earl's Automobile Works, liked Harley and respected his unique skills, so he bought the company in 1919, incorporating it into his dealership. By 1925, under the younger Earl's direction, Lee's business was selling three hundred customized cars per year to a clientele that included Hollywood's A list. Tom Mix, Fatty Arbuckle, Douglas Fairbanks, and Mary Pickford all bought customized cars from Earl's. The unique styles of these cars caught Sloan's attention, and in 1926 Harley took temporary leave from Don Lee's company to design a luxury LaSalle for GM. Larry Fisher, head of Cadillac, and Alfred P. Sloan were so impressed with the work that Harley's temporary assignment turned into a permanent job. In 1927, Harley moved to Detroit to take the reins of the Art and Color Section that designed the look and feel of GM cars.

With his strong sense of aesthetics and his drive to design cars with elegant, streamlined contours, Earl was rankled at being blamed for the Pregnant Buick. "Unfortunately," he said, "the factory, for operational reasons, pulled the side panels in at the bottom more than the design called for. In addition, five inches were added in vertical height, with the result that the arc I had plotted was pulled out of shape in two directions, the highlight line was unpleasant and the effect was bulgy."

Earl's design had fallen victim to the "Get it fast and get it easy" play in the brain's playbook. The factory decided that to make the new Buick resemble previous models was quicker and cheaper than to implement Earl's novel concepts, so they sacrificed streamlined design in favor of streamlined production. From the factory's point of view, this made perfect sense because of yet another play in their brain's playbook: "Repeat behaviors that are rewarded and avoid those that are punished." Factory managers were promoted—or fired—based on how *efficient* their production lines were, not on the aesthetic appeal of the cars they produced.

The Pregnant Buick disaster taught Harley the importance of controlling design all the way through production. Employing the clay modeling technique to rapidly move through different designs until discovering styles that were just right, he played a major role in helping GM pass Ford in sales in 1931, with sleek new designs. Based on this success, Earl asked for, and was granted, final say on all production designs.

He retained the final word on GM designs until retiring in 1959.

The story of how Earl, whose motivation was aesthetics, managed to maintain iron control over design for almost three decades in a corporation whose motivation was profit, illustrates how to get one set of plays in the brain's playbook to finesse, and ultimately overcome, another set of plays. Although Earl was no neuroscientist, he intuitively understood that the brain has more plays than the "got to have it fast," "got to have it easy," and "repeat behaviors that are rewarded" scripts that led to the profit-motivated Pregnant Buick debacle.

Growing up in Hollywood, Earl had seen firsthand the awesome power of visual images to create emotional experiences that profoundly moved people. He knew the importance of sensory reactions, and he translated this knowledge into a car design concept that not only co-opted GM's here-and-now profit instincts for almost thirty years, but also permanently changed the way cars were designed everywhere.

THE CONCEPT OF THE CONCEPT CAR

No one had ever seen anything like it. Gone were the running boards, separate bumpers, and large wheels that were standard on cars of the era. Gone too were the traditional automotive right angles and flat planes. In place of a flat windshield rising straight up from the body was a wraparound windshield. Curved—rather than straight—front and rear bumpers clung to the car's boat-tail body. And headlights, which in previous cars had been mounted outside the car body, above the front bumper, had disappeared entirely, hidden inside motorized recesses in the front fenders. The body of the car itself was streamlined to such an extent that it was hard to distinguish the front of the car from the rear. Finally, the car was much lower and longer than conventional cars, giving it an ultra-sleek aerodynamic look. You could never accuse this elegant sculpture on wheels of being pregnant.

The car was Harley Earl's 1938 Buick "Y Job."

Although it never went into production, the Y Job was a historic achievement because all the basic features of modern car body design—fenders integrated into the body, wraparound windshield and bumpers, recessed door handles, integrated headlights, hidden trunk, and spare tires—can trace their origins back to the Y Job. It didn't trouble Harley Earl that his Y Job never went into production, because he never intended that it should. He wanted the car to serve as a platform for promoting his concepts for what future automobiles should look like. The 1938 Buick Y Job, which got the Y from the experimental Y series military airplanes, was the world's first concept car.

Today, we take for granted that auto manufacturers will roll out a new batch of eye-catching, futuristic cars at auto shows to excite our imaginations, but auto shows before 1938 provided just the boring stock production variety.

The term "concept car" gets its name from the fact that these futuristic models each embodied a new "concept," such as airplane fins, an all-plastic body, or solar power. In the case of Earl's Y Job, his "concept" was lower, wider, longer. So with this revolutionary new Buick, Harley Earl and his GM team had not only invented many of the features that make modern cars modern, but they had also invented the concept of the concept car.

The world's first concept car was actually the culmination of a long series of Earl's experiments in evangelizing revolutionary ideas. Asked to show "something eye-catching" at the 1933 Century of Progress Exhibition in Chicago, Harley's team built a model Cadillac that had the world's first "turret top." These roofs, unlike traditional designs made from canvas-wrapped wooden frames, were built from a single, formed sheet of steel. The excitement and buzz generated by the turret-top Cadillac showed Earl that life-size models were much more effective at selling new ideas than drawings or scale models. This insight proved very useful when GM's top brass decided to discontinue the LaSalle line in 1934. Upon learning of the decision, Earl instructed his shop to build a full-scale wooden model of a new LaSalle, complete with first-ever airplane-like features. Earl hid the model behind curtains in the GM auditorium, then assembled GM's top leadership there. With a great flourish, he parted the curtains, exclaiming, "This is the car you've decided not to build next year." The executives were stunned, first into silence, then into action. With the Y Job, Harley's team had graduated from full-scale models that showed what new cars could look like, to fully functioning prototypes that people could actually drive. Drivable models were much more effective than static models in capturing the interest of auto executives and consumers, because hands-on experience made the futuristic cars seem real. The Y Job was so drivable that Harley used it as his personal transportation for another twelve years.

Harley remained in charge of design at GM until 1959, introducing innovations such as two-tone paint, hidden convertible roof wells, telescoping radio antennas, electric windows, heated seats, concealed gas caps, steering wheel horns, keyless entry, and double taillights, just to name a few.

A NEW VISUAL VOCABULARY

Auto manufacturers build concept cars because the direct sensory experience that futuristic prototypes provide exploit plays in the brain's playbook: direct sensory experience exerts heavy influence over our emotions, motivations, and behaviors. A quick look at the brain's anatomy gives the first clues as to why sensory experiences are so important. About 40 percent of the neocortex—that convoluted mass of cerebral sausage that comprises the surface of the brain—is devoted to processing visual, acoustic, and tactile information. With such a heavy investment in sensory processing, our brains place great importance on sensory experience. Well-worn phrases give us clues about just how much priority we give to our senses. When we understand a new concept, we say, "I see." Conversely, when we don't understand an explanation we might say, "I can't see it." Something that's "out of sight" is also "out of mind." In writing classes, aspiring authors learn to "show, don't tell." Rare individuals who have accurate intuitions about the future are called "visionaries," who "see" what others cannot. Those of us who are not visionaries are "shortsighted." Missouri is the "show me" state because its residents are, according to legend, notoriously skeptical. Finally, we all know that "seeing is believing," which implies that not seeing is not believing.

Vision isn't the only sense that serves as a metaphor for comprehension and belief. We signify that we understand and agree with something by saying, "I hear you." Things that don't seem quite right "smell," and if a new situation is alien to us, we don't have a "feel" for it. When we finally comprehend an unfamiliar concept, we "grasp" it.

These idioms suggest that the sensory regions of our neocortex do much more than process real-time visual, acoustic, and tactile information. Conscious sensations, which arise in the sensory cortex, are also the building blocks of comprehension, belief, memory, and imagination. Close your eyes (after finishing this sentence) and conjure up a past experience or imagine a new one. What are you actually aware of? Almost certainly, your mind's eye will "see" images. You might also remember or imagine spoken words, touches, smells, and tastes. Perhaps you are remembering what it feels like to walk, run, swim . . . or drive.

Functional magnetic resonance imaging (fMRI) studies pinpoint the different parts of the brain that turn on when we sense, think, remember, and solve problems. These studies reveal that we activate the same regions of the brain whether we recall past events, imagine new ones, or experience these corresponding events "live." For example, when college students in the labs of Kathleen McDermott and Karl Szpunar at Washington University were asked to visualize themselves in a new situation similar to one they had previously experienced, such as getting lost, fMRIs showed that the sensory brain regions activated were identical to those that "turned on" when the students originally experienced the situation or when the students simply recalled the original experience. Our real eyes turn on the same neocortical neurons as our mind's eye. When we hear ourselves think, the same part of our cortex is active as when we hear others speak. An imagined caress turns on the same cells as a real caress.

In addition to serving as a sort of TV screen and loudspeaker to play real-time sensations, our sensory cortex acts as a tape recorder that stores sensory experiences, and a video game machine that synthesizes new images and sounds on command. The intensity of experience that our sensory cortex either plays back or "plays forward" will be proportional to the vividness of the experiences that originally stimulated the cortex. For example, a life-size car stimulates a wider swath of nerve cells in the visual cortex than a scale model of the same car. Cars with novel colors, textures, and flourishes similarly elicit more sensory neural activity than monochrome cars lacking special details. Thus, when we see a colorful, life-size version of a car that we also get to touch, smell, and drive, the car is much more memorable than a dull, scale model, because the memory of the flashier, larger car will reactivate a larger population of neurons. A vivid memory is like replaying a recording of many voices shouting at the top of their lungs, as opposed to a few voices that are whispering.

The fact that we use the same sensory cortex to imagine future events and to recall past experiences implies that past experience constrains our imagination. If our cortex has never been exposed to a sensory pattern, how can it conjure up that pattern to "play forward"? Try to imagine a color you've never seen before or a sound you've never heard before. Hard, isn't it? That's why Harley Earl's fully functioning concept cars were so important to transforming the look and feel of automobiles. They presented vivid new multisensory images that helped the brains of auto executives and consumers imagine new experiences with cars. Before the advent of concept cars, automobile designs were based on the familiar features of horse-drawn carriages, including tall planar carriages, large-diameter wheels, and running boards. The Y Job introduced an entirely new "visual vocabulary" that allowed people to remember and imagine cars that looked nothing like horse-drawn carriages. Earl's pioneering use of modeling clay, which enabled his stylists to experiment quickly with an infinite variety of shapes, played a major role in creating this new vocabulary.

THE BABY-STEP PRINCIPLE

Inventing a new visual vocabulary was a critical first step to getting consumers to imagine themselves in novel-looking cars. But this new vocabulary only solved part of GM's problem: the company also had to make consumers *want* the new experiences they imagined.

Earl's concept cars proved highly effective at arousing such desires. The full-scale prototypes inspired much more awe than scale models, and the throaty growl of real engines and the smell of fine leather interiors created a sense of excitement. Our brains etch such experiences deep into memory, because recalling emotional events is important for survival. We won't forget a cave where a bear almost killed us, or a potential mate who aroused us when we first met them. It's hard to overstate the importance of evoking strong emotions for persuading people to embrace new ideas. Our brains evolved in dangerous environments that discouraged taking risks with unproven ways of doing things. Therefore, we need powerful emotional reasons to let go of old habits. Harley Earl understood this, which is why his concept cars maximized the emotional impact of new designs.

But Earl's understanding of his audience went deeper than knowing he had to excite their passions. Earl wouldn't have thought of consumers as

Paleolithic risk avoiders, but he seems to have viscerally understood that humans have a certain behavioral inertia that makes them change in small steps, even when they are moving toward something that excites and inspires them: "Consumers could be prepared by measured steps for more radical changes in styling," he said.

Under Earl's guidance, GM didn't introduce all the features of the Y Job in one model year, but gradually added one or two new features a year to get consumers comfortable with them. The 1940 Buicks had headlights integrated for the first time into the car's body (as opposed to standing alone above the front bumper) but retained planar windshields and running boards. The next model year, Buick's running boards and fenders began to fuse with the car bodies, but were still recognizable in vestigial form. The 1942 Buicks had no hint of a running board, and distinct fenders on some models began to fade, fusing into the car's body. GM made very few changes to its designs during World War II, but after the war, they continued to incorporate features the Y Job had anticipated. Some of the Y Job innovations, such as hidden headlights, showed up in GM cars as late as 1963, when the first Corvette sported the feature.

The baby-step principle of bringing about radical change has been repeated with other innovations, such as motion pictures, radio, television, computer software, and the Internet. The first motion pictures were simply filmed stage plays, while the first TV shows were televised radio programs. The earliest commercial Web pages were electronic versions of printed magazines. New software programs put commands such as File and Edit in the same place as older programs, because these placements had become so familiar in Windows software. Locating File and Edit commands in different places would have made them unfamiliar and unusable. Each of these new forms of media evolved in many small steps into the forms you see today, as designers bent, but did not break, consumers' expectations. For example, George Méliès's 1902 motion picture *A Trip to the Moon* adhered to many accepted norms of theater, such as distinct acts and a familiar narrative arc. But Méliès also introduced new storytelling devices, like time lapse, dissolves, and special effects, that were unique to film. Second-generation television shows such as *I Love Lucy* told stories in familiar ways, but improved on first-generation television by fully exploiting the uniquely visual potential of TV through Lucy's animated expressions and slapstick antics.

As TV technology continues to evolve, we can anticipate gradual, but ultimately major, changes in the TV viewing experience. Today TV shows viewed on the Internet, cell phones, and Internet-enabled TVs are identical to those shown on conventional TVs in that they lack any interactive capability. But just as magazine publishers eventually discovered that the Web was a different medium than print and added social networking and blogs to stories published there, sooner or later TV studios and networks will change not only the electronic devices on which TV shows are consumed, but the very nature of the shows themselves. For example, as all TV viewing devices, including TV sets, turn into interactive devices with high-speed connections that allow viewers to upload audio, video, and text to TVs in real time, TV news shows might increase the amount of audience-generated news, such as cell-phone videos of fast-breaking stories.

Similarly, as consumers shift from reading books on printed pages to reading them on devices such as Amazon's Kindle and Apple's iPhone, the very nature of books may change to take advantage of the audio, video, and interactive capabilities of the new platforms. Readers of nonfiction could simply click on the names of people to summon up images, videos, and sound recordings of them. Illustrations and photos could be replaced by videos; tables of data and statistics could be continually updated and refreshed—transforming books from a static medium into a dynamic, ever-changing medium such as today's Web pages. These descriptions of possible futures for TV and books use words such as "might" and "could" because history has shown that it's extraordinarily difficult to predict where the big wins with new technology will be. Over the past fifteen years, many attempts—such as Microsoft's ill-fated Web-TV initiative—to add interactivity to the TV viewing experience have failed because consumers rarely adopt new technologies and new behaviors simply because the technologies are available. Harley Earl said:

> You will never know what the industrial products of the future will be like, but the secret is to keep trying to find out. . . . I'd rather try crossing a river on a path of bobbing soap cakes than make predictions about the car of tomorrow. The footing would be far safer.

In reviewing Earl's successes in automotive design, and the way that electronic media evolved over the past century, we see that there are two distinct ways to develop big bang products. Earl's method was to start in the distant future, discover a big bang, then work toward the future he'd discovered, in a long series of baby steps. The other approach, adopted by motion picture and television innovators, was to start in the present, incrementally tweak offerings that were already available, then gradually move forward. Although Earl's approach started in the distant future, while media innovators started in the present, human nature—which embraces change grudgingly—dictates that both approaches advance at the same pace, in baby steps.

As powerful as Earl's baby-step methods were for fostering big-bang innovations, they relied on a design approach that falls short in today's world of accelerating change. Earl's team built the Y Job, for example, with off-the-shelf components that pushed the state of the art in visual design but not the technology under the hood. Today, as big bang innovations such as the iPhone emerge from advances in technology, a purely aesthetic approach to imagining the future no longer works. It's also necessary to design, build, and demonstrate new concepts that actually work "under the hood" the way they will in the future. The only way to demonstrate technology that hasn't been invented is to travel to the future and bring the technology back with you—in a time machine.

WHERE ART, SCIENCE, AND TECHNOLOGY MEET: FERREN'S TIME MACHINES

Ten-year-old Bran Ferren decided to humor his father. An abstract expressionist artist, the elder Ferren wanted to expose his only child to the world of architecture. So he'd taken Bran to Rome in the summer of 1963 to show off the Forum and classics like the Colosseum. But Bran was a technology enthusiast who was more interested in looking at TV and radio antennas on building roofs, than at the buildings themselves. Old buildings were . . . well . . . old. Bran was excited by new things.

For that reason Bran only agreed to go inside the Pantheon out of politeness. The round building was very different from others he had just been dragged through, but it was still old. "Borrrring," thought Bran. "Borrrring." Then Bran noticed the ceiling. From the outside, the Pantheon looked like a lot of other classical buildings—Corinthian columns supporting a triangular attic. But the rear of the pantheon was circular, topped by a domed roof with a large hole, called an oculus, in its center. A shaft of sunlight streamed through the oculus, providing the room's only illumination. Bran was curious.

"How old is this?" he asked his father.

"More than eighteen hundred years," came the reply.

Bran tried again. "No, I mean the roof. That must be much newer."

Bran couldn't understand how ancient architects, with only rudimentary knowledge of mechanics, could have built an enormous domed roof with a large hole in its center. Bran's father smiled.

"The whole building was built at the same time."

He went on to tell Bran that the Romans had used forced perspective to make the ceiling appear much more curved than it actually was and had constructed the roof from poured concrete. The concrete was a special mix, composed of lightweight but incredibly strong volcanic pumice.

Bran was flabbergasted. He'd thought of concrete, especially the light-weight variety, as a modern invention. And it was common knowledge that artists didn't discover forced perspective until the Renaissance. Clearly he had to reexamine some of his fundamental assumptions.

The most important assumption that Bran reevaluated that day was that art and science were separate entities. It was obvious to Bran that consider-able architectural science had gone into the Pantheon's artistic design, not to mention a deep understanding of light and human perception. With the shaft of sunlight that filled the Pantheon's interior, the ancient Romans had mastered a kind of alchemy, turning insubstantial light into a solid object that was as much a part of the Pantheon as its walls.

When Bran returned home to Manhattan's Upper West Side, he couldn't get the idea of light as a solid object out of his head. Light was really cool. Light was something you could play with, mold, shape, and create exciting new things with. Bran began to tinker with light. He learned how to use a camera and to develop film. In high school Bran started up a business, Syn-chronetics, that designed lighting for rock bands and live theater.

But Bran was never interested in designing show lighting the way other people had before him. The solid shaft of light pouring through the Pan-theon's oculus had shown him that light could do far more than illuminate props and characters: treated imaginatively, light could take on weight and substance of its own, and *become* a prop or a character. His attitude toward conventional thinking is best illustrated by answers he gave to a question on a high school physics exam. The test asked "How would you measure the height of a building if you only had a barometer?" The correct answer was to measure the difference in air pressure at the top and bottom of the building, then use the change in air pressure with altitude to compute the height of the building. Bran gave two different answers: "You could drop the barometer from the roof and time how long it took to hit the ground, or you could offer the barometer to the building's custodian to get him to tell you how tall the building was." The teacher gave Bran full credit for his answers.

Despite passing many tests with answers like this and earning grades good enough to get him into MIT, Bran never finished high school, entering college at sixteen without a diploma. Bran never finished college either, having gotten bored after a year in Cambridge and returning to New York to expand his lighting and design business. Over the next few years, he branched out into set design, sound, lighting, and effects for TV commercials and feature films.

Bran's penchant for doing things that had never been done before got him noticed. After breaking new ground synchronizing lighting, pyrotechnics, audio, and video projection for the rock group Emerson, Lake & Palmer, he was asked by the director of a new Broadway show, *Crucifer of Blood,* to apply his technical wizardry to live theater. Bran rose to the challenge, blending sound and light and set design to create a storm that was so compelling that it became one of the show's main characters. The new effect drew rave reviews and the attention of Hollywood. Ken Russell, dissatisfied with progress on special effects for his new film *Altered States,* had heard about Bran's work on Broadway and asked him for new ideas. Bran created a creeping flesh effect that became the film's major icon and has been much copied in later science fiction and horror films.

For the next twenty years, Bran continued his work with Broadway, rock-and-roll bands, television, and film, designing visual effects for projects such as *The Manhattan Project, Star Trek V,* and *Little Shop of Horrors. Little Shop* earned Bran an Oscar nomination to go with his earlier Technical Achievement and Science and Engineering awards from the Academy.

By the early 1990s, he had built up a company, Associates and Ferren, that was world-renowned for technical innovation in show business. The company's novel approach to blending art, science, and technology into a seamless, pleasing whole appealed to Walt Disney Imagineering, the Glendale, California, studio that designs and builds Disney theme parks. After contracting with Bran's company to build prototypes of new rides such as Hollywood Tower of Terror, Imagineering was so pleased with Bran's approach that they bought his entire company in 1993, making Bran a Disney senior vice president. Shortly thereafter, Disney promoted him to executive vice president and put him in charge of research and development for the Walt Disney Company. Michael Eisner described Bran as "our de facto CTO [chief technology officer]."

HOW TOMORROWS EXIST TODAY

I started working for Bran after his elevation to head of R&D. For the next six years I watched him perfect the "time machine" method of innovation. This method is similar to Harley Earl's concept car approach, with a major twist: Bran didn't stop with creating artistically pleasing designs for new Disney rides, shows, and interactive applications. He also made the underlying technology work the way it was likely to work several years into the future. This was no mean feat; how do you demonstrate technology that doesn't exist?

Bran solved this problem two ways. First, he understood that pieces of tomorrow always exist today in disguised form. With digital computers, for example, the government and large commercial users, like banks, always have cutting edge high-performance machines, costing millions of dollars, that have computing power that desktop PCs will have ten years later. This migration of high-performance computing from specialized government use—such as nuclear weapons design—to ordinary PCs, follows Moore's law, where computers of a given power drop in size and cost by a factor of two every eighteen months. Following the math of exponents, a computer that costs a million dollars today will only cost $3,900 twelve years from now.

Bran capitalized on this "technology trickle down" phenomenon by directing his Imagineers to buy today's state-of-the-art technology and use it to simulate tomorrow's consumer technology. For example, Imagineers simulated television viewing experiences of the future by lashing together high-performance graphics computers, disc storage systems, studio video effects generators, and other exotic technology to emulate a cable set-top box with performance that would be routine ten years later. We placed all the exotic computer and video equipment in a large, air-conditioned room, behind a mocked-up living room, and had our creative team develop and test futuristic ideas for interactive television. Viewers who "guest tested" our ideas never saw the mountains of high-tech gear that made it possible, just a standard-looking set-top box driving a large-screen TV. From the viewer's perspective, the simple, consumer-grade set-top box actually worked the way real set-top boxes would work ten years later.

A second way that Bran brought technology back from the future was to abuse high-performance machines in creative ways. After buying state-of-the-art technology, Bran always pushed us to make the high-tech equipment perform as far beyond its specifications as we could. In the mid-1990s, Bran decided that digital projectors would one day replace film in theme parks and cinemas, and he wanted to prove this idea to skeptical Hollywood cinematographers, directors, and producers. The stakes were high because Disney and other motion picture studios could save hundreds of millions of dollars each year by eliminating costs for developing, copying, shipping, and insuring film. Digital Cinema would also create new business opportunities for live entertainment and interactive audience participation.

But film projectors had been around since Thomas Edison invented them a century before, and they could not be equaled—so conventional Hollywood wisdom went—by the dim, blocky, faded images of digital projectors. And in the mid-1990s, conventional wisdom was correct. Even the most expensive digital projectors were too dim for all but the smallest cinema screens. Bran solved this problem by having his Imagineers build special optics and lamps that increased the brightness of state-of-the-art projectors by almost a factor of ten. The project was very challenging because the brighter lamps generated extra heat and ultraviolet radiation that damaged the delicate liquid crystals of the image source. I remember calling Bran to tell him we could reduce, but not eliminate, this harmful radiation, and he answered, "So what? The light valves [sensitive imaging components] don't have to last forever, just long enough to convince DPs [directors of photography]."

This last comment carries an important insight about how Bran used technology time machines: he focused more on the emotional and perceptual impact of new technology than on the technology itself. The technology only had to last long enough to produce the desired impact, so Bran urged us to push technology well beyond its normal limits, in order to travel as far into the technology future as possible.

This approach didn't always work, but with digital cinema, it succeeded spectacularly. Cooperating with other studios such as Paramount, Disney demonstrated the new technology in a large theater in Hollywood and convinced directors, cinematographers, and production executives that a digital future was not only possible, but inevitable. As a direct result of these demonstrations, Hollywood filmmakers and their exhibitors embraced digital projection and began to replace film projectors with digital counterparts. By 2007, there were more than five thousand cinema screens worldwide using digital projection technology.

Before Bran left Disney in 2000 to start the company Applied Minds, his R&D team had developed dozens of time machines. Just as with concept cars, these time machine prototypes rarely turned into actual products, but they gradually introduced elements of revolutionary new ideas into more modest new product offerings. In 1996, for example, Bran envisioned that future theme park guests would bring their own supercomputers into the parks—in the form of cell phones. Moore's law dictates that high-performance computers don't stop in their migration from government laboratories to desktop PCs, but keep shrinking and getting cheaper until they find their way into mobile devices. A 2008 model iPhone, for example, has more computer power than a $10 million supercomputer of the 1980s. Bran asked me to lead a team to build and demonstrate a time machine model of a mobile device for theme park guests. The performance of the futuristic device would be typical of the cell phones or personal digital assistants (PDAs) that theme park guests would carry with them ten years later.

The R&D team of engineers and show designers bought expensive miniature high-performance computers to simulate a futuristic PDA/cell phone. Then, with thousands of guests in Disney's Animal Kingdom, we tested applications that relied on this ultra-high-performance technology. As often occurs with such experiments, consumer reactions to the new technology surprised us. The most exotic, high-tech applications, such as mobile video conferencing with a restaurant reservation desk, had little appeal. Rather, simple, low-tech applications, such as text messages informing guests where Mickey was signing autographs, turned out to be "killer apps." Over the next few years, we deployed a half dozen simple mobile applications similar to "Where's Mickey?" with great success. For example, we sold guests a "Pal Mickey" plush toy with sophisticated electronics that sensed the toy's location in the park, alerted the guest that Mickey had something new to say about that location, and had Mickey whisper the new information in the guest's ear. Pal Mickey helped the parks address an age-old problem: keeping guests entertained while waiting in line. None of the applications that grew out of the park PDA applications, such as Pal Mickey, resembled our exotic time machine technology, but all were inspired by it.

The time machine efforts that Bran directed in his years at Disney shared one thing in common with Harley Earl's concept cars: they aimed for maximum emotional impact. Bran, like Earl, understood that people buy new products because they find them exciting, fun, or inspiring, not because the products are practical. Harley Earl's highly successful use of airplane fins on GM cars of the fifties amply illustrated this point. Bran constantly told his teams "avoid subtlety at all cost" in creating powerful emotional impacts. We didn't use ordinary speakers for the sound systems in our time machines, but ultra-loud, high-performance speakers with incredible range. We made our video displays as large and bright as possible, borrowing from Earl's principle that "bigger is better." Sometimes, as in our mock-up of the Alien Encounter ride at Florida's Magic Kingdom, we even used exotic smells to evoke strong emotions.

Working with Bran and others at Disney for ten years, I learned important lessons about the brain that I never got in graduate school, or my postdoctoral fellowship in Neuroanatomy. Immediately after my formal training, I viewed the brain as a collection of marvelously complex special purpose computers, each of which performed a dedicated function such as hearing, vision, smell, movement, control of appetite, body temperature, heart rate, and so forth. The most important of these special purpose processors, I believed, was the frontal lobe of the neocortex, the seat of reason, foresight, and logic. If you wanted to influence a person's behavior—for example to adopt a radical new technology—you persuaded that person's frontal lobes that the behavior was logical. But at Disney, I learned that the frontal lobes do not have the decision-making power I thought they did and that the brain is more than a collection of separate parts toiling away in isolation of one another. Rather, the brain is like an orchestra, where different instruments synchronize and harmonize to produce melodies that are greater than the sum of their parts. To influence the brain, we don't ask one instrument—such as the frontal lobe—in this neural ensemble to play a solitary tune, we get all the instruments to play together.

Bran understood this when he directed us to build prototypes of novel experiences that stimulated all of the senses and emotions simultaneously, and asked us to study the techniques of Disney Feature Animation. The animation group, who produced such hits as *The Little Mermaid, Beauty and the Beast, Aladdin,* and *The Lion King,* were masters at creating multisensory experiences that moved audiences. They carefully crafted the musical scores as well as lighting, color, and shading of each scene to evoke emotions such as affection, fear, and anger in audiences. For example, in early scenes of the feature *Aladdin,* animators get us to like the characters not only through what the characters say and do, but also by the way the characters are drawn and illuminated. The lines that define the characters are soft and rounded, the lighting gentle and warm. To reinforce our positive feelings, the musical score is playful and bright. But later in the feature, when the main characters conflict with the evil Jafar, they are drawn with more angular lines and lit more harshly, reinforcing the tension in each scene. The musical score also grows more strident, to amplify the conflict and suspense of the story. Audiences are usually not aware of all of these separate details, but they are acutely aware of the emotions that these details evoke.

My take-away lesson from working with Bran and Disney Feature Animation was that we can be profoundly moved without our frontal lobes knowing *why* we are moved.

And the most effective way to influence emotions and motivations—whether in a compelling movie or an exciting demonstration of a radical new product—is to orchestrate a coordinated attack on the senses. This does not mean that in persuading the brain to let go of its natural resistance to change, we should overwhelm it with complex sights, sounds, and smells. Rather, multisensory experiences should flow seamlessly together, creating harmonious experiences that are *rich,* not complicated. Harley Earl's Y Job contained a diverse array of innovations, such as recessed headlights and wraparound windshields, but Earl ingeniously blended all these novel features to emphasize a single concept: streamlined elegance. Our futuristic mobile device for theme parks had many different features, such as games, teleconferencing, and video playback, but we took great pains to simplify our users' experience to embody one idea: portable fun.

Bran constantly reminded us to "make the technology work hard so our users don't have to" and to avoid making cool new technology an end in itself. "The definition of technology," Bran observed, "is stuff that doesn't work yet."

LOOKING LONG AND ACTING SHORT

Bran's time machine method was never intended to invent new shows and applications that would take a decade for technology to catch up to. Rather, his intent from the start was to uncover elements of a futuristic design that we could roll out as soon as possible. I call this approach "looking long and acting short."

Looking long and acting short caters to the corporate brain's craving for instant gratification by delivering a series of short fuse, small bang wins. But these short fuse victories—discovered through a "time machine"—often lead eventually to big bang successes because they grow out of real experiences with real consumers interacting with real technology. When, after many trial-and-error experiments with time machines, you know where a new product ultimately should go, you can develop a step-by-step road map that moves each new generation of product inexorably toward big bang versions of that product.

Apple's latest big bang product, the iPhone, gradually came into being by just such an incremental process. The revolutionary new phone can trace its roots all the way back to a time machine project led by Alan Kay, who's widely regarded as the father of personal computing.

In 1968, fresh out of grad school at the University of Utah, Alan mocked up a concept called the Dynabook, which was a small tablet computer with a flat screen and a graphical user interface. Alan's ultimate goal was to invent a computer small enough, simple enough, and cheap enough for kids to use. The Dynabook wasn't just futuristic, it was pure science fiction. In the late 1960s computers weighed thousands of pounds and cost millions of dollars. The idea that one person—especially a kid—could own a computer for his exclusive use and carry it around with him was laughable. Flat screens and real-time graphics were also far over the horizon. But Alan lived in Silicon

Valley, where Moore's law was the eleventh commandment, so he believed the Dynabook would one day be feasible.

Alan helped found Xerox's Palo Alto Research Center (PARC) in 1970, hiring a team of computer scientists to make the Dynabook a reality. Kay knew that personal computers wouldn't be possible for more than a decade, but his team proceeded to experiment with personal computing experiences because PARC's philosophy was to pursue visions of the future, not products. Alan's vision was to create an entirely new electronic medium—as revolutionary as Gutenberg's mass-produced books—that would promote learning and literacy among children.

Using expensive high-performance computers designed for "time sharing" by many people at once, the Xerox group developed and tested software designed for individuals who used their own computers. Kay's team wrote software that allowed users to interact with computers with simple icons and graphics instead of text. To help kids navigate a computer's complex file system and applications, the Dynabook "emulations" (fully functional simulations of the look and feel of a Dynabook personal computing experience) replaced complex text commands with simple pull-down menus that could be easily manipulated with Englebart's recently invented interface, "the mouse." Kids could keep track of multiple documents and applications that were open at the same time through a "desktop" that had overlapping "windows" containing the different documents and applications.

If these features sound familiar to you, they should. All of the major elements of personal computing today, including desktops, windows, graphical user interfaces, pull-down menus, and the use of a mouse, trace their origins to PARC's Dynabook simulations. Kay and the Xerox team had traveled to the future in their time machine and brought back a PC.

Kay carried this vision to Apple Computer in 1984, where his transplanted Xerox team continued to work on a book-size computer for kids. As part of this work, in 1987 they developed a new kind of time machine, the concept video. Kay's video, like the concept car from which it derived its name, didn't actually implement futuristic technology, but it showed how the future technology would function. The video was called *Knowledge Navigator* because it demonstrated how people could tap into vast stores of information, communicate, and plan their day through a futuristic book-size computer.

The mock-up of the device used in the video had a camera, a voice interface, and a touch screen. If you own an iPhone, many of the Knowledge Navigator's features would look very familiar to you.

Like Earl's concept cars and Ferren's time machines, Kay's *Knowledge Navigator* video aimed to evoke a strong emotional response in its audience. The video transmitted a sense of optimism and excitement about how mobile computing could make our lives less complicated and more fun. The concept video worked. Popular reaction was overwhelmingly positive, and Apple got thousands of calls asking where people could buy the nonexistent Knowledge Navigator.

Encouraged by the buzz the video had created, Apple started development on an entirely new class of personal computing device they called a "personal digital assistant" or PDA. In 1988 they marketed the first ever PDA, the Apple Newton. The Newton had a touch screen that offered handwriting recognition, personal calendars, audio, and productivity applications such as text editing. The Newton product line continued for another decade, until a financial squeeze forced Apple to discontinue PDAs and concentrate on their core PC business.

Around the time Apple dropped Newton, Alan Kay took his team to Disney, where they went to work for Bran Ferren for another five years, pursuing their vision of computer learning for kids.

But Apple's interest in palm-size computing devices didn't end with Kay's departure and the demise of the Newton. When Steve Jobs returned as the company's CEO in 1997, he began to talk publicly about reviving the Newton or a similar product. Apple had learned some hard lessons with the Newton, however, among them that you couldn't cram too many features into a device without a large display keyboard or mouse. Although Apple had tried to make the Newton as simple as possible, most users found it too difficult and time-consuming to exploit all the PDA's "bells and whistles." Apple's Newton experience taught them that a personal computing device that did one, and only one, thing would probably sell much better than the complex Newton. After surveying the market for digital music, Jobs decided that the just-one-thing "killer app" would be music. In 2001, Apple introduced the first such product, the Apple iPod.

Over the next five years, Apple harnessed Moore's law to slowly expand the iPod's features to include photos, games, and ultimately video. Finally, in

2007, when multi-touch technology and small, high-resolution displays finally made it easy for users to navigate complex information spaces, Apple added a cell phone and PC-like features to their product line and called the new device the iPhone.

Looking back over the iPhone's decades-long evolution, it's hard to overstate the importance of time machines for keeping Apple on their successful trajectory toward the revolutionary new product. Alan Kay's time-machine vision, of what a small personal computing experience should be, acted as a compass that guided Apple along each incremental step of their journey. The overarching concept of Kay's vision was "keep it simple, keep it simple, keep it simple."

Having established this futuristic vision, Apple stuck to it as much as possible on the long journey from Dynabook to Knowledge Navigator to Newton to iPod to iPhone. Steve Jobs, who rarely talks about how Apple innovates, underscored the importance of time machines and concept cars in a 2005 interview: "You know how you see a show car, and it's really cool, and then four years later you see the production car, and it sucks? And you go, 'What happened? They had it! They had it in the palm of their hands! They grabbed defeat from the jaws of victory!'

"What happened was, the designers came up with this really great idea. Then they take it to the engineers, and the engineers go, 'Nah, we can't do that. That's impossible.' And so it gets a lot worse. Then they take it to the manufacturing people, and they go, 'We can't build that!' "

Jobs went on to explain that he'd had to strong-arm his own engineers into adhering to the design vision embodied in an iMac "concept car" prototype.

"When we took it [the iMac concept] to the engineers, they said, 'Oh.' And they came up with thirty-eight reasons. And I said, 'No, no, we're doing this.' And they said, 'Well, why?' And I said, 'Because I'm the CEO, and I think it can be done.' And so they kind of begrudgingly did it. But then it was a big hit."

Harley Earl, Bran Ferren, Alan Kay, and Steve Jobs all succeeded in lighting long fuses to big bangs because they had good working knowledge of the brain's playbook. They understood that our brains struggle to imagine what they've never seen before, and therefore have to be shown vivid, compelling visions of radical new concepts. The more hands-on and experiential these new visions, the better. And our Paleolithic brains are so risk-averse, they have to be taken by the hand (as it were) and led in small steps toward these radically new experiences.

A final lesson emerging from use of concept cars and time machines is that radically new ideas should evoke strong positive emotions. Without awe, excitement, or a sense of fun, people are unlikely to overcome the behavioral inertia that keeps them using tried-and-true ways of doing things.

Walt Disney stated this more eloquently when he told his animators: "You can speak to people's hearts, or you can speak to people's minds. But there are a lot more hearts out there than minds."

RECAP

Inventing the Future

Fiction-writing classes teach aspiring authors that "show is better than tell." So, for example, instead of telling readers that a character is compassionate, authors should show that character volunteering at a soup kitchen. At Disney Imagineering, working under Bran Ferren, I learned to take this theory one step further: "Show is better than tell, but *experience* is better than show."

We understand and accept unfamiliar concepts best when we immerse ourselves in experiences that stimulate our senses of sight, sound, and touch, *and* that move us emotionally. Although mavericks are well advised to hide their early work from naysayers, sooner or later all innovators need to sell their big bang ideas. Our brains crave sensory stimulation, so the best vehicles for selling novel ideas are "concept cars" that create immersive sensory and emotional experiences. Concept cars also let us see into the future. Alan Kay, father of desktop computing, said: "The best way to predict the future is to invent it."

CHAPTER 8

The Language of the Heart

THE FEAR FACTOR

Lurking just below the surface of our brain's overwhelming preference for near-term rewards is fear. Fear that we'll starve to death. Fear that predators will do us harm. Fear of losing our home. Our brains fear that tomorrow may never come, so they compel us to make the most of today. In the modern world, we rarely experience the kind of mortal fear that drove our ancestors; nevertheless, our brains keep us in a constant state of implicit fear that unconsciously drives us to grab up everything we can while the grabbing is good. When we're agonizing over whether to eat that extra donut during a coffee break, for example, fear of starvation may not factor into our thought process. We're more likely to be thinking of how good the donut will taste, or how hungry the donut makes us feel, but we don't fear that passing up an extra donut will put an end to our gene line. If we consciously fear anything, it's that our waistline will expand. Still, while the ancient fear of starvation doesn't factor into our thought process, it does subconsciously factor into our ultimate decision, which is why all too many of us watch our hands, seemingly of their own volition, reach out and grab that second donut.

If there's a practical reason behind ancient fears our brains hide from us—and there is—why not go a step further? Why not bring these ancient anxieties to the surface, where they can exert maximum influence? If a fear-driven behavior—such as bingeing on donuts—makes evolutionary sense, why not pull out all the emotional stops to motivate that behavior?

The reason is that the energizing effects of overt fear come with a price. Constantly revving up your engine to run away from threats or to attack them is hard on your engine. Hormones, such as cortisone, that flow into our bloodstream during fear responses not only depress our immune systems, they damage our hearts and brains when secreted too frequently.

Chronic stress can lead to cardiovascular disease, cancer, memory loss, and depression. Sure, predators can kill you, but so, it seems, can the constant stress of *worrying* about predators.

Because our brains understand this, they dial down to subliminal levels the vestigial fear that's left over from our evolutionary past. A desire to minimize damage from stress hormones also drives our brains to ignore potentially bad news so that we see what we want to see and don't see what we don't want to see. Thus, emotional blind spots may protect us from too many stress hormones, but they may also cause us to overlook big bang opportunities.

When you think about the daily pressures that our Paleolithic ancestors faced, with environments that neuroeconomics suggests were six times riskier than today, it makes sense that our brains evolved ways of coping with stress. Pushing anxieties below the surface is one of these coping mechanisms, but there are others. To balance negative emotions such as fear and anger, our brains also let us experience positive emotions such as joy and contentment. Just as negative emotions cause release of stress hormones that tear down our bodies, positive emotions release substances that build our bodies back up. Stroking a pet, for example, elevates the number of natural killer T-cells circulating in your blood. So does laughter. Enjoying friends and family lowers your blood pressure and heart rate.

THE POWER OF POSITIVE EMOTIONS

Barbara Fredrickson, head of the Positive Emotions and Psychophysiology Lab at the University of North Carolina, argues that positive emotions have been hardwired into us to offset the damaging effects of negative emotions. Feelings such as excitement, joy, serenity, and gratitude charge up our emotional batteries so that we have something left when, inevitably, those batteries discharge while coping with stressful situations. Some of the benefits of positive emotions are immediate. Relaxing after work or playing board games with close friends gets us ready to cope with a demanding schedule the next day.

But positive emotions also lead us to engage in behaviors with benefits that extend far beyond the next day. These activities, which Fredrickson calls *broadening and extending*, are among the very few behaviors that our brains engage in naturally that garner long-term versus near-term rewards. An example of broadening is the valuable training that results from joy. Joy drives a desire to play, which is often excellent preparation for future combat. Puppies at play bite, claw, and maneuver for advantage exactly as adult dogs do when they actually fight, the only difference being that puppies engage in mock combat, whereas adults play for keeps. Mock combat strengthens puppies' muscles and teaches them which tactics work and don't work on other dogs. Playful young monkeys learn to use tree branches as springboards to propel them rapidly away from playmates in hot pursuit, a skill that comes in handy later for avoiding predators. And what kinds of play are common among young boys? Wrestling, cowboys and Indians, cops and robbers, and fight-oriented video games. The play of many young girls—pampering dolls, cooking, and bonding with close friends—anticipates more serious adult activities such as caring for children, nourishing families, and strengthening the cohesion of social groups. Adult play, especially sports, also prepares our bodies for emergencies. Exercise strengthens our immune systems to help us cope with infection and builds our muscles and cardiovascular system, preparing us to combat threats or run from them.

Our ability to cope with the world is also highly dependent on the quantity and quality of relationships we have with others. The more people we know and trust, the more people we can draw on in a pinch. Our ancestors used their social networks to share food, tools, and child rearing chores. Today we draw upon our friends to help us expand our business, find a new job, or find the right doctor. According to Fredrickson, joy-driven playfulness extends this beneficial social capital by making us interact with people we don't know and strengthening bonds with people we do know.

Positive emotions can extend our intellectual capital as well as our social capital. When we are relaxed and feeling interested or curious, we open ourselves up to new experiences that broaden and extend our store of useful knowledge and ideas. We read books and magazines, surf the Web, take a class, or chat with friends. All of these activities increase our intellectual resources and effectiveness at coping with the world. One can easily imagine that our ancestors discovered how to make fire, use new tools, or sew clothes while in a relaxed, curious state. The same broadening behaviors that make us more effective today helped our ancestors survive yesterday. Fredrickson believes that such intellectual broadening counterbalances the narrowing of focus that accompanies negative emotions. When we're afraid, we shut out any information that's not relevant to escape; when we're angry, we focus all our attention on the object of our wrath. However, our ancestors wouldn't have survived a changing world if they only paid attention to a narrow, unchanging set of information. Broadening activities such as exploration, experimentation, and invention must also have been part of our ancestors' behavioral repertoire, or humans would never have invented better tools, clothing, shelter, or other revolutionary, big bang advances that helped us cope with everything from droughts to ice ages.

Viewed from this perspective, we can see that negative emotions such as fear narrow our focus to short fuses, while positive emotions such as curiosity draw our attention to long fuses. If this is true, then one way to find and light long fuses to big bangs is to make the brain feel good about itself and the world around it. In a relaxed, affable, curious state, the brain will open itself up to new ideas and experiences and even look into its emotional and perceptual blind spots.

If you think about problems that you've experienced in your own life, it's easy to see why countering the narrowing effects of negative emotions with the broadening effects of positive emotions makes sense. If, for example, like most people, you occasionally have trouble falling asleep, the most likely reason you stay awake is that your mind gets locked into a narrow grove of negative emotion. These emotions may be anxieties over current or future problems or, more commonly, fear of insomnia itself. Perversely, most insomnia results from a fear of insomnia! We can't get to sleep because we worry about getting to sleep. No matter how logical we are in reasoning with ourselves, having one part of our brain tell another part that it's illogical to let fear of insomnia keep us awake, we can't seem to escape the narrow groove of fear that traps and obsesses us. In short, reason and logic are ineffective antidotes to the toxic effects of emotions. The only cure for one emotion is another emotion. That's why therapists tell insomniacs not to fight the insomnia with logic, but to break the vicious cycle of fear by substituting positive emotions for negative ones. Therapists tell insomniacs to get out of bed and take a walk, watch TV, or read a book, relaxing activities that are incompatible with fear.

It's also nearly impossible to reason your way out of anger. No matter how persuasive you are in telling yourself that there's no point in staying mad at someone, you won't be able to let go of your anger until you switch gears and focus on something else. Anger management specialists teach their patients guided imagery, deep breathing, muscle relaxation, and other techniques that create a sense of serenity that is incompatible with anger.

These examples reinforce common sense experience that emotions are more powerful than logic. But why should our brains give such greater weight to emotions than to reason? Don't both faculties help us survive? The answer to this question provides a useful model for thinking about how to get your brain, and those around you, to light long fuses to big bangs. If we posit that emotions arise in the ancient limbic system, whereas reason resides in our more recently evolved neocortex, the anatomy and physiology of these two distinct brain regions tells us why emotions exert more influence on behavior than reason. Structures in the limbic system, such as the amygdala, have a direct, physiologically potent connection to the motor centers of the brain that tell our muscles to move and our glands to secrete hormones such as adrenaline and cortisone. Regions of the limbic system also receive sensory inputs that arrive before sensations reach our neocortex. This raw sensory information is much cruder than the refined sensory data that the neocortex "sees," but the limbic system is more interested in speed than accuracy, and acts on incomplete information. Thus, even though the limbic system has a narrow, fuzzy view of the world, it occupies a privileged position that lets it command us to run from predators or eat donuts, before the neocortex has a chance to weigh in.

The limbic system outputs are stronger, as well as faster, than those of the neocortex. For example, the neocortex and the amygdala "talk" to each other through nerve fibers that pass to and from the amygdala and the neocortex. The conversation between the two parts of the brain goes something like this.

AMYGDALA: *ALERT! ALERT! INCOMING THREAT! SNAKE! SNAKE!*

CORTEX: Hold on just a second. Yes, I see it now. Well, I have a much clearer picture of this thing than you do, and I'm not at all convinced it's a snake in the grass. It looks much more like a garden hose to me. And besides, we've never had a snake in our backyard before. I'll analyze the images further, cross-reference them with my extensive data store, and get back to you.

AMYGDALA: *NO TIME FOR ANALYSIS PARALYSIS,*
   I'M GETTING US OUT OF HERE!

CORTEX: Calm down, you could be wasting precious calories if, as
   I now think likely, the object turns out to be nothing more than
   a harmless—

AMYDGALA: *TOO LATE, WE'RE MOVING!*

CORTEX: (Sigh.) What's the point? I never win.

One reason the neocortex loses this argument is that the nerve fibers that come to it from the amygdala are much more developed than the fibers it sends down to the amygdala. Metaphorically, the amygdala speaks through a bullhorn while the neocortex whispers. Your own subjective experience of thoughts versus feelings should reflect the relative power of the limbic system and the neocortex. Feelings, such as fear, anger, and lust, that originate in your limbic system are far more intense than routine thoughts that rise in your neocortex. Adding considerably to the power of emotions are the bodily sensations that accompany them. When your limbic system "shouts" at your neocortex, it simultaneously commands your stomach to clench, your heart to race, and your breathing to quicken. As a result, you are *aware* of cortically generated thoughts, but you literally *feel* limbically generated emotions.

Here's a useful model to keep in mind when trying to convince someone to let go of negative emotions so that he can shift his attention from short fuse threats to long-term opportunities. The brain is like a ship that has a bridge manned by a highly educated captain and an engine room manned by working-class seamen. The bridge is analogous to the neocortex, while the engine room is analogous to the limbic system. The bridge has a clear, panoramic view of the world, while the engine room sees things through a smudgy porthole. This ship is unusual in two respects: seamen in the engine room see the outside world before the captain does and can steer the ship without the captain's orders. The captain's job is not to give orders, so much as it is to observe, draw on past experience, plan ahead, and offer helpful suggestions. In the absence of urgent threats, seamen in the engine room obey the captain because they see no reason not to. But the engine room workers are not of one mind about the best way to navigate. One group only pays attention to developing bad news and swiftly takes control of the tiller and engine to move away from (or toward) near-term trouble. The other group only looks for good news and takes control in a more leisurely way to steer the ship toward opportunity.

In this loosely run ship, it's pointless for the captain to order the "bad news" seamen to take their hands off the engine room controls. If these workers think there's trouble ahead, no amount of cajoling from the bridge will change their behavior. The captain's only hope is to persuade "good news" seamen to muscle the controls away from their "bad news" counterparts. From his elevated perch, the captain can supply the "good news" seamen with positive developments that they can't see through their smudgy porthole. The captain can explain that the ship is near the equator, where there are no icebergs, making it safe for "good news" seamen to wrest the controls away from their "bad news" brethren. The captain can also point out that there are plenty of tropical islands nearby for shore leave, and that one of those islands makes the best rum in the world. Such arguments stand a good chance of getting the "good news" seamen to accomplish something that the captain cannot: take direct control of the ship.

In harnessing positive emotions to achieve long-term success, it's better to think of the brain as an ally than as an opponent. Positive emotions naturally move us in directions that prepare us for long-range success, so our task is not to deflect and channel these emotions, but to reinforce and strengthen them so that they can take over from the negative emotions. Psychologist Daniel Goleman, coauthor of *Primal Leadership*, argues that the most effective leaders adopt this strategy. Instead of motivating through rational arguments that appeal to the logical but ineffectual neocortex, good leaders exude contagious enthusiasm that evokes strong positive emotions in the primal but potent limbic systems of their subordinates and peers. The most effective leaders are also scrupulous in eschewing fear as a motivational tool. Goleman calls these managers "resonant leaders" who reinforce and amplify the better half of the brain's mixed intentions.

PROJECT HOPE

The British Airways flight from London to Johannesburg was a long one, so Prasad Nimogagadda, a drug company executive, didn't immediately ask his seatmate what was troubling him. The melancholy Kenyan next to Prasad had started drinking heavily soon after takeoff and looked like he wanted to unburden himself. But Prasad thought it wise not to make the first move. Several hours into the flight, when it was clear his seatmate wasn't going to open up on his own, Prasad overcame his natural shyness and asked the man if he was OK.

The Kenyan looked at him with watery eyes and began to cry as he poured out his story. He worked for the Kenyan government in London and had recently taken on the task of buying up real estate in his country—from landholders in South Africa and elsewhere—to serve as new cemeteries for Kenya's fast-growing population of AIDS victims. Every time the government official returned to his homeland, he learned that more of his friends and relatives had died of the disease, and the job of finding resting places for so many loved ones was proving more painful than he could bear.

Prasad listened to the man for most of the remaining hours of the flight, then asked, "Why do all these people have to die? There are now 'cocktails' of antiviral medication that can extend HIV patients' lives for up to a decade or more."

The man looked pained. "Yes, but they cost up to fifteen thousand dollars a year. Kenyans don't have that kind of money."

Prasad thought about the man's answer. As a chemist and pharmaceutical executive, he knew something about how antiviral medications were manufactured and was puzzled why they should cost so much. He suspected that part of the answer was that drug companies who made anti-HIV agents had patents that restricted who could make the drugs, allowing the patent holders to charge monopoly prices.

Prasad told the Kenyan, "I run a small drug company in India. Let me see what I can do to get the prices down."

The Kenyan regarded Prasad with skepticism. "This is just a nice story for you to tell your friends."

Prasad was stung by the implication that he would not follow through on his promise. The Kenyan's words stayed with Prasad as he deplaned and went to his hotel. The next day, and the day after that, images of the bereaved man, and also the phrase *This is just a nice story for you* kept coming back to him. Prasad resolved *not* to let the Kenyan's narrative become *just a nice story*.

Prasad returned to Hyderabad a few days later, where he ran Matrix, a small company that he partly owned, which manufactured generics such as ibuprofen and the antiviral drug Indinavir. As soon as he got into the office, he started searching the literature on HIV drugs to learn how they were made and why they cost so much. He focused on four drugs: zidovudine (AZT), lamivudine, stavudine, and nevirapine, all reverse transcriptase inhibitors that prevented the HIV virus from converting its RNA into DNA, which would splice its way into an infected cell's healthy DNA. These reverse transcriptase inhibitors were commonly administered in LSN (lamivudine, stavudine, nevirapine) or LZN (lamivudine, zidovudine, nevirapine) cocktails because three-drug combinations worked much better than single drugs. Prasad also read everything he could about the disease itself—where it was spreading fastest and the economic resources of stricken populations.

Based on this research, Prasad concluded that his original hunch was right: most of the price of these four drugs was comprised of royalty payments to patent holders. The pure manufacturing costs of a year's dosage of an LSN or LZN cocktail was less than $1,000. Through his firm's work with Indinavir, a protease inhibitor that stops retroviruses like HIV from chopping up proteins into manageable pieces, Prasad knew that the World Trade Organization had special emergency provisions that allowed companies to manufacture drugs for low-income countries without paying royalties to patent holders. Matrix already sold Indinavir to the Brazilian government at a steep discount under this provision. Prasad speculated that it was possible Matrix could get a similar WTO emergency exemption from royalties for drugs sold to Kenya and other African countries, driving the yearly price of the drugs down below $1,000 per person.

But Prasad's analysis suggested $1,000 was still too high a price in countries where per capita income was only a few hundred dollars per year. Matrix would have to get the cost down to about $150 per year so that charities, governments, and "wealthier" patients in Africa could afford the antiviral cocktails. From his analysis of the chemical structure of the drugs "L, S, Z, and N," Prasad suspected that a more efficient synthesis process might be possible, and that it was conceivable Matrix could make a small profit selling the drugs—without royalty payments—for about $150.

When he'd lined up all his facts, he convened a meeting of Matrix's leadership and presented his findings. He asked his team whether they would be interested in adding L, S, Z, and N to their product line. The reaction was overwhelmingly negative. Some managers didn't agree with Prasad that Matrix could invent new chemistries for synthesizing the drugs more cheaply. Others thought adding four new drugs was too big a risk for such a small company. Prasad backed off in the first meeting, but he didn't let the idea go.

In a series of management meetings over the next few months, Prasad tried different arguments. He reminded his team that they were in the health care business, not the chemical business, and it was their job to tackle important health problems if doing so could add to Matrix's bottom line. His troops were unconvinced, so Prasad changed tactics, pointing out that there was no competition in the discount HIV drug market and that Matrix could enjoy a first mover advantage that would give them a lion's share of a large, fast-growing market. Still, his team resisted.

The reluctance of Prasad's managers only strengthened his resolve. The more he studied the market for HIV drugs, the more convinced he became that Matrix could make money on the one hand, and save many lives on the other. Moreover, the Kenyan's taunt—*This is just a nice story for you*—still echoed in Prasad's head. Prasad tried one more time to sway the people who worked for him. He suggested that the company had too narrow a product line and needed to "de-risk" its portfolio by expanding the number of drugs it sold. Adding new HIV drugs to their repertoire would insulate Matrix from downturn in demand for their traditional products, he argued. His team didn't budge.

Frustrated as Prasad was, it never occurred to him to order his managers to add the four new drugs to Matrix's product line. Prasad adored his grandfather, a landowner in Andhra Pradesh Province in eastern India who had prospered by treating his farmhands as equals. His grandfather had also taught Prasad to be generous with subordinates, observing that whatever he gave to his own farm workers, such as gifts during the yearly Diwali festival of light, came back to him severalfold in increased productivity. Following his grandfather's example, Prasad was the first CEO in Hyderabad to give employees stock in their company. Prasad also saw himself less as a boss and more as a facilitator, who stimulated discussion and built consensus. He rarely issued direct orders. Prasad, like his grandfather before him, believed this democratic management style was "good for the heart, and good for business." But this benevolent leadership technique was not moving Matrix in the direction he wanted it to go. Prasad was in conflict. He would have to abandon either his dream of saving millions of lives or the family tradition of treating employees as equals.

Prasad ultimately decided to stay with his family's egalitarian tradition. However, having failed to bring his managers around after repeated attempts, he gave a great deal of thought to his next move. Looking at the world from his subordinates' point of view, he could see two good reasons *not* to take on the ambitious HIV project. First, Matrix had only recently emerged from bankruptcy after Prasad, a turnaround specialist, had purchased it two years earlier and gotten the company to drop unprofitable old product lines in favor of lucrative new ones. As a result, Matrix was in the black, but just barely. A heavy R&D investment that wouldn't pay off for several years could fatally drain the company's precarious cash flow. In addition to this big negative, the Matrix management team had scant reason to believe the HIV project had any strong positives. Given the extreme price sensitivity of the low-income market Prasad proposed to enter, Matrix couldn't expect to make a profit unless they somehow lowered manufacturing costs by almost a factor of ten.

To address these valid concerns, Prasad realized that he needed simultaneously to dial down the negatives of the HIV plan, while ramping up its positives. At the next management meeting he pitched a two-prong approach.

First, he dropped the suggestion that Matrix launch four new drugs. Instead, he proposed an inexpensive eight-month R&D project to determine whether or not it was possible to synthesize the drugs for a few hundred dollars a year. If the study failed to quickly find inexpensive chemical processes, Prasad would abandon the idea. But if the R&D effort proved that profitable low-cost production was feasible, Matrix would retool its production and get into the reverse transcriptase inhibitor business. The drain on cash flow would be modest, and the HIV project would stop if it couldn't find a way to make a profit quickly.

The second facet of Prasad's new approach was to name the R&D study "Project Hope." If the R&D effort succeeded, millions of doomed patients in Africa and other developing countries would live more normal lives. At the same time, Prasad refrained from making the usual "logical" arguments about the importance of achieving first mover advantage in the discount HIV drug market and lowering the risk of declining sales of current Matrix products by adding a completely new product line. To build up the positives of the HIV project, Prasad had switched from talking to his workers' minds, to talking to their hearts.

It's important to point out that although he is naturally shy, Prasad is a passionate man. His dark eyes crackle with energy and he speaks with conviction. He uses a rich variety of gestures to explain his ideas about what a company should be. "It should have the vision of an eagle, the speed of a cheetah, and strike like a cobra." He smiles as he makes this pronouncement—as if he knows it sounds over-the-top but he doesn't care. He means every word of it, and everyone around him knows it. Prasad's enthusiasm, energy, and optimism are infectious. I once left a three-hour lunch with him convinced that several of my own projects that I'd thought were marginal were suddenly very doable.

I wasn't at the 2004 meeting where Prasad finally convinced his managers to agree to Project Hope, but having seen him in action, I can imagine how powerful the combination of Prasad's dynamic personality and uplifting message of hope were. Shortly after his management group and board of directors finally gave their approval for the project, Prasad addressed his R&D team, explaining that they had a unique opportunity to change the world. He told them he was confident in their abilities and that he believed they would succeed.

Six months later—sixty days short of Project Hope's eight-month deadline—the R&D team proved Prasad right. The Matrix chemists and manufacturing experts developed and demonstrated a new chemical process that would—in high-volume production—make a three-drug cocktail for about $180 a year. Less than a year after Prasad's flight to Johannesburg with the grieving Kenyan official, Matrix had proved it was possible to slash the price of HIV drugs by almost a factor of a hundred.

As encouraging as these laboratory results were, Matrix was still $30 short of the $150 target for the cost of a yearly dose of drugs. This gap was small in comparison to the $15,000 starting point, but the enormous quantities of HIV drugs needed in Africa alone made each extra dollar add up quickly. By late 2004 about 20 million Africans had contracted HIV and roughly 2 million African AIDS sufferers died each year. With 20 million HIV patients needing treatment, an extra $30 a year would add $600 million a year to the cost of reaching Africa's infected population. It wasn't clear where cash-strapped nongovernment organizations (NGOs) and governments were going to get that kind of money. Prasad realized that Matrix would need outside help to lower the price of the HIV cocktail enough to be affordable in low-income markets.

In the course of his work in Africa, Prasad had heard that the William J. Clinton Foundation wanted to increase access to antiviral medication for low-income HIV sufferers worldwide. The foundation had established the Clinton HIV/AIDS Initiative (CHAI) to make HIV drugs much more affordable. One of CHAI's initiatives helped drug companies pool many small orders for simple bulk chemicals and more complex active pharmaceutical ingredients (APIs) into a single large order that earned steep volume discounts. CHAI also had found very low-cost suppliers in China for both the chemicals and the APIs. This supply chain project allowed small drug companies to enjoy economies of scale that normally were the exclusive preserve of pharmaceutical giants such as Merck, Bayer, or GlaxoSmithKline. CHAI instituted a similar supply chain program for NGOs and governments who bought finished HIV drugs, allowing many small buyers to pool their purchases to earn volume discounts from drug companies. Prasad knew CHAI's supply chain programs could help Matrix by lowering the cost of its bulk chemical ingredients and APIs and improving the efficiency of converting those ingredients into finished drugs. Making drugs was like baking bread in a commercial bakery: the bigger the batch, the lower the unit cost of each loaf.

Meeting with Ira Magaziner—who had spearheaded the Clintons' abortive attempt at health care reform in the 1990s and now ran CHAI—Prasad got Matrix into CHAI's supply chain programs and lowered the projected cost of a three-drug cocktail to $140. The Kenyan's heartrending tale had not been *just a nice story*. It was about to change the world.

In late 2004, true to his promise to make Matrix swift as a cheetah, Prasad's company went to market with LSN and LZN cocktails. Rock-bottom prices made possible by Matrix's new manufacturing process and CHAI's supply chain programs drove Matrix's sales through the roof. By 2009 Matrix was supplying 40 percent of the world's HIV drugs, providing life-extending treatments to more than 2 million low-income HIV patients across the globe. The meteoric rise in sales and profits allowed Prasad to sell Matrix—a company that had cost him $2 million when he'd bought it in bankruptcy in 2001—for over $1 billion in 2006.

Long fuse. Very big bang.

HEARTS OVER MINDS

Prasad's two-pronged approach to convincing his managers to explore reverse transcriptase inhibitors took advantage of one familiar play and one new play in the brain's playbook. The familiar play was "Get as much as you can as soon as you can." Limiting the first phase of Project Hope to eight months, with the intention of going to market quickly if the project succeeded, catered to the brain's inherent desire to avoid risks and capture rewards quickly. By dialing down the risk of the HIV project, Prasad soothed the implicit (and possibly explicit) fears of his subordinates.

But it was Prasad's skillful emphasis on the HIV project's positives that is most noteworthy, because his pitch was a textbook example of "primal leadership." Naming the HIV study "Project Hope" took advantage of a play in the brain's playbook that essentially says "Pay much more attention to your limbic system than your neocortex." As Barack Obama found out in 2008, there are very few words that carry as much emotional impact as "hope," because in one form or another, hope is the primary drive that keeps us going. We hope to live our dreams someday. We hope our loved ones will thrive. We hope to make a difference and leave a mark when we're gone. So just naming the project "Hope" was guaranteed to move the limbic systems of Matrix employees to action.

Prasad did more than say the right words, however. The *way* he conveyed his message was very compelling. He delivered it with passion and rock-solid conviction. His voice, facial expressions, and gestures carried rich sub-verbal messages that evoked powerful emotions. Sub-verbal messages are very important because both our limbic system and our neocortex have "mirror neurons" that turn on when we observe other people's behavior. If we watch a tennis coach demonstrate the correct way to serve, "mirror neurons" in our own motor cortex turn on in the same way that they would if *we* were serving. Essentially, our brains perceive movements by acting them out.

The same is true of our perception of emotions. Mirror neurons in our amygdala, for example, turn on when we observe the fearful facial expressions of others. These are the very same neurons that fire when we experience fear for ourselves. When we see joy or anger on the face of another, our limbic system literally feels these emotions as well. This means that emotional words such as *hope* are much more impactful if they are delivered with facial expressions and other sub-verbal cues that powerfully excite limbic neurons.

The term *resonant leadership* is a particularly fitting description of the way that the passions of one person turn on the limbic system of another. When we radiate enthusiasm, energy, and optimism, as Prasad does, it's as if we are playing pure tones of music that create sympathetic vibrations in the limbic systems of others, just as a tone of the right pitch will cause a wineglass of a certain size to resonate at that pitch. Thus, the most effective way to communicate with a limbic system is not to speak to it in a level voice, but to passionately sing to it. It's no accident that common English idioms say emotions *move* us.

Using the "good news seamen, bad news seamen" model of the limbic system, let's replay the meeting where Prasad finally convinced Matrix's leadership to embrace Project Hope. Prasad "sang" to both types of seamen. By dialing down the project's negatives with confident assurance, he hummed a lullaby that soothed the "bad news" seamen to sleep. At the same time, he "sang" a stirring melody filled with pride and hope that roused the "good news" seamen into action.

Prasad's managers didn't act irrationally (either before or after they changed their minds), nor did Prasad somehow cheat by shifting from logical to emotional arguments. To the contrary, the managers would have been irrational if they had *not* let emotions sway their decisions. Neurologist Antonio Damasio says that we can't make rational decisions without tapping into our emotions, because the human brain is ill equipped to consciously sort through the complex combinations of risk and reward that confronted Matrix.

Consider the number of different questions Matrix's leadership had to consider at the same time: How likely was it that the company could invent the required new chemistries? If new chemistries could be found, how much time and money would it take to discover them? Would NGOs and governments be able to afford the drugs even at $150? Would large pharmaceutical companies, who enjoyed economies of scale that Matrix did not, drive their costs below Matrix's? What if newer, better drugs came on the market soon after Matrix spent millions gearing up to produce an older generation of drugs? Human consciousness is like a small Post-it note that only has room for a few pieces of information. It is simply too limited to hold so many ideas in one place at one time.

Unconscious processes, however, store vastly greater amounts of information. If the conscious mind is a Post-it note, then, by comparison, the unconscious is the Library of Congress. Pause for a moment and consider the full extent of your knowledge about people, places, and things, and how little of that knowledge actually rises to the level of consciousness at any given time. Damasio believes that in making decisions on complex questions, we tap into this vast store of unconscious memories through emotional hooks associated with each memory. When we store away new facts that we've just learned, we tag the memory of each fact with an emotion. If we meet someone we like, we color our memory of them with positive feelings. If we experience a painful event, our memory of that event is tagged as negative. Decision making, according to Damasio, is a process by which we sum up all the emotional pluses and minuses associated with relevant memories to calculate net negative or net positive feelings about options we are considering. With emotion-based reasoning, Matrix's managers wouldn't have consciously added up all potential outcomes, along with the probabilities and payoffs of those outcomes. Rather, Prasad's managers had either experienced (or heard about) similar situations in the past and had unconsciously tagged each of those recollections with emotions. They made decisions by unconsciously weighing a collection of negative emotions, such as fear, against an array of positive emotions, such as hope. The net output of that process was a single positive or negative emotion that triggered subtle body sensations of joy or fear when they thought about each choice. For example, managers might have known they didn't like the HIV proposal from a sensation of tension in their stomach. Similarly they knew they *did* like the proposal from a lack of visceral tension combined with excited, expansive sensations in their chests.

This is what gut feel is all about. The unconscious, emotional part of our brain adds up all the pluses and minuses of a decision and reports its findings to the conscious part of our brain through an intermediary—our body.

Our body, then, is the landscape on which the battle between short-term thinking and long-term thinking plays out. Because evolution has taken the side of short-term thinking, making our "guts" naturally feel uneasy about risky, long-range payoffs, we won't normally pursue long-range opportunities unless passionate visionaries like Prasad overcome our latent fears with powerful messages of hope. Walt Disney was no brain scientist, but he got it right: speaking to the heart works much better than speaking to the mind.

Other facets of Prasad's story also provide useful hints about how to light long fuses to big bangs. Notice that Prasad improved his odds of success by exploiting more than one play at a time. He supplied the brain quick wins at the same time he made those wins seem emotionally satisfying. A lethal one-two punch.

Prasad also didn't let repeated failures faze him. When plan A failed, he tried plans B, C, and D until he finally hit on the right combination. Such persistence is an essential part of making the brain's playbook work for you. It's quite rare—even for exceptional leaders such as Prasad—to hit on the right formula for persuading people to embrace radical ideas on the first try. Although all of our brains follow the same basic plays in one form or another, there is tremendous variation from one person to the next—and from one situation to the next—in when and how the brain calls these plays up. For example, the leadership at Matrix had just escaped bankruptcy, so it was only natural that they would be more risk-averse than managers at a company that was flush with cash. Groups also have different cultures and team dynamics that heavily influence their reactions to long fuse, big bang ideas.

At Disney Imagineering, for example, it wasn't hard to get employees excited about risky, revolutionary ideas, because Imagineering hired artists, engineers, and designers who were future-oriented. Revolutionary ideas were harder to sell in the Intelligence Community, where failures could get people killed.

BIG BANGS IGNITE FROM BIG NEEDS

A final lesson to be drawn from Prasad's story is that the developing world holds many big bang opportunities for profitably selling new products and technologies. By 2004, wealthy nations in Europe and North America could treat most of their HIV patients with expensive antiviral cocktails, but impoverished countries—especially in sub-Saharan Africa—couldn't afford the drugs. This inequality of access to HIV therapy, which created enormous pent-up demand for low-cost antivirals, was a big bang waiting to happen. The magnitude of the bang was so great that sooner or later, someone was going to find a way to ignite it.

That the first "someone" turned out to be Prasad was no accident because of the unique way he looked at the world. Perhaps because his grandfather was such a strong believer in equality, Prasad had developed a keen eye for the inequality that surrounded him. The small rice-farming village where Prasad was born had no electricity, but he noticed that a town of the same size just six miles away was fully electrified. That same town had full-time teachers, but the elementary school in Prasad's village had to get by with a single teacher who bicycled from village to village. In Delhi, you could buy high-quality pasteurized milk out of Mother's Dairy vending machines that were available nowhere else in India. Just as some kids wondered why the wind always seemed to blow from the same direction or the moon changed appearance throughout the month, Prasad was curious why two villages of the same size so close to each other had such a wide disparity in quality of life.

After becoming a successful businessman, first with the Indian Molasses company, then with the pharmaceutical company Vorin Labs, Prasad continued to be sensitive to the stark contrasts in quality of life between the rich and poor of India. But his attitude toward these inequalities was complex. On the one hand, Prasad considered himself a socialist who wanted to even out the distribution of wealth, providing quality health care, nutrition, education, and opportunity for all Indians. On the other hand, he saw himself as a capitalist intent on making money and securing the future of his own family. "My head wants to make money, my heart is compassionate, and my belly is filled with passion," Prasad said. "I struggle to keep these forces in balance." At Matrix, Prasad found a creative way to balance his capitalism and his socialism: making a profit from "democratizing" the distribution of HIV drugs. After selling Matrix in 2006, he maintained the balance between his head and his heart by dividing proceeds of the sales into three parts: one third went to a trust fund for his family, one third went to new "capitalist" ventures, such as a TV station, and one third went into establishing the Nimogagada Charitable Foundation, whose goal is to cure childhood blindness in India.

In reconciling his conflicting drives, Prasad applied a formula that characterizes a fast-growing category of long fuse, big bang successes: he harnessed the power of science and technology to accomplish what Harvard Business professor Clayton Christensen calls "serving the underserved."

Looking ahead at both demographic and technology trends, the number of big bang opportunities for serving the underserved is going to multiply rapidly. The global distribution of wealth, already disproportionately concentrated in North America and Europe, is projected to become more uneven as populations in Asia, Africa, and Latin America continue their exponential growth. At the same time, Moore's law, and rapid advances in non-digital technologies such as nanomaterials, new chemistries of the kind Matrix developed, and green energy will drive down the costs of improving the quality of life in low-income countries. Thus, opportunities for marrying fast-paced "technology push" to accelerating "demand pull" in developing countries will abound. To the Prasads of the world, such opportunities will be easy to spot, but they won't be so obvious to the rest of us, especially those of us who live in wealthy nations.

It follows then that in looking for your own long fuse, big bang wins, you'll discover unexpected opportunities by putting yourself in Prasad's place and finding modern solutions to age-old problems in disadvantaged markets. C. K. Prahalad, author of *Fortune at the Bottom of the Pyramid,* says that in the past, new technologies always "trickled down" from wealthy countries to poorer countries as cost of the technologies dropped. But increasingly, due to the large size of markets in countries like China, India, and Indonesia, global companies are designing products specifically for "the bottom of the pyramid" then migrating those products into high-income markets. Companies who adopt this "trickle up" approach not only accelerate their international growth, but also reap economies of scale in the third world that open up new markets and make their products more competitive in the first world. General Electric, for example, designed an electrocardiogram (EKG) machine specifically for the Chinese market that GE later sold in the West, quickly grabbing 20 percent of the market share for EKG machines. This EKG device didn't have all of the features of machines used at major Western hospitals, but it greatly increased the quality of cardiac care at Chinese hospitals that didn't have the money for more sophisticated technology. After a successful deployment in China, GE then sold the machines in the West, to small medical clinics, visiting nurses, and general practitioners who had wanted EKG machines but couldn't afford them. The Dannon yogurt company experimented successfully with small-scale unrefrigerated "microplants" in Bangladesh that later enabled the company to launch a new, low-cost Eco-Pack product in France. Nokia developed a cell phone for Ghana and Morocco with a special speaker that allowed groups of people to huddle around the phone and participate in a single conversation. That same speaker later turned out to be popular with teens in the West, who liked to listen to MP3s as a group.

The trickle-up phenomenon suggests a different way to build time machines to anticipate future big bang opportunities. Instead of using today's ultra-high-performance industrial technology—such as supercomputers—to emulate tomorrow's sophisticated consumer technology, time machines could emulate much less sophisticated, much less expensive products for low-income markets. For example, Imagineering would have taken a very different approach to simulating a PDA of the future if its goal had been to launch mobile services in low-income markets. Rather than simulating a device with more than ten times the performance of PDAs available at the time, we would have simulated the look and feel of devices that had one tenth the *cost* of contemporary PDAs. We might have made the device with a simple black-and-white display and no touch screen, no camera, and no GPS, and simulated only one feature, such as a very high-speed wireless connection, that wouldn't be deployed in the low-income countries for many years.

If Prasad's story is any guide, time machine simulations of futuristic products for disadvantaged consumers could be much more effective at motivating organizations to pursue long fuse, big bang opportunities than simulations of more exotic, high-performance products for high-income markets. Cool, high-performance technologies will make organizations feel good about their products; simple technologies that improve the lives of the poor will make organizations feel good about themselves.

RECAP

Schindler's List and Big Bangs

Oskar Schindler, the main character in Spielberg's movie about the German industrialist who saved Jewish workers from the Nazis in World War II, observed that selling an idea "is all in the presentation." One way of interpreting Schindler's advice is that generating *excitement* about an idea can be much more important than convincing people of the *logic* of the idea.

Antonio Damasio and other neuroscientists have discovered the reason for this is that our brains do not dispassionately weigh hard facts in order to make logical choices, but instead rely heavily on the *emotional* content of information to decide what to do. Thus, to persuade our naturally risk-averse, here-and-now brains to embrace risky, there-and-then ideas, it's necessary to evoke strong positive emotions—such as hope and compassion—that replace our unconscious fears about the future with *conscious* passions for it.

CHAPTER 9

Light Long Fuses
and Leave

FREEDOM TO FAIL

No human endeavor drives innovation more than warfare. World War II spurred development of groundbreaking technologies such as V2 rockets, radar, sonar, and smart weapons (such as Bill McLean's BAT missile). Today's digital computers trace their origins to the code-breaking engines that America and Britain used to decipher encrypted German messages. World War II also gave us nuclear weapons, the ultimate Big Bang.

The technological legacy of the Cold War was equally impressive, including satellites, manned space flight, and miniature, lightweight electronics that made satellites and space travel possible and that fuel today's digital revolution. To better understand how big bang advances happen, it's useful to ask, "Where did breakthrough Cold War technologies such as spy satellites, unmanned air vehicles, and stealth aircraft actually come from?" The answer is, not the aerospace and defense companies that built these technologies, not the labs of the U.S. armed services that use these technologies, not academic settings or industrial R&D organizations such as Bell Labs. The long fuses that led to all of these revolutionary breakthroughs were lit in a single place—DARPA (Defense Advanced Research Projects Agency).

Since its creation in 1958, DARPA has ushered in more long fuse, big bang successes than any other organization in history. In addition to breakthroughs in spy satellites and exotic aircraft, DARPA created global positioning satellites (GPS) as well as the Galliun Arsenide technology (transistors that communicate with light instead of electrons) that enables much of today's wireless and fiber-optic communications. And DARPA was the birthplace of the Internet, which grew out of an experiment to build a communications network that could survive a nuclear war.

One of the reasons that DARPA has produced so many outstanding successes is that it has also produced a large number of failures. DARPA's Orion project sought to propel interplanetary spacecraft by "pushing" the space vehicles through explosions of nuclear weapons. Orion never overcame the formidable problems of how to get very heavy nuclear weapons into space in the first place, how to protect crews from radiation, and how to get around treaties banning nuclear weapons in space. DARPA also violated the laws of physics when they tried to use the radioactive compound halfnium to build nuclear weapons the size of hand grenades. DARPA's experiments in extrasensory perception never panned out, because the actual science of ESP did not measure up to its hype. Finally, DARPA's recent attempt to create futures markets to predict terrorist attacks by letting people buy "puts and calls" on future terrorist events failed spectacularly when public outrage at the idea of profiting from terrorist attacks killed the project. The fact that no one at DARPA has ever been punished for these failures has contributed to a "freedom to fail" culture where taking extreme risks in pursuit of extreme rewards is encouraged. If military R&D were the game of baseball, DARPA would be the power hitters in the lineup. They hit more home runs than anyone else on the team because they swing for the fences and strike out more than other players.

But the agency's history has much more to tell us about how to light long fuses to big bangs than "always swing for the fences." Over a period of fifty years, the agency has learned to orchestrate many different plays in the brain's playbook, some of which are obvious, and others of which are not.

FRAGMENTED SPECIALIZATION

If you look closely at a deciduous tree, you'll notice something interesting. The geometric pattern formed from the large branches emerging from the trunk is repeated in the much smaller branches that grow out of each main branch. The same pattern of branching continues in the stems that emerge from the smaller branches. But the branching pattern does not stop there. The leaves themselves have large veins that split off into a series of smaller veins in geometries that mirror the branching pattern of the tree's trunk, large branches, and smaller branches. Individual large branches, small branches, and leaves all look like scaled down versions of the tree on which they live.

If you could see below the ground, you'd observe that tree's branching geometry is also preserved in its roots. Larger roots split into smaller roots, which in turn split into still smaller rootlets, in the same pattern as large branches, smaller branches, twigs, and leaves.

Mathematicians call such patterns of self-similarity *fractals,* a term derived from the Latin word *fractus* which means "broken" or "fractured." We don't yet know exactly why trees grow in fractal geometries, but nature must have a good reason for using self-similar patterns, because they show up in many biological forms. Arteries and veins in animal (and human) circulatory systems obey fractal geometries, as do the shells of sea creatures such as the nautilus. Neurons in the brain sprout processes called dendrites, which receive inputs from other nerve cells and branch into fractal geometries that look exactly like those of certain trees.

Groups of organisms also organize themselves into repeating patterns-within-patterns. Bacteria cultures in petri dishes branch into fractal patterns. The very building blocks of life, DNA, and the chromosomes into which DNA cluster also resemble fractal geometries And if you look at the organization chart of most Fortune 500 companies, you'll find that large organizations divide into smaller organizations, that branch into still smaller organizations in patterns that look similar from top to bottom. Individual boxes on org charts, for example, will typically have a maximum number of smaller boxes reporting to them, reflecting a limitation in the number of direct reports that leaders can effectively manage. This last example, where humans organize themselves into self-similar patterns, is worth dwelling on because it partly explains why DARPA succeeds.

A clue to DARPA's unique ability to solve hard problems can be found by looking more closely at the smallest unit of human problem solving—an individual neuron in the human brain. Nerve cells do not have simple shapes, like single-celled organisms, but are broken into several parts, each of which performs a special function. The dendritic trees of neurons receive inputs from other nerve cells, while the bloblike cell bodies of these neurons are metabolic engines that convert sugar to energy to operate the cells, manufacture proteins, regulate growth, and generally serve as the "nerve center" of each nerve. Finally, neurons have sprouts, called axons, that sometimes branch into fractal geometries. Axons conduct electrical nerve impulses generated in nerve cells' bodies down to connections or "synapses" with other nerve cells, where information is transmitted from one nerve cell to another through secretion of chemicals called neurotransmitters. Adrenaline, which kicks off our fight-or-flight response, is an example of a neurotransmitter.

The essential pattern of nerve cell organization (which is repeated at higher and higher levels of the nervous system), and ultimately *collections* of nervous systems in groups of humans, is fragmented specialization. Just as individual nerve cells are broken into different parts—axons, dendrites, and cell bodies—that excel at specific tasks, so too do populations of neurons in a given region of the brain take on different forms to perform different tasks. For example, in the neocortex there are large *pyramidal* cells (with pyramid-shaped cell bodies) that have axons that travel long distances to other regions of the brain, as well as much smaller *granular* cells that have short axons that connect only to nearby cells in the cortex. The pyramidal cells perform computations of inputs from widely separated parts of the brain, while granule cells perform calculations only among local populations of cortical neurons. This division of labor lets pyramidal cells do what they do best—communication and computation with distant parts of the brain—while leaving granule cells to specialize in communication and computation within local regions of the neocortex. The pattern of fragmented specialization of local regions of the neocortex holds true for the cortex as a whole. Cells in the visual processing regions at the very back of the brain are organized very differently from cells at the very front of the cortex that initiate movement and plan future courses of action. Form follows function.

Evolution has decided that, at all levels of brain organization, it's better to have specialists than generalists. We know from the population genetics of personality and intelligence that this principle of fragmented specialization creates individual differences within groups of humans that persist from one group to the next and from one generation to the next. Thus when grouped together, a collection of human brains acts like a single uber-brain that optimizes its performance by assigning unique tasks to each constituent brain according to the special skills of that brain. The brain's playbook contains plays that govern not only how individual brains should respond under different circumstances, but also how *teams* of brains should organize themselves to achieve the best results. In this case, the playbook says, "Groups of individuals should divide and conquer."

DARPA has extended this principle of fragmented specialization from groups of individuals to groups of *groups*. Just as fragmented specialization will produce an occasional Bill McLean or Don Burke in a group of individuals, the principle of fractal self-similarity dictates that large organizations comprised of many groups will have at least one group that specializes in out-of-the-box thinking. This is DARPA's role within the mammoth Department of Defense. Other defense research organizations, such as the army, navy, and air force labs, also do some high-risk research, but these armed services labs are under intense pressure to deliver near-term solutions to pressing military problems, so they focus more on evolutionary advances, as opposed to revolutionary advances, in military technology.

The short-term focus of the armed services labs caused President Eisenhower to create DARPA (then simply ARPA) in the first place. The Russian launch of Sputnik in 1957, which caught America by surprise, had rattled the Eisenhower administration to its core. The President wanted to know how it was possible for the backward Russians to beat America into space, given America's vastly superior science and technology base and the billions of dollars it spent each year on R&D.

The reason, Eisenhower's advisors informed him, was that the armed services labs, who were doing the bulk of defense R&D, were focusing too much on near-term mission requirements and too little on long-range needs, such as monitoring the Russians. Another reason the Russians caught America's defense establishment by surprise was that the service labs were inventing too few surprises of their own. These labs had been focusing heavily on the needs of risk-averse military customers who were asking for incremental versus radical improvements to their weapons systems. The military in the late 1950s was asking its own research labs for improved versions of tried-and-true technologies such as jets, tanks, and submarines, not entirely new classes of technology such as spy satellites.

A former five-star general, Eisenhower was intimately familiar with military thinking and decided that it was unlikely the armed services would change their ways fast enough—or ever—to meet the growing threat of Soviet science and technology. Adhering to the dictum "It's better to change people than change minds," Eisenhower created the Advanced Research Projects Agency (ARPA) with the charter to "prevent surprise."

Anticipating—correctly as it turned out—that generals and admirals would pressure ARPA to focus on their immediate needs, and thereby undermine ARPA's high-risk, high-reward mission, Eisenhower made the new agency completely independent of the armed services. ARPA would be accountable only to the secretary of defense, and their own consciences. In short, ARPA not only could ignore their ultimate customers, but were encouraged from the start to do so.

Looking at Eisenhower's actions from an evolutionary perspective, it seems that the President created a beneficial mutation designed to help the larger organism (America) grow a new part of its collective brain to counter a dangerous new predator (the Russians). This move added an element of fragmented specialization to the government bureaucracy that had been sorely lacking: exclusive focus on surprise. Up until 1958, breakthrough military innovations had come, almost by accident, from a few random individuals, such as Bill McLean, who were scattered around the country in different organizations. Eisenhower thought avoiding surprise was too important to be left to a few isolated mavericks. America needed innovation by design, he believed. Not by chance.

In creating an entire group of mavericks to implement Eisenhower's vision, ARPA, and later DARPA, took advantage of the same population genetics that produced Bill McLean, hiring almost exclusively from an elite group of risk takers who were passionate about creating long fuse, big bang surprises. From DARPA's very beginning, very few of its scientists and engineers were interested in mundane problems of the type conservative military commanders wanted to solve. As a result the military has never viewed DARPA as "customer focused."

NO PASSION, NO PROGRESS

George Heilmeier was a gifted athlete. In high school he excelled at both basketball and baseball, and hoped that one day his talent would take him all the way to the major leagues. Maybe he would even get to play for his hometown Philadelphia Phillies.

George liked sports so much that when he got a full scholarship to the University of Pennsylvania, he decided to major in Physical Education while pursuing his twin dreams of getting a college degree and playing professional baseball. However, George's ambition to major in PE hit two stumbling blocks. His father, a janitor who never got past the eighth grade, was adamant that his only child get a degree that would earn him a decent living.

George's father wasn't as sure as George that he'd make it to the major leagues, and he wanted his son to have more to fall back on than a PE coach's salary. The second obstacle was even more formidable: Penn didn't offer a Physical Education degree.

Caving in to his father's desires and the reality of Penn's curriculum, George majored in Engineering, choosing Electrical Engineering because it didn't require drafting. "This was important to me," George later said, "since I did not excel in this area in high school."

Heilmeier did excel in Electrical Engineering, however, earning a bachelor's degree in the subject from Penn, then a master's and PhD from Princeton. Much to his dismay, George's athletic career did not fare so well: he was forced out of competitive baseball when a fastball struck the side of his head, robbing him of his memory for several weeks.

George's first job after finishing college in 1958 was at RCA's David Sarnoff Research Lab, where he worked on semiconductor technologies, lasers, and a new class of electronic materials called liquid crystals. George's 1964 discovery of novel applications of liquid crystals would ultimately earn him the Japanese equivalent of the Nobel Prize, the Kyoto Prize, for developing the first viable liquid crystal displays. To get a sense of how important George's discoveries were, consider that all laptop computers, the majority of cell phones and PCs, and a fast-growing percentage of TV sets use liquid crystal displays that trace their origins back to George's work at RCA.

Despite his successes there, George soon grew impatient with the slowness with which RCA moved its discoveries out of the lab and into the marketplace. George felt that the glacial pace at which RCA commercialized his discoveries in liquid crystal displays robbed him of the fun and excitement of his work. "I had lost my passion and excitement for liquid crystal display work," he said. "It's my view that when your passion and excitement for work in a specific technical field leaves you, you should leave the field with it."

Here was another example of the key role that emotions play in motivating people to pursue long fuse, big bang advances. Where there's passion, there's progress; where's there's no passion, there's no progress.

Because of his loss of passion, when the opportunity arose in 1970 to serve as a prestigious White House fellow, George grabbed it, leaving RCA for the nation's capital. During his one-year fellowship, George served as special assistant to the secretary of defense, helping to develop long-range plans for research and development. That work led naturally to his next post in the Defense Department as assistant director of defense research and engineering, and ultimately to an appointment in 1974 as the director of DARPA.

Having spent the previous four years looking into the military's future, George had strong opinions about what DARPA's long fuse, big bang priorities should be. He identified six "silver bullets" that America would need in the coming decades to cope with the increasing sophistication of Soviet technology. Thirty years later, when these ultra-classified silver bullets were made public, George described them as follows:

- Create an "invisible aircraft" (undetectable by Soviet radars and other sensors)
- Make the oceans "transparent" (to find Soviet submarines)
- Create an agile, lightweight tank armed with a tank-killer "machine gun"
- Develop new space-based surveillance and warning systems based on infrared focal plane arrays
- Create command and control systems that adapted to the commander instead of forcing the commander to adapt to them
- Increase the reliability of our vehicles by creating onboard diagnostics and prognostics

An aircraft that was invisible to Soviet sensors was at the top of the list because of recent experiences in Viet Nam and the 1973 Arab-Israeli conflict. In both theaters of war, Soviet air defense radars and surface-to-air missiles, used by the North Vietnamese and Arabs, had proven devastatingly effective at finding and shooting down American fighters and bombers. Russian air defenses had gotten so good that in Viet Nam the U.S. bombing missions had to use a large number of unarmed electronic warfare planes to try to overwhelm North Vietnamese defenses with electronic jamming. This tactic was costly, inefficient, and ultimately only partially effective.

Looking ahead to a possible Soviet invasion of Western Europe, George saw disaster. The Russians and their Warsaw Pact allies had many more tanks and troops than NATO. NATO's only alternative to using nuclear weapons to stop an invasion was to strike Warsaw Pact forces from the air on their home turf, before the Soviets and their allies could reach West Germany. But Soviet air defenses were so effective that NATO's conventional (non-nuclear) air power was unlikely to stop an invasion of the West. NATO would then be faced with the agonizing choice of whether to start a nuclear war or let Russia take over Europe.

George realized that if America had aircraft that were invisible to Soviet air defense radars and radar-guided surface-to-air missiles, NATO would not have to make this choice. NATO air forces could penetrate deep into Warsaw Pact territory and stop an invasion before it got started.

However, cloaking devices and invisibility were the stuff of science fiction. No one knew if it was even possible to build a radar-invisible plane. This excited Heilmeier and his team: invisibility was a typical "DARPA hard" problem that no one else in the government would dream of tackling. It was exactly the kind of "surprise" that Eisenhower had created DARPA to invent.

Under George's direction, DARPA took on the invisibility challenge using a methodology that dated back to its earliest days. DARPA and their scientific contractors began with a *gedanken,* or thought experiment, in which they assumed that a particular phenomenon was possible, then worked backward to identify all of the physics that must be true to make that phenomenon a reality. The way that NASA got Apollo 13 safely back to Earth after an oxygen tank explosion crippled the spacecraft was a simple illustration of the start-at-the-end-and-work-backward process that DARPA used. NASA flight controllers assumed that Apollo *could* be brought home, then took an inventory of every piece of hardware on the vehicle to explore how these pieces of hardware could be adapted to keep the astronauts alive. By tinkering on the ground with replicas of gear on Apollo, NASA engineers discovered that they could use a space suit's air hose to plug incompatible air purifiers together, giving the crew enough breathable air to get home. In the case of aircraft "invisibility," scientists working for DARPA listed all of the features an airplane would have to have to escape radar detection. A stealthy airplane would have to radiate very little heat for enemy thermal sensors to pick up, and would also need to communicate with ground controllers with hard-to-detect radio signals. Most important, the skin of a stealth aircraft should absorb radar energy so that enemy radars, which sent out high-power radio waves then listened for reflected returns, would not get enough energy back to detect a signal. Because it was unlikely any material could absorb 100 percent of the radar energy that struck it, DARPA's contractors—such as Northrup and Lockheed—believed that invisible aircraft would have to have exotic shapes that reflected radar energy at odd angles, such that very little of that energy would bounce back at radar receivers.

After listing all of the attributes that were both necessary and sufficient for radar invisibility, DARPA's contract scientists then examined each attribute carefully. Would any of these attributes violate the laws of physics? If so, keep looking for science that did work. If not, which of the properties had already been developed elsewhere and which had not? Ultimately, the DARPA team concluded that the laws of physics did not preclude radar invisibility, but several key problems remained to be solved, chief among them identification of complex aircraft shapes that would direct radar energy away from radar receivers. DARPA then focused its attention on finding solutions to this key "technology bottleneck," as well as several others, some of which remain classified even today.

DARPAs methodology for developing radar invisibility took the time machine method of innovation one step beyond Bran Ferren's approach. Bran created a vision of the future by stretching the art of the possible as far as it would go using expensive, state-of-the art technology. But DARPA imagined a future, then tried to invent it with new solutions that were completely *impossible* with even the most expensive technology available at the time.

If pressed, most technology executives will admit that the biggest challenges to developing innovative technologies have nothing to do with technology. Protection of organizational turf, resistance to change, and bureaucratic red tape kill many more technology projects than scientific hurdles ever do. Acutely aware of the need to overcome such hurdles to developing stealth technology, Heilmeier also took on "impossible" bureaucratic obstacles, such as long-standing Defense Department contracting rules that threatened to slow projects like Stealth to a crawl. Issuing contracts quickly was crucial to DARPA because the agency didn't perform its own research, instead issuing R&D contracts and grants to universities and companies such as McDonnell Douglas, Northrup, and Lockheed. George called his approach to cutting through mountains of red tape "no excuses management," signifying that the only thing that DARPA would let stand in the way of one of its visions was scientific infeasibility.

Throughout 1974 and 1975 DARPA's contractors studied the math, physics, and material science of radar stealth, concluding that what had been previously impossible for aircraft stealth might now be within reach. Ironically, it was a Russian scientist who made the key breakthrough that fueled George's optimism. Peter Ufimetsev, a physicist who'd only been allowed to publish because the Soviet government thought his work was useless, wrote a book in 1962 entitled *Method of Edge Waves in the Physical Theory of Diffraction* that laid out basic principles for estimating how much electromagnetic energy would bounce off different geometric shapes at different angles. Although Ufimetsev did not concentrate on radar energy per se, his work was highly relevant to stealth because radars emit electromagnetic energy. Ufimetsev's theories were applicable to all such energy, from low-frequency radio waves all the way to ultra-high-frequency gamma rays. Guided by Ufimetsev's equations, DARPA's contractors developed computer simulations describing how surfaces of different shapes would reflect radar energy away from radar receivers.

By late 1975 DARPA's engineering contractors had, with paper-and-pencil calculations, invented about as much "impossible" stealth technology as they could without experimenting with real hardware. So DARPA's Tactical Technology Office (TTO) issued contracts to Lockheed and Northrup to design and build full-scale aircraft models with skins that both absorbed radar energy and directed it away from radar receivers. The two companies built aircraft models mounted on poles in special test ranges that measured the strength of radar signals returned from the models at different angles. DARPA then conducted a "pole off" competition to determine which of the two designs had the lowest radar "signature." Lockheed's entry in the competition, which had a blocky, faceted, distinctly non-aerodynamic shape, won.

George and his TTO team were enthused. Lockheed's design returned so little radar energy that it would be effectively invisible to Soviet air defense radars and radar-seeking missiles. The time had come to move out of the analysis, simulation, and laboratory phase and have Lockheed build a real airplane. But, having turned the impossible into the possible in just two years, DARPA faced a new, seemingly insurmountable challenge: the biggest customer for stealth technology, the U.S. Air Force, didn't want it.

True to its charter, DARPA ignored the air force's wishes in undertaking the stealth project. The air force brass believed that the answer to potent Soviet defenses was not a science-fiction cloaking device, but straightforward technical advances that made air force jets more maneuverable or that allowed American planes to fly higher and faster than Soviet air defenses could cope with. The air force leadership also wanted improved electronic warfare systems for jamming Soviet radars and better missiles to home on radar signals and destroy air defense radar installations. DARPA's stealth technology, which produced planes with bizarre, diamond-faceted shapes that reduced aircraft speed and maneuverability, seemed like a really bad idea. Even if the ugly, ungainly stealth aircraft somehow got built over the air force's objections, the expensive planes were bound to divert funding from much needed upgrades to electronic warfare and anti-radar missile technology. The air force dug in its heels and refused to cooperate.

Lack of air force support in early phases of the stealth project hadn't slowed DARPA down because paper-and-pencil studies and laboratory experiments didn't cost much, and they didn't require air force cooperation. But building and testing operational aircraft would require DARPA to spend serious money that would be hard to justify without air force backing. Also, DARPA would need the air force's help testing experimental aircraft. Pentagon politics threatened to do something that the laws of physics had not—kill the stealth airplane before it could get off the ground.

George tried unsuccessfully for several months to convince senior air force officers that stealth was an essential part of their future. Running out of options, he decided to violate military protocol and go around the one-, two-, and three-star generals who'd been opposing him, appealing directly to the four-star general, David Jones, who ran the air force. This was a highly risky maneuver. In the stratified Pentagon, going around officers who opposed you rarely worked, because senior officers like Jones routinely delegated decisions to lower echelons and considered it very bad form to second-guess subordinates. Also, although George reported to the secretary of defense, he didn't have the same bureaucratic throw weight as the chief of staff of the air force. It was therefore unseemly for him to approach a de facto superior as an equal. Violating the Pentagon's pecking order was the equivalent of breaking the glass on a fire alarm: you only did it in emergencies.

But George believed the need for stealth technology was an emergency, so he asked for, and was granted, an audience with General Jones. George expected vigorous resistance from the assembled generals, but he plowed ahead with his briefing, describing the test results from the radar range and explaining the value of stealth for stopping a Russian invasion of Europe. To George's surprise, at the end of the briefing General Jones turned to a senior general who'd vigorously opposed the stealth project and said, "We're going to help these guys." The senior general knew better than to argue. He said simply, "Yes, sir!"

From that day forward, the air force cooperated closely with DARPA, setting up a program office at Wright-Patterson Air Force Base to oversee Lockheed's construction and testing of two prototype stealth aircraft. Having started the project in April 1976, Lockheed took just nineteen months to design and build the first fully functional stealth aircraft. The aircraft, code-named *Have Blue,* took off from a secret desert runway on December 1, 1977, flying into the history books of military aviation. A mere three years after putting stealth at the top of the silver bullet list, DARPA had made the impossible possible.

By "breaking glass" and violating Pentagon protocol to get stealth technology off the ground, George Heilmeier took advantage of a variant of the play in the brain's playbook that says, "Groups of brains should divide and conquer." Just as this play insures that most groups will have one or two maverick outsiders, it also pushes groups to have at least one risk-taking *insider.*

Consider the roles of leaders at different levels of an organization such as the air force. Officers at the bottom of the command pyramid and those in the middle have the job of running day-to-day operations and paying attention to details. But leaders at the very top, at least in theory, are not supposed to concern themselves with day-to-day operations and small details, but to focus on really big questions, such as "Which direction should this enterprise go in the next five to ten years?"

CEOs and four-star generals spend very little time addressing such long fuse, big bang questions, due to the constant pressure of here-and-now emergencies such as budget or earnings shortfalls, irate stakeholders, or bad press of one kind or another. Many of these leaders feel guilty about spending more time on "fighting fires than on fire prevention" and welcome opportunities to do the long-range thinking they're paid to do. So when someone like George Heilmeier comes to them with a genuine long fuse, big bang opportunity—even one that's risky—they can ease their guilt about neglecting their organization's future by saying yes.

The take-away here is that long fuse, big bang opportunities have two kinds of natural allies: mavericks at the fringe of an organization and leaders at the very heart of the organization. More conservative than the mavericks, top leaders such as General Jones can be slow to embrace radical new ideas. But almost all top executives have latent guilt that you can exploit to keep these ideas alive . . . *if* your passion for the ideas is great enough to risk your job.

Breaking glass in emergencies can produce fatal cuts!

FIRE YOUR SUPERSTARS

In 2006 my deputy at ODNI, Steve Nixon, and I wanted to create our own DARPA for the Intelligence Community. We believed that the bulk of R&D taking place at the CIA, the NSA, and elsewhere had a short-term focus and that agencies absorbed in prolonged wars in Iraq and Afghanistan were unlikely to shift their priorities from evolutionary to revolutionary advancements in technology. Steve and I were convinced that the Intelligence Community badly needed radically new solutions to cope with terrorists on the one hand and more traditional targets such as nation states on the other. Over the past three decades, America had lost its near monopoly on high technology, as countries such as China, Korea, Taiwan, and Japan took manufacturing of all-important digital electronics away from us. Also, just as America faced threats in the new domain of space in the 1950s, in 2006 it faced a growing threat in the new domain of cyberspace. We had become entirely dependent on the Internet for running both businesses and government and were more vulnerable to cyber attacks from criminals, terrorists, and traditional adversaries than any other country in the world. Finally, the Intelligence Community needed to ramp up its work on "soft sciences" that would help us address the root causes of threats such as terrorist IEDs.

In sum, the Intelligence Community in 2006 needed the same infusion of new ideas that the military had needed in 1957.

In order to benefit as much as we could from DARPA's experience, Steve interviewed the current director of DARPA, Tony Tether, as well as several former directors. In each interview, Steve asked what the key ingredients to DARPA's success were, as well as what pitfalls we should avoid in setting up our own R&D agency. Steve compiled answers to these questions into a single list of prioritized "do's and don'ts," then went over the list with me after finishing his interviews.

Much of the advice on the list came as no surprise: "Make sure you stay independent of operators (intelligence agencies)," "Get your own budget," "Hire the best people on the planet to run your research and development programs," and "Get authority to bypass red tape in hiring and purchasing." But one item, near the top of the list, caught me by surprise: "Fire people after five years." Steve smiled when I asked him about this. "Apparently, even DARPA program managers get stale after a few years," Steve said. "The only way to insure a steady stream of new ideas is to insure a steady stream of new people."

Having run R&D organizations myself for almost thirty years, and thinking I knew everything there was to know about R&D management, I was shocked. The DARPA directors were saying that we should hire only superstars, then turn around and fire them. This ran counter to my experience at Hughes, Disney, and NSA, where less than 10 percent of my research staff—the superstars—had produced nearly 100 percent of the big breakthroughs. Superstars were incredibly hard to find; when you got your hands on one, you pampered him, reassured him, and worked around his (often numerous) interpersonal shortcomings. But you never, ever fired him!

DARPA directors were not unanimous on the wisdom of shedding top talent after five years. George Heilmeier, for example, said, "People should be measured by their contributions, not the amount of time they were at DARPA."

But the more Steve talked, and the more I thought about my own experiences, the more sense firing superstars made to me. By the end of our discussion, when I agreed that our own version of DARPA, IARPA, should also hire top-notch scientists and engineers for single five-year terms, I realized that I had learned some important new plays in the brain's book.

One of the consequences of humans' strategy of surviving by sharing useful information is that our brains place tremendous value on this information. For example, life lessons and values that our parents pass down to us become an integral part of our identities. We often define ourselves by our parents' religious beliefs, political party, or favorite sports team. Similarly, we want to pass on our values and affinities to our own children and give them every advantage from the hard lessons we have learned.

Our attachment to cherished ideas goes far beyond the cultural information and life experiences that we share in our families. Consider what happens in most meetings in your workplace. People consume a great deal of time explaining and justifying their own ideas or attacking someone else's. We cling to and protect our ideas as if they were our children. In Paleolithic times we competed for status and reproductive rights by proving that our genes for hunting, gathering, and fostering healthy children were superior. In today's world we more commonly compete for status through the superiority of ideas, or what Richard Dawkins calls "memes" (derived from the Greek word *mimema* for "something imitated"). Humans are hardwired to imitate one another's constructive behavior, so we intuitively understand that we can advance our cause, and that of our progeny, by feeding people's innate desire to imitate and pass on new and useful information.

According to Richard Dawkins, Susan Blackmore, and other biologists and evolutionary psychologists, another good reason to defend and propagate our own unique "memes" is that memes give us greater immortality than genes. Socrates' genes, for example, were diluted by half in his children, by 75 percent in his grandchildren, by 87.5 percent in his great-grandchildren, to the point where his genes have completely disappeared today. But Socrates' ideas, by virtue of mass media, have a much wider distribution today than when the great philosopher first published them more than two thousand years ago.

Our brains have an ancient script that says, in effect, "Propagate your memes as well as your genes." This script, when played out too long, can be very damaging to the productivity of R&D organizations such as DARPA. When research superstars succeed, they gain prestige, position, budget, and power. They accumulate support staffs, sit in judgment over the work of others, and gain tremendous influence with the boss. In short, after years at the top, these superstars are in an excellent position to make their memes outcompete those of other researchers. And that's exactly what superstars usually do. They garner a disproportionate share of research budgets and get good at shooting down promising new ideas. Like many viruses and bacteria that have successfully infected a host, they are adept at killing competing organisms (mold organisms, for instance, secrete antibiotics such as penicillin that kill competing germs).

As long as the superstars' ideas help the organization thrive, such competitiveness does no harm. But even the most innovative researchers, after making a big discovery, are prone to incrementally milk it for years, tweaking this and slightly improving that, even when the organization's environment changes, making the big discovery less and less relevant. At Disney I fell into this trap myself. My early technical work, from 1992 through 1994, successfully applied optical beam-splitters (partially mirrored see-through glass) to create both a new type of virtual reality display and an innovative drawing tool for animators. But after these initial successes, I continued to invent gadgets with beam-splitters long after new technologies, such as large flat-panel displays, made them obsolete. A colleague at Disney Feature Animation accused me of being "a hammer that sees the whole word as a nail." Another Disney colleague, Alan Kay, who had more than forty years of experience in research labs at Xerox, Apple, and Hewlett-Packard, told me: "The names of the research projects change to include the latest buzzwords, but the actual research never does."

I have known a few superstars who really did change their research to adapt to changing environments, but these individuals were the exception to the rule. As a consequence, R&D labs frequently ossify with old ideas that are—owing to the political power of their exponents—nearly impossible to shed. The same is true of superstars themselves who have outlived their usefulness; you simply can't get rid of them.

DARPA avoids all of these pitfalls by automatically getting rid of superstars after five years. It doesn't matter how successful, persuasive, politically adept, or powerful DARPA program managers get, after five years, they have to move on. Far from discouraging new talent from applying for jobs at DARPA, this unusual policy actually enhances DARPA's recruiting. Successful scientists and engineers, who are usually well aware of the stultified superstar phenomenon that plagues many research labs, are drawn to DARPA because its policies prevent stagnation. Potential recruits know that all of their colleagues will be "new blood" and that their ability to compete for resources will only be limited by the power of their ideas.

As we saw with the stealth program, which produced a successful prototype in just three years, superstars can accomplish a lot in five years. Ironically, you may be able to recruit more of these superstars if you promise to fire them a few years later.

BACK TO SHORT FUSES

George Heilmeier's comment that he lost his passion for liquid crystal technology when RCA took too long to commercialize his discoveries reveals something interesting about the motivation of many DARPA employees: although they work exclusively on long fuse, big bang pursuits, DARPAns from top to bottom like quick payoffs as much as anyone. The difference between DARPA and most of the rest of the world is that DARPA program managers get quick rewards from lighting long fuses, not setting off quick bangs. These quick rewards are both intrinsic and extrinsic.

Intrinsic rewards are those we give ourselves. We kick up our feet at the end of a long day and congratulate ourselves for starting down the right path, solving an important problem, or helping a friend. We derive satisfaction from overcoming obstacles. DARPA employees are typically self-starters who are often more interested in pleasing themselves with these kinds of intrinsic rewards than in pleasing others. This doesn't mean DARPA scientists are selfish, only that they have very strong internal compasses that dictate what they will find rewarding. These internal compasses usually point in specific directions, such as "invisible airplanes" or "intelligent robots." DARPA program managers derive tremendous near-term satisfaction just from setting out in the right direction. DARPA scientist Dr. Amy Kruse told me that she gets a thrill from starting important research programs that "would never happen without me." She also said that DARPA colleagues are "addicted to novelty." The organization only pursues revolutionary advances in technology, so its employees are guaranteed a steady diet of novelty as they venture far beyond the realm of the practical in search of the impossible.

DARPA program managers also receive extrinsic rewards, in the form of praise and bigger research budgets based on the quality of their ideas and the progress of their programs. If they manage their contractors well (DARPA contracts out all R&D) and meet milestones, they don't have to wait years for "attaboys" and financial rewards for outstanding performance, even though the military might not benefit from their work for a decade or more. It's very rare for any DARPA employees to see their projects all the way through to finished products during their five-year tenures. At DARPA you get rewarded for lighting long fuses, then leaving.

Thus, even the most farsighted, risk-taking, maverick-laden organization in the U.S. government still goes by the play in brain's playbook that says, "Grab what you can, while you can." Except DARPA grabs for big pieces of tomorrow, not small pieces of today.

SOLVING ONE PROBLEM CREATES ANOTHER

It's no accident that almost all of the technologies that have been big wins for the military over the past fifty years, such as stealth, GPS, and unmanned air vehicles, came out of DARPA, despite the fact that DARPA spends less than 4 percent of the Defense Department's total R&D budget. DARPA's performance, pound for pound, far outstrips that of other defense labs because the agency gives military customers what they need, not what they want. The vast majority of these military customers demand that their own "captive" R&D labs create better versions of weapons the service already has—the equivalent of Henry Ford's "faster horse." And the armed services labs, entirely dependent on the goodwill of their military masters, are in no position to refuse. They salute, say "yes, sir," and crank out one incremental improvement after another.

This is not to say that DARPA only hits home runs and that armed services labs only hit singles. DARPA has rolled out a number of ho-hum innovations (such as the Phraselator, which helps soldiers crudely communicate in foreign languages such as Arabic), just as the service labs (as in the case of the navy's Sidewinder missile) have occasionally made huge advances. But on balance, DARPA outperforms the much better funded armed services labs year in and year out when it comes to groundbreaking innovation.

DARPA's enviable track record has implications that extend beyond national security. Any enterprise that wants to radically improve its products or services, or invent entirely new kinds of products, must follow at least part of DARPA's formula for success. The most important element of this formula is organizational independence. An R&D lab, new product group, or "skunk works" (a group of out-of-the-box thinkers and inventors) that reports to an organization with operational or profit responsibilities, will inevitably behave like an armed services lab and help its conservative masters take small steps instead of quantum leaps. Unable to boast a record of revolutionary breakthroughs, such a development group will not be able to recruit and retain the kind of self-motivated, curiosity junkies that make DARPA so successful.

The trend in American business over the past thirty years has been to shift almost all R&D from independent organizations, such as AT&T's Bell Labs, into R&D labs that report to profit-and-loss business units. These moves have succeeded in making American R&D labs more responsive to internal customers—and in increasing near-term earnings—but the long-term effect of "customer friendly" R&D has been a loss of American leadership in many technologies.

In my consulting business, where I help Fortune 500 companies find major new avenues of growth, I counsel corporate executives to set up small, independent innovation cells that don't have to please operating business units. A basic play in the brain's playbook is "Repeat behaviors that are rewarded; avoid behaviors that are punished." Therefore, I tell top corporate leaders that if the leaders want to increase their home run production, they—not the business unit heads who report to them—must hire power hitters and reward them for swinging for the fences. Sooner or later, under intense pressure to deliver next quarter results, most business unit leaders will punish their home run hitters for striking out too much and replace them with players who reliably hit singles.

DARPA has proven that organizational independence, coupled with a risk-taking mentality, can produce a steady stream of groundbreaking inventions. But the agency constantly struggles to find customers for innovations such as stealth, because organizational independence comes at the price of customer buy-in. In the R&D field, this phenomenon is called "the valley of death," where inventions fly out of new product organizations, only to crash and burn in the wide chasm that separates new product developers, who follow their hearts, from no-nonsense managers, who follow the bottom line. Most business managers will embrace new products that they originally asked for, but they rarely accept "gifts" that outsiders think they need.

It's only human to like your own ideas more than someone else's. This not-invented-here syndrome also creates a valley of death for new start-up companies. Many of these risk-taking ventures "build it hoping they will come," only to find out that no one ever comes.

In addition to rejecting ideas that aren't our own, we also tend to mistrust people outside of our immediate circle. This animosity flows directly from ancient scripts in our brains that drive us to organize ourselves into tribe-like units who compete with other tribe-like units for scarce resources.

Such tribalism makes new product development groups and their internal customers mistrust each other, extinguishing many long fuses as they burn their way through the valley of death. For instance, managers of profit-and-loss business units usually question the motives of in-house R&D labs, suspecting that researchers are more interested in pursuing their dreams than in pursuing profits for the company. Therefore, business units are typically skeptical about any new product emerging from the company's R&D labs. Conversely, R&D employees often perceive profit-and-loss managers as shortsighted, unimaginative Luddites, who are incapable of seeing the potential of any new invention. As a result, many researchers don't "waste time" explaining or selling their new products to internal customers. Communication breaks down, mistrust grows, and the valley of death gets deeper and wider.

Tribally motivated mistrust and antagonism is so deeply ingrained in our psyches that it inhibits communication and transfer of new ideas, not just between R&D groups and their internal customers, but between any two groups, whether the groups are separated by religion, race, family, geography, age, nationality, or organizational structure. Thus, any two groups that work in close proximity are certain to have some level of antagonism. In southern Indiana, natives look down on and tell jokes about residents of neighboring Kentucky, and Ketuckians reciprocate. The same regional tensions exist between Minnesotans and Iowans and between Northern Californians and Southern Californians. Factory managers often dislike the salespeople who sell their products and salespeople dislike marketers. In publishing houses the editorial staff lives in constant conflict with the production group. The U.S. Army has active rivalries with the Navy and Air Force that go far beyond good-natured sports competitions among the service academies.

Such rivalries very often kill long fuse, big bang ideas, whether these ideas are grounded in technology, ideology, business, or politics. No matter how many promising ideas you discover by following the brain's playbook—pursuing big opportunities in quick and easy steps, looking into blind spots, finding discomfort zones, mavericks, or Lagrange points—sooner or later you usually have to sell your big bang ideas to other tribes. Big bang ideas by their very nature have a broad sweep that changes the lives of many different groups and therefore requires their buy-in. The idea of an independent country called the United States had to be patiently socialized among all thirteen colonies. The United Nations, which traces its roots all the way back to the League of Nations in 1919, is a big bang idea that is very much a work in progress as diverse "tribes" of the world slowly figure out where their common interests lie.

As with other plays in the brain's playbook, the best way to cope with the "tribal" play that deepens such divisions is not to fight the play, but to go with it. The next chapter shows how.

RECAP

Big Bangs Require Critical Mass

An atomic bomb will explode if it contains enough radioactive material to generate a runaway chain reaction—that is, if a fast-rising wave of neutron collisions triggers a cataclysmic release of energy. However, if the amount of radioactive isotopes inside a weapon is less than "critical mass," a bomb, when triggered, will get very hot, but never explode. The same is true for innovators and mavericks inside an organization. Like a "subcritical" mass of enriched uranium that generates plenty of neutrons and heat—but no big bang—individual mavericks can throw off many great ideas that won't produce explosive results unless these mavericks work alongside a critical mass of *other* mavericks who also generate big ideas.

CHAPTER 10

In Defense of Tribalism

GETTING TO US

It's tempting to blame our ancient tribal instincts for modern ills far more serious than the "valley of death" problem. Ethnic violence in Indonesia, Rwanda, the Balkans, the Middle East, and Sri Lanka, as well as the global struggle between the West and fundamentalist Islam, suggest that tribalism is a universal and immutable downside of human nature that will promote violence between different "tribes" forever. If only we could get rid of the powerful urge to divide ourselves into "us" versus "them," we would not only enjoy many more big bang advances in technology, business, and government, but the world would be a much safer place.

Or would it?

Tribalism is hardwired into our genes because it improved our ancestors' chances of survival. Cohesive groups of humans—tribes—stood a far better chance of finding food, warding off predators, and raising their young than isolated individuals. So natural selection favored the survival of humans who had an affinity for bonding with people outside their immediate families. Tribalism, then, had as much to do with cooperation *within* groups as it did with competition *between* groups.

One reason that tribalism thrives inside modern institutions is that tribally motivated cooperation has as much value today as it did in Paleolithic times. Whether we work in a company, a government, or a nonprofit organization, we are more productive when we team up with people we like and trust to achieve common goals. A sense of group identity and strong emotional bonds among members of modern "tribes" motivates individuals who belong to these tribes to share information, help one another, and stick together during tough times. The U.S. Army, for example, trains its recruits to be loyal not only to the army as a whole, but also to much smaller groups, such as squads comprised of about ten soldiers. Squads heighten their shared identities and cohesiveness by working together as a unit and pitting their skills, such as marksmanship, against other squads.

The army's purposeful pitting of one artificial tribe—a squad—against another in competitions such as marksmanship, physical fitness, and war gaming highlights an interesting facet of tribalism: competition *between* groups increases cooperation *within* groups. When we share a common rival, we tend to forget differences among ourselves. Tribally inspired competitions can be a net positive if the resulting benefits of increased cooperation outweigh the costs of competition. Over its two-hundred-plus-year history, the army has learned how to strike the right balance between cooperation and competition, in a manner that makes the army as a whole come out ahead. The same squads who compete with one another, also cooperate when they band together into multi-squad platoons competing against other platoons. Similarly, competing platoons later cooperate with one another when they form companies that compete with other companies. The process repeats itself as companies form into battalions, battalions form into divisions, and so forth. By the time soldiers finish training and reach the field, they have forged emotional bonds and a sense of belonging that extends from the lowest unit to the highest unit of organization in the army. All of the repeated competitions do leave a residue of antagonism that hampers cooperation and communication between different units at all levels, but on balance the army gets more internal cooperation from carefully fostering tribalism than it loses from competitive friction.

The army's success forging teams has a lot to teach us about how to exploit the brain's ancient tribal scripts to foster cooperation. The first lesson is that even a few months of shared training and competition can turn complete strangers into comrades—even close friends. The second is that it's possible for rival groups to compete with one another at the same time they cooperate, with the result being a net increase in cooperation. Finally, and most important, the army has proven that it's possible to get people to continually expand their definition of what constitutes "us." When a soldier enlists, "us" includes himself and maybe a friend or two. Then "us" becomes a squad, a platoon, a company, a battalion, and on up to the army as a whole. In times of war, an army soldier's definition of "us" can even include armies of allied nations (and in very rare cases, the U.S. Navy and Air Force).

Getting people to redefine "us" is crucially important for keeping long fuses burning to big bangs, because the kind of people who most often come up with revolutionary, big bang ideas rarely belong to the same "tribe" as the people who must implement or accept those ideas. In the Department of Defense, DARPA invents the majority of paradigm-shifting technologies, such as stealth, but the armed services have the job of turning DARPA proto-types into production systems, then buying, deploying, and operating the new technology. In corporations, R&D groups develop new products and solutions, but engineering, manufacturing, and sales organizations must make these new solutions a reality. The jobs of product creation and product implementation are segregated this way because the temperament and skills of idea creators and idea implementers are vastly different. Idea creators are usually—but not always—divergent, unconventional, big-picture thinkers who are best managed with loose goals and flexible deadlines, while idea im-plementers are often convergent, detail-oriented thinkers who are best man-aged with specific goals and well defined deadlines and budgets.

Even between tribes comprised of like-minded people, there will be natu-ral resistance in one group to ideas created in another group. In modern organizations, departments who perform similar functions such as sales are supposed to share "best practices" with one another, but they rarely do. And the bigger the idea, the less its chances for crossing the "valley of death" that separates two entities: big ideas entail big changes, and big changes require big movements away from comfort zones.

The solution to keeping long fuses burning as they cross between groups is to get rival tribes to redefine "us." Strong leaders, such as General David Jones, Jack Welch, Lou Gerstner, Sam Walton, and P&G's A. J. Lafley, succeeded largely because they got their subordinates to break down tradi-tional barriers and embrace ideas of other "tribes." Jones ordered his generals to accept DARPA's stealth technology. When Jack Welch took the helm at GE, he required executives to share best practices and to foster a "horizon-tal" organization that shared products, markets, employees, and customers. Corporate turnaround specialist Lou Gerstner pulled IBM out of a down-ward spiral by creating positive incentives for cooperation, and *disincentives* for competition among IBM's different businesses, while P&G and Wal-Mart CEOs A. J. Lafley and Sam Walton mandated radical redefinitions of their organization's boundaries with their suppliers.

Steve Nixon used his authority as leader of science technology for the Intelligence Community to move promising new technologies across the "valley of death" that separated Intelligence R&D labs from Intelligence operations. For example, in his Rapid Technology Transition Initiative (RTTI) Steve provided financial incentives that encouraged operational intelligence collection and analysis units to adopt new technologies that had been languishing in their own agency's R&D labs (or even labs of other agencies). The Biometric Quick Capture System, which allowed FBI agents and Special Operations units to quickly identify terrorist suspects anytime, anywhere on the globe, was a prominent example of the success of RTTI, but there were others.

Starting in 2000, Disney's corporate CFO, Tom Staggs, increased the transfer of technology from the company's R&D labs into Disney's operating businesses by earmarking portions of the corporate R&D budget to be directed according to the wishes of different businesses. By allowing individual businesses to "redeem" research funds to solve technical and business problems that were not a fit for their own internal development groups, this program caused an important shift in the way some (but unfortunately, not all) businesses viewed corporate R&D. Instead of looking at corporate research funds as "someone else's budget," a few of Disney businesses, such as cable network ESPN, came to view the special funds as "our budget," and therefore engaged with corporate R&D labs to develop solutions that ESPN quickly deployed in their business. High-quality video on ESPN's Web site, which was free for the first time of jerkiness and other image artifacts, was an example of an important new product that emerged from the program.

In each of these cases, big bang ideas crossed over the tribally inspired "valley of death" because a leader at the top strongly encouraged cooperation among rival tribes. The same is true for the army's methods of getting recruits to constantly widen their definition of "us": soldiers cooperated in large part because they were ordered to. Although such top-down approaches have produced dramatic results in the military, and at firms such as Disney, GE, and IBM, they won't work everywhere. Many organizations don't have a leader at the top who believes that breaking down tribal barriers is important *and* has the skill and willpower to damp down the competitive instincts of subordinates, so the benefits of top-down cooperation are usually temporary: when the strong-willed leader departs, so does the spirit of cooperation. Another limitation of the top-down method is that it requires competing tribes to all report to a common leader. There are many situations—for example relations between completely independent companies or countries—where rival tribes don't share the same leader. And even in hierarchical organizations where there *is* theoretically a single person in charge who can mandate cooperation, in practice most leaders are so consumed with short-fuse emergencies that they let underlings figure out how to break down organizational barriers.

So, is it possible to redefine "us" when a leader at the top doesn't mandate cooperation? And if it is possible, can the new definition of "us" survive the departure of the parties who somehow managed to foster voluntary cooperation?

LEADING FROM BELOW

Despite its fame as the home of France's premier brandy, the town of Cognac in southwestern France is a small village of only 10,500 people. At one time, Cognac had double that population, but over the past fifty years, as its youth moved to urban centers such as Paris and Lyon, the city has been in steady decline. However, those who remain in Cognac are proud of their village, its heritage, and of the famous Frenchmen who were born there. Francois I, king of France from 1515 to 1547, was born in the castle at Cognac in 1494. The poet Octavien de Saint-Gelais and Paul-Emile Lecoq de Boisbaudran, discoverer of the elements gallium and samarium, were also born and raised in Cognac, as was Claude Bouche, inventor of the glass blowing machine that revolutionized bottle making. But Cognac's most famous son is Jean Monnet, who forever transformed European's definition of "us" without ever holding major political office.

Born into a merchant family in 1888, Monnet as a young boy developed a keen interest in numbers, which would stay with him and shape his approach to solving problems throughout his life. Jean loved to sit with his father, who'd built up a prosperous wine and spirits business, and pore over the company's balance sheets. His natural affinity for business and finance led him to join his father's firm immediately after finishing secondary school. The decision to skip college wasn't a difficult one. Monnet said, "There are two kinds of people: those who want to be someone and those who want to do something." Jean fell firmly into the second category.

Monnet's desire for action took him all over the globe selling brandy. After two years in London learning English and looking after the family's UK interests, Jean took frequent business trips to Egypt, Russia, Scandinavia, America, and Canada. Jean loved international travel, meeting new people, and being exposed to perspectives that were very different from those he'd experienced in rural France. Monnet said of those early years in the family business:

> Through this thing [cognac], we had an immense field of observation and a very active exchange of ideas. . . . I learned about people, international business, more than I would have with a formal education. All I had to do was to watch and listen. Why should I have taken a detour studying law in a student's room in Poitiers, when I could easily enter the school of life and visit the world?

The lesson in "the school of life" that influenced Jean the most was the principle of "co-authored action." Especially in what he referred to as the "Anglo-Saxon" world of the UK, America, and Canada, Monnet said he experienced a level of consensus building, compromise, and communal thinking that he had not seen in his native France. Monnet illustrated this "Anglo-Saxon" approach by describing an encounter he had with a Canadian while traveling from Medicine Hat to Moose Jaw, Canada, on a sales trip. Stuck in Calgary without a horse or buggy, Monnet asked a blacksmith where he might rent a horse. "Take my horse," the man said. "When you're through just hitch it up here."

Whether or not Anglo-Saxons deserved all the credit Monnet gave them for being team players, his perception that they had a culture of "co-authored action" motivated him to seek out strong partnerships with them throughout his career. When the world war broke out in 1914, Jean was dismayed over disorganization and waste in France's approach to acquiring, moving, and managing supplies for the war effort. Having seen much more efficient approaches to managing supply chains in his business dealings overseas, Monnet used his family connections to gain a meeting with France's leader, René Viviani, to propose that France, the UK, and other allies pool their resources for the common good rather than act as completely independent countries.

To Monnet's shrewd business eye, the war amounted to a battle of balance sheets. Germany and its allies had so many troops, artillery, trucks, and supplies that were pitted against those of France, Britain, and its allies. Whoever's balance sheet was healthiest would win the war. In 1914, the allied balance sheet was decidedly unhealthy. Monnet told Viviani:

> "There is an immense waste, the merchant fleets have not been requisitioned for understandable reasons, but the present competitive situation [France competing with Britain for scarce resources] is not without absurdity. No priority has been defined. . . . The interallied cooperative bodies are insufficient."

Monnet proposed that France and Britain unify their purchasing and shipment of supplies such as food, coal, and iron to make better use of scarce resources. For example, it was common for British ships to arrive with a full load of cargo at French ports, unload, then leave empty, while at the same time French ships were leaving British ports empty after unloading their cargo. Thus, the allies were taking two trips instead of one at a time when U-boat attacks were making shipping a precious commodity. The French and English were also bidding against each other for purchase of fuel, combat equipment, and food, driving up prices of critical supplies for both parties. Monnet argued that only cooperative planning and control could eliminate these dangerous inefficiencies and build up the allies' collective "balance sheet."

Although Monnet was only twenty-six, Viviani accepted his proposal and sent him to London to sell the English on this idea. Working with France's trade representative, Etien Clementel, Monnet undertook the daunting task of persuading the English to coordinate shipping and purchase of supplies. France and England had fought each other for more than one thousand years, creating deep-seated mutual suspicion. The French had a popular phrase, *"Perfidious Albion,"* to describe their neighbor (Albion was the Latin name of the British Isles) across the Channel, expressing the widespread perception that Englishmen were treacherous. This perception grew out of the English response to the French Revolution. Instead of following their stated liberal, egalitarian values, the English had sided with European monarchies to help undermine the revolution. The English, for their part, also had long memories of French bad behavior. The French, having suffered a humiliating

defeat by a much smaller English force of longbowmen at Agincourt, threatened to amputate the bow fingers of any English archers they captured. After-
ward, Englishmen were fond of giving Frenchmen "two fingers," a sign that
was at the same time vulgar and a reminder of French barbarity.

Monnet's job was made even more difficult by England's long-standing
belief that its power and prestige were rooted in its navy and merchant ma-
rine. The refrain in England's iconic patriotic song "Rule Britannia" said it all:

> *Rule Britannia*
> *Britannia rule the waves*
> *Britons never never never shall be slaves*

Such pride made it very difficult for the English to give up sovereignty
over their maritime fleet.

Finally the English believed in a free market economy in which the
government had little say in how businesses behaved, whereas the French government often dictated the priorities of key industries. Thus, even though the
French agreed to pool resources, there was no single business or government
organization that had the authority to unify supply and shipping, even if the
English government wanted to cooperate.

Monnet and Clementel struggled for two years to unify Allied shipping
and purchase of supplies. Finally, in late 1916, after two years of debilitating
conflict on the continent, with food supplies growing short in both France
and England, the two former rivals agreed to cooperate with Italy in forming
the Wheat Executive. This joint body fell far short of the total unification
that Monnet had wanted, but its modest approach—voluntary, loose coordination of shipping and pooling of purchases of wheat and other staples—
helped reduce food prices and increase availability of food for civilians. This
success, together with deepening privation and hardship, eased England's
mistrust of the French to the point where they agreed to set up the Allied
Martine Transport Council (AMTC) in November 1917, with Jean Monnet taking the lead role for France. The AMTC, which included England,
Italy, France, and the United States, had much broader authority than the
Wheat Executive, serving as a cartel that carefully controlled prices for key
commodities as well as the priorities and availability of all allied shipping.
The added efficiency of the AMTC allowed the Allies to compensate for

their heavy losses to German U-boats and played a pivotal role in forcing the Austro-Hungarian Empire to surrender a year after AMTC was formed.

Impressed with Monnet's extraordinary contributions to the war effort, in 1919, England's foreign secretary, Lord Balfour, and French prime minister Georges Clemenceau appointed Monnet deputy secretary general of the League of Nations at the age of thirty-one. Monnet later explained how he accomplished so much at a young age, despite his lack of formal education. One key ingredient to his success was that Monnet was not a politician. In his view, politicians had to spend so much time acquiring and protecting power that they had no time to develop big ideas of their own. Monnet said of politicians, "When ideas are lacking, they accept yours with gratitude—provided they can present them as their own."

Recognizing that accepting ideas was only a first step, Monnet knew he also had to motivate politicians to *act* on those ideas. He said: "People only accept change when they are faced with necessity and only recognize necessity when a crisis is upon them."

Monnet understood that, even in times of war, shortsighted leaders can be slow to comprehend the full magnitude of the crises facing them, so he learned to push for changes that only went as far as politicians' *perceptions* of crisis. In 1916, when the British saw a food crisis, Monnet proposed the Wheat Executive. A year later, when continued U-boat predation and the cumulative effects of three years of war had deepened the supply crisis, Monnet proposed a much wider scope of collaboration in the AMTC.

We see in Monnet's methods an intuitive understanding of how to get brains (in this case, politicians' brains) to change their behavior without fundamentally changing the scripts by which they operate. Monnet understood that brains ignore all but obvious here-and-now problems, so he proposed obvious here-and-now solutions. He also knew that risk-averse brains only change behaviors in small steps, so each of Monnet's here-and-now solutions was more evolutionary than revolutionary. Finally, with both the Wheat Executive and AMTC, Monnet did not try to get different nationalities to drop tribalism altogether, but to *shift* their tribal loyalties from individual nation states to an allied collective of nation states. By the end of the war the brains of British and French politicians were as shortsighted, risk-averse, and tribal as they were before the war, but Monnet had managed to steer those natural tendencies into highly productive directions: a classic example of brain judo.

SHORT FUSE, BIG BANG

In his senior post at the League of Nations, Monnet tried to apply the principles he'd learned during the war to increase the scope of "co-authored action" to the entire world. The League enjoyed some success recruiting countries on all continents (though not the isolationist United States), setting up precursors to important bodies that are preserved to this day in the World Health Organization, UNESCO, and the World Court. But on balance, Monnet was disillusioned with the League. Cooperative efforts that had begun during the war floundered. Monnet wrote: "During the war, the pooling of resources and the Allied organization resulted from a joint effort, but I had forgotten that this joint effort resulted from the war, from the absolute necessity to agree."

Realizing that the key ingredient for success—a shared crisis—was lacking, Monnet resigned from the League in 1923 to look after his family's struggling business. He remained in the private sector for the next sixteen years, shifting to international finance after getting his Cognac business back on a sound footing in 1924.

Three months after the Second World War began in September 1939, Monnet re-joined the French government as the president of the Franco-British Coordination Committee. The British, having seen the benefits of co-operation in the previous war, understood the need to unify supply and shipping of critical goods. They quickly agreed to share fuel, arms, raw materials, food, shipping, and other supplies under the auspices of Monnet's committee. However, despite this attitude of cooperation, Monnet still found that he constantly had to sell big ideas. French and British financial interests balked at combining a very large order for American warplanes until Monnet presented them with one of his famous balance sheets showing that German fighters and bombers outnumbered the combined Franco-British air forces respectively 1.5:1 and 2:1. Presented in such stark, simple terms, the need to buy warplanes jointly in bulk became obvious, and governments and financiers on both channels agreed to order 7,400 planes and 8,000 aircraft engines.

When, in the spring of 1940, it became clear that these cooperative efforts might not stop a German overthrow of France, Monnet proposed a much more radical approach to Franco-British cooperation: the complete union of the two nations into a single country. By early June, de Gaulle, Churchill, and Monnet had finished a draft of a document spelling out the "indissoluble union" of France and Britain into "not two countries, but one." However, even though the Germans had forced French President Reynaud to flee Paris for Bordeaux, Reynaud refused to sign the document. Within days, Germany effectively took control of France.

Although Monnet fully embraced the idea of a Franco-British union, it's unclear whether Churchill and de Gaulle ever saw the move as more than a symbolic, last-ditch attempt to forestall a German takeover of France. Shortly after the war, de Gaulle observed that Monnet always tried to "mix the unmixables."

Despite de Gaulle's cynicism, Monnet enjoyed considerable success doing just that during the war. Immediately after the fall of France, Monnet offered his services to Churchill securing desperately needed supplies from the Americans. Taking his balance sheets to America, Monnet showed Roosevelt the relative quantities of aircraft, tanks, artillery, and ammunition possessed by the British and Axis powers, again revealing the numerical inferiority of the British and the Russians. These balance sheets demonstrated that America needed to quickly ramp up its war production if it hoped to prevent its English friends from becoming a vassal state of Germany. Monnet also pointed out that volume purchases from Britain would prepare America for war if the country's fragile peace with the Axis powers ever collapsed. Monnet's arguments and simple balance sheets played a major role in helping Roosevelt persuade an isolationist Congress to authorize a rapid expansion of America's war machine. This expansion prepared America for war to such an extent that the economist John Maynard Keynes later said that "Monnet had shortened the war by a year."

Pleased that Roosevelt had gotten America's "Victory Program" together, Monnet dubbed the country "The Arsenal of Democracy." Roosevelt liked this phrase so much that he borrowed it as his own, sending word through aides that Monnet should stop using it lest the phrase's authorship be in doubt. Monnet, adhering to his policy of selling big ideas by giving them away to politicians, quickly complied. Monnet stayed in Washington three more years, becoming a close confidant of Roosevelt and helping keep British and Russian troops supplied with American planes, tanks, artillery, and ammunition. In 1943, Monnet rejoined the provisional French government in Algeria, where he worked until the end of the war securing American loans and equipment for France.

Although Monnet had learned a great deal about overcoming tribal instincts during the First World War, he gained more insight during the Second. One of these lessons was that it was always better to appeal to selfishness than selflessness. Instead of leading off a pitch by emphasizing the communal good for multiple parties, Monnet always started by describing how his proposals would satisfy the proprietary interests of each party. For example, Monnet told the Americans that ramping up war production would kickstart their flagging economy while getting someone else—the British and the Russians—to help pay the capital costs for tooling up new factories. This would lower America's own production costs if they ever needed the factories for their own war effort. Thus, Americans—especially isolationists in Congress—perceived the "Victory Program" as an initiative that primarily helped America. If the program also helped the Brits and the Russians—so American thinking went—well, no harm in that. But helping others was not the prime motivator. Here was another example of "brain judo." In getting the "Victory Program" started, Monnet persuaded the Americans to cooperate with other tribes by going *with* their natural instincts to look after the interests of their own tribe.

Another important lesson that Monnet learned in World War II was that Western leaders failed to learn from experience. Even with Hitler threatening to take over Europe and North Africa, and the Japanese threatening to take over China and the Pacific, many Allied statesmen and businessmen did not grasp the extremity of the cooperative measures that would be required to defeat the Axis powers, despite the spectacular successes of the AMTC twenty years earlier. The Allies were run mostly by History majors who had forgotten history. Monnet used another play in the brain's playbook—heavy reliance on direct sensory experience—to overcome the short memories of politicians through his skillful use of simple, visually compelling balance sheets.

Monnet did not have to wait long after the Second World War ended to see more evidence of the short memories of Western leaders. Instead of reaching across the channel to cooperate with continental Europe on re-building their ravished economy, the British turned back to the traditional source of economic power, their colonies. Although many of these colonies had gained independence, and others—such as India—were in the process of breaking away, Britain spent more energy fostering economic cooperation among their colonies and former colonies, collectively called the British Commonwealth, than it did fostering cooperation with its historic rivals France and Germany.

France also was falling back into a familiar pattern. At France's urging, the Allies forced Germany to give France administrative and economic control of two border regions, the Saar and the Ruhr, as a precondition for the establishment of an independent German state. France wanted control of these regions because the Saar and the Ruhr produced most of the coal and steel that Germany would need if they ever decided to re-arm. Also, France badly needed German coal and steel to rebuild its own devastated economy. France's control of the Saar and the Ruhr greatly weakened Germany and strengthened France; from the French point of view, what wasn't to like?

Monnet, who was in charge of rebuilding France's economy after the war, was uneasy about the Ruhr and Saar arrangements because he saw in them a repeat of the Versailles Treaty, which had imposed steep war reparations and other harsh conditions that fueled German economic collapse and Hitler's rise to power. Monnet also saw continued rivalry among European states as a missed opportunity for the whole of the continent to be greater than the sum of its parts. As early as 1943 he had written:

> There will be no peace in Europe if the States rebuild themselves on the basis of national sovereignty, with its implications of prestige politics and economic protection. . . . The countries of Europe are not strong enough individually to be able to guarantee prosperity and social development for their peoples. The States of Europe must therefore form a federation or a European entity that would make them into a common economic unit.

But Monnet was not in a position to do much about his concerns, as anti-German sentiment ran high and France's top priority was reconstruction. Therefore, from 1945 to 1949, Monnet focused his energies on modernizing and rebuilding French industry and trade as commissioner of France's economic plan.

Toward the end of 1949, with France's economy well on its way to full recovery, Monnet saw a convergence of factors that would help him reinvigorate the spirit of "supranational" cooperation that he had so thoroughly embraced throughout two world wars. First, tension between France and West Germany over control of steel and coal production was beginning to mount, once again raising the specter of conflict between Europe's two largest countries. Monnet, whose role rebuilding France's economy brought him into frequent contact with Germans in the Saar and the Ruhr, summed up the "German problem" in a note to French foreign minister Robert Schumann: "Peace must be based on equality. We missed peace in 1919 because we have introduced discrimination and the spirit of superiority. We are now beginning to make the same mistakes."

In parallel with mounting animosity between France and Germany, the United States had concluded that Germany must re-arm to bolster Allied forces against Soviet expansion into Western Europe. The United States was also concerned that France's exploitation of German steel and coal would create a combination of ill will and economic stagnation in West Germany that would drive the country closer to the Soviets. In early 1950, U.S. secretary of state Dean Acheson strongly suggested that his counterparts in Britain and France, Ernest Bevin and Robert Schuman, develop a strategy for bringing Germany more closely into the European fold. With tensions mounting on the Korean Peninsula, and the looming drain on American military forces there, Acheson was in a hurry. He asked for a draft plan to be ready at the May 1950 meeting of the three foreign ministers. Schuman understood that lurking just below the surface of Acheson's request was an implied threat: if France and Britain didn't make Germany a strong bulwark against the Soviets, America would. The prospect of a re-armed Germany that harbored deep resentments over loss of its steel and coal regions was too horrible to contemplate. Schuman was desperate for creative solutions that would strengthen Germany without threatening France.

Monnet, who had been waiting for five years for a crisis that could propel European states toward a federation, was well prepared. He quickly presented Schuman with a plan that would build up West Germany as the Americans wanted, but in a way that would prevent the former rival from using its newfound might against its French neighbor. The plan called for a unification of French and German coal and steel production and consumption under an independent, supranational authority that France and Germany would influence equally. This arrangement would benefit France by ensuring it access to German coal and steel when France's own resources were inadequate to meet the needs of its aggressive industrial modernization campaign. And if domestic demand for coal and steel ever fell below France's production capacity, France could keep its coal and steel workers fully employed by selling to Germany, whose need for coal and steel after the war far outstripped France's. Monnet's plan also prevented Germany from focusing their steel production on construction of armaments that could be used against France. Germany liked Monnet's plan because it gave the country back influence over its own coal and steel assets, while opening up new markets and sources of labor (French workers) and affording Germany greater power in the international marketplace by making Germany's coal and steel industries part of a larger French-German conglomerate. In business as in war, size matters. The bigger you are, the more favorable a deal you can strike with a negotiating partner. Larger size also helps you realize economies of scale that lower your costs and raise profits.

Due to pressures of time and rising tensions with Germany, Schuman was inclined to go along with the plan, but Monnet wanted to insure that France didn't squander a rare opportunity to advance the cause of supranationalism, so he increased the appeal of the coal and steel plan by suggesting it be named "The Schuman Plan." Schuman accepted both the plan and the name, secured the necessary endorsements for it in both Paris and Bonn, and presented the proposal at the London foreign ministers' conference in May 1950. Acheson and Bevin gave their approval, and serious negotiations soon got under way for creation of the European Coal and Steel Community (ECSC).

It's hard to overstate the historic importance of the foreign ministers' agreement. A peacetime "supranational" entity, with real economic power, was unprecedented. As later events proved, the Schuman Plan was a crucial first step in getting European states to relinquish some of their sovereignty for the greater good of Europe as a whole.

Monnet's behind-the-scenes orchestration of the May 1950 foreign ministers' agreement on the Schuman Plan represented an important advancement in methods for overcoming the tribal instincts of Europeans. His experience in two wars had taught him that European leaders would only let go of their powerful nationalistic urges in times of crises, and even then the leaders needed to be continually reeducated on the aggressiveness of cooperative measures required.

Therefore, Monnet realized that there was no point wasting energy or influence trying to damp down nationalistic/tribal rivalries in the absence of a crisis. He would have to bide his time. In his memoirs, Monnet wrote that growing up in the brandy business had given him exactly the right temperament for waiting for the correct moment to act.

> Events that strike me and occupy my thoughts lead me to general conclusions about what has to be done. Then circumstances, which determine day-to-day events, suggest or supply the means of action. I can wait a long time for the right moment. In Cognac, they are good at waiting. It is the only way to make good brandy.

Monnet had learned how to set off big bangs—not by lighting long fuses—but by preparing short fuses and waiting patiently for the big bangs to come to him. Through his experiences with the Allied Maritime Transport Council in World War I and the Franco-British Cooperation Committee in World War II, Monnet had developed clear ideas about how nations could pool their resources in peacetime to mutual benefit, but he had kept these ideas largely to himself until the looming crisis over German rearmament amid Franco-German tension over coal and steel created just the right moment. Although Monnet did not tell Schuman this, key elements of the soon-to-be-famous plan that bore the foreign minister's name had been sitting in Monnet's back pocket since 1943.

There are two important take-aways from Monnet's success setting up the ECSC. First, discomfort zones, such as acute material shortages that arise during a world war, are not always available, so you sometimes have to prepare the fuse to a big bang well in advance of the time it can be lit. Second, while some big bangs, such as America becoming the "Arsenal of Democracy" before it entered World War II, are best ignited through a long series of interconnected smaller bangs, other types of big bangs occur quickly or not at all. This second category of revolutionary change comes about when a crisis demands solutions that are both far-reaching and extremely fast.

In times of crisis, anxious leaders who are under intense pressure to act are drawn to plans that have been worked out in advance and can be implemented quickly. And the most important attribute of any plan for quick execution, Monnet knew, was simplicity. As with all of his proposals, Monnet pushed the small team of collaborators who developed the Schuman Plan to eliminate as many complications as possible. For example, even though he ultimately wanted to include all of Europe in a supranational economic entity as a first step toward a European Federation, Monnet thought the ECSC should initially encompass only France and Germany in order to streamline and shorten the negotiating process.

In the end, Monnet was only partially successful in making the Schuman plan simple. He was able to keep Britain out of the initial ECSC agreement, but not Italy, Belgium, Luxembourg, and the Netherlands. Also, a charter that Monnet had hoped to restrict to a few articles ballooned into a hundred separate articles encompassing far-reaching issues such as a European Court. To Monnet's relief, these complications slowed but did not kill the agreement, and in April 1951 six nations signed the Treaty of Paris establishing the ECSC, which began full operation in July of the following year. Most important to Monnet, the treaty gave ECSC considerable power to set prices, allocate scarce resources, make investments, and punish member states who erected barriers to free trade, or engaged in predatory pricing, dumping, or other anti-competitive behaviors. The ECSC would *not* be just another toothless body like the League of Nations.

The Treaty of Paris was written in French with German ink on Dutch vellum, then bound in Belgian parchment, glued with paste from Luxembourg, and tied with an Italian ribbon. Preparation and speed had been important in getting the historic agreement adopted, but so had symbolism.

A THOUSAND YEARS OF PROGRESS IN ONLY TWENTY

Monnet took charge of the governing body of the ECSC, the High Authority, as the organization's first president in 1952. The position afforded him an excellent opportunity to implement another strategy for overcoming tribal rivalries he had been incubating since the end of the war: putting cooperation in the hands of institutions instead of men. From long experience, Monnet knew that individual leaders would stop working together as soon as the urgent need to cooperate vanished. But Monnet theorized that a supranational institution that had real power to enforce its decisions would be motivated—crisis or no—to continually expand its reach and influence, and along with it, the cause of international cooperation. Although he never described the ECSC in tribal terms, Monnet wanted members of the ECSC to change their definition of "us" from French, German, Dutch, Belgian, Italian, or Luxembourger tribe to "ECSC tribe" or, better still, "European tribe." As with his efforts setting up the AMTC in World War I, he did not try to eliminate tribalism, just to change its scope to encompass an ever larger group. Instincts that drove individuals to seek advantage for their tribe, could be put to good use as employees of the new ECSC "tribe" naturally sought to expand the bureaucratic power of their institution.

From the very beginning, although he confided his true intentions to a small circle of confidants, Monnet intended that the ECSC should be the seed from which a fully unified Europe would grow. So he insisted that the ECSC be given a fifty-year charter that extended far beyond the crisis that had spurred its creation. Even though ECSC was a big bang in its own right, Monnet saw the coal and steel cooperative as merely the first step in a long journey toward the complete political and economic union of Europe. He would use a connected string of big bangs—not small ones—to set off the biggest bang of all time: the peaceful unification of an entire continent.

A detailed examination of the way in which the ECSC advanced the selfish interests of each of its members—and ultimately paved the way for the modern European Union that Monnet envisioned in 1950—provides important insights about how to spot certain types of big bang opportunities and make them a reality.

Before the Second World War gave France control of much of German coal and steel production, the segregation of coal and steel production into separate national markets had created major inefficiencies in both supply and demand of these critical commodities. For example, if French factories needed more steel than the French steel industry could supply, they had to import steel from abroad and pay steep tariffs designed to protect French steel interests. This raised their costs and made their products less competitive. Conversely, if French steel producers had excess capacity, other nations' protectionist policies and duties made it difficult for them to export their products. Both undersupply and oversupply of steel-making capacity stunted economic growth, fueled unemployment, and restricted funds available for modernization. If France—under pressure from America to strengthen Germany—were forced to lessen its control of coal and steel in the Saar/Ruhr regions and return to the prewar way of doing business, its economic recovery, heavily dependent on coal and steel, would falter.

The situation in other European countries mirrored that in France. The coal and steel industries in each nation effectively owned 100 percent of the "pie" in the country, but each pie was small, and it was very difficult to make the pie much bigger. Without enlarging this local "pie," each nation would struggle to create new jobs and grow their economies. The trade barriers that produced inefficiency and stagnation in coal and steel represented a latent big bang opportunity in the following sense: when coal and steel could move without restriction into the markets where they were needed most, both oversupply and undersupply of the materials would be greatly reduced. A stable, cost-efficient supply chain increased production, created new jobs, and made funds available for industrial expansions that drove production and employment still higher. With higher employment, consumer demand for products containing steel or manufactured with coal power increased. A virtuous circle of steadily increasing production and consumption was created that made the size of the total "pie" for coal and steel for cooperating nations much larger than the combined "pie" would have been without the lowering of trade barriers. Paradoxically, each nation advanced its own selfish economic interests by opening its domestic markets up to other nations, swapping 100 percent of a small, fixed pie for a smaller percentage of a much larger, fast-growing pie.

Combining all coal and steel into a larger "common market" gave member nations other important benefits. ECSC imposed levies on all member nations to pool funds for investment and modernization. With these pooled resources, ECSC was able to fund modernization and expansion projects in member states that would have been impossible without the common market. Also, due to its massive size, ECSC was able to borrow at favorable rates, then turn around and offer low-cost loans to member nations. During recessions and times of overcapacity, ECSC imposed quotas that insured that each nation got its fair share of production, and funded retraining and employment programs to help displaced coal and steel workers.

The ECSC lived up to its big bang promise. From 1952 through 1960 coal and steel production in member nations rose 75 percent and industrial production as a whole went up 58 percent. Although coal production started to decline in the 1950s worldwide, as alternative fuels such as oil, natural gas, and atomic energy became more cost-effective, intra-European trade in coal increased tenfold, greatly reducing Europe's need to import costly coal from North America. Finally, ECSC helped its less efficient members, such as Belgium, recover from economic downturns, such as the recession of 1959, by providing grants and training programs that helped displaced workers find new jobs.

Wherever you see artificial barriers, such as protectionist trade policies, you will also see ready-made big bang opportunities that await the demolition of those barriers. One of Monnet's favorite quotes was from King Ibn Saud, who had united the many tribes of the Arabian Peninsula into the modern nation of Saudi Arabia. Saud said that Allah had appeared before him in the desert and told him, "For me, everything is a means, even the obstacles."

In setting up the ECSC, Monnet had taken this idea one step further, making everything a means, *especially* the obstacles. Major obstacles to intra-European cooperation that remained after the establishment of ECSC provided still greater opportunities. As ECSC member nations learned that they could safely drop trade barriers and grow by exchanging small "whole pies" for large slices of much bigger "pies," it became obvious that barriers to the movement of products and services other than coal and steel, as well as of people and capital, were limiting growth of the European economy. Capitalizing on the early success of the ECSC, Monnet and his "tribe" of supranationals worked with politicians in each member country to widen cooperation among the six founding nations. These efforts culminated in the 1957 Treaties of Rome that established the European Economic Community (also called the Common Market), which eliminated tariffs, quotas, and customs duties for all goods, agricultural products, and services, and for the first time allowed citizens of one member state to cross the borders of other member states without going through lengthy checks at Customs and Immigration. Investment capital could also flow without restrictions across borders of member states.

In the decade after the formation of the Common Market, Monnet and his supranational allies kept the momentum building toward full European unification. In 1967, the Treaty of Brussels merged the ECSC, the Common Market, and other cooperative bodies, such as EURATOM, into a single administrative entity with a unified budget. In 1973 Denmark, Ireland, and the United Kingdom joined the European Common Market, followed by Greece in 1981, and Portugal and Spain in 1986. In 1990, as part of German unification, East Germany also joined. The 1992 Treaty of Maastricht formally created the European Union and mandated a single currency for adoption by 1999. As part of this restructuring, the EEC was renamed the EC (European Community), signifying that the federation was no longer primarily an economic entity, but now also a political entity, in which member nations closely coordinated defense, foreign policy, and legal matters. So-called "enlargements" added Austria, Finland, and Sweden in 1995 and Cyprus, the Czech Republic, Yalta, Latvia, Lithuania, Estonia, Malta, Poland, Hungary, Slovakia, and Slovenia in 2004.

Monnet, who died in 1979, did not live to witness the birth of the European Union, but he is widely regarded as its father. In a letter to Monnet in 1963, John F. Kennedy wrote: "Under your inspiration, Europe has moved closer to unity in less than twenty years than it had done before in a thousand."

ALL THE PLAYS IN THE PLAYBOOK

We have seen that working with the brain's ancient scripts can produce spectacular innovations such as HIV drugs and iPhones. Using the brain's playbook helped Sam Walton build the largest company in the world, just as it helped Lou Gerstner save IBM. And America's military has an awesome array of cutting edge technology thanks to playbook practitioners such as DARPA's George Heilmeier. But Jean Monnet's accomplishment founding the European Union stands out as the most spectacular of all of these long fuse, big bang achievements. Not only does the European Union have an impressively long fuse—beginning with the establishment of the Wheat Commission in 1917 and continuing through the founding of the ECSC in 1951 and the European Union in 1992—but the magnitude of the EU big bang dwarfs the other accomplishments. The establishment of the EU has made it unlikely that European nations will continue with their three-thousand-year-old tradition of warring with each other, and will probably enhance the prosperity and well-being of Europeans far into the future. Finally, the success of the EU has shown the rest of the globe what humans can achieve when they co-opt their tribal instincts to transform "them" into "us." In sum, Monnet's big bang literally changed the world.

It's instructive to ask, "What made Monnet's accomplishment stand head and shoulders above the other achievements that we've explored?" Timing was certainly a factor; it's hard to imagine a unified Europe in the Napoleonic era, or in the Middle Ages. Also, Monnet thought big. His goal was not to grow a company or introduce a revolutionary new product, but to irreversibly improve the human condition. Although his focus was Europe, Monnet harbored global ambitions for the cause of transnationalism. Toward the end of his life he wrote: "The Community we have created is not an end in itself. The sovereign nations of the past can no longer solve the problems of the present; they cannot control their own future. The European Community should only be a stage on the way to the organised world of tomorrow."

But fortuitous timing and sweeping ambition do not explain all of Monnet's success. A major reason that Monnet fathered the EU was that he simultaneously exploited most, if not all, of the plays in the brain's playbook, creating a kind of perfect storm in which the brain's hidden scripts built upon and mutually reinforced one another in powerful ways. For example, the establishment of the ECSC was, considering Monnet's ultimate ambitions for global union, a relatively modest advancement that catered to the brain's affinity for taking small, low-risk steps that produce instant gratification. But the ECSC also moved France and Germany out of a discomfort zone of rising political tension over the coal and steel producing regions of Germany, while speaking to the hearts of Europeans, instilling a sense of hope that stirred strong emotions in a continent recovering from a devastating war. The ECSC also cleverly channeled Europeans' tribal instincts in ways that broadened but did not eliminate "we-they" distinctions. In pursuing his objectives, Monnet exploited the diversity of population genetics by allying with like-minded, supranational mavericks in different countries.

Monnet's masterful orchestration of basic human nature teaches us a final, crucial lesson about exploiting the brain's playbook to achieve big bang results: the whole of the playbook is much larger than the sum of its individual parts. Just as the depressant effect on the brain of simultaneously consuming alcohol and barbiturate can be far more devastating than a simple addition of the separate effect of each of the two powerful drugs, combinations of powerful emotions such as hope, discomfort, and impulsiveness can produce disproportionately large changes in human motivation and behavior. For example, Bill W. discovered that to let go of their addiction alcoholics often need a 12-step program that simultaneously harnesses the small-step principle, hope, discomfort zones, group culture, and other plays in the playbook. The brain, it turns out, has its own peculiar arithmetic where $1+1=3$, $1+1+1=7$, $1+1+1+1=15$, and so on. This means that in using the brain's playbook to achieve big bang results in our own worlds, we should find creative ways to combine multiple plays. If we want to develop killer new products, we should chart a gradual course that takes many quick, small steps away from acknowledged discomfort zones, at the same time keeping an eye out for opportunities to redefine "we" and "they," while appealing to hearts over minds. Campaigns to re-engineer an organization should harness not only the brain's instinctive affinity for cultural learning, but also its diversity: effective use of mavericks such as Don Burke and Bill McLean is often essential to any major business transformation. Or if we seek to improve our individual lives, we should look for big opportunities in our emotional and perceptual blind spots and plot a practical series of small steps that will lead us toward those big opportunities, producing a long chain of small payoffs along the way.

The common thread that ties together all of the techniques for creating synergies among the brain's different plays is *internal focus*. While it's natural to look for big bang opportunities in *external* sources such as advancements in technology, changes in demographics, or shifting political landscapes, in reality all progress begins and ends inside our own brains. Our brains spot opportunities, invent opportunities, and ultimately enjoy the benefits of fully realized opportunities. In other words, big bangs live within, not outside of, ourselves.

RECAP

Surfing Human Nature versus Drowning in It

Successful visionaries such as Jean Monnet deal with people as they *really* are, not as they are *supposed* to be. We are *supposed* to cooperate with one another, but ancient tribal instincts drive us to fight one another, even when we are theoretically on the same team. When I joined the NSA shortly after 9/11, an unusually candid colleague at the CIA told me "Al Qaeda is our target; *you* [NSA] are our enemy." I soon discovered that the CIA wasn't the only agency that harbored officers who held on to their territorial instincts: equal proportions of such individuals remained at *all* the agencies. The fact that an attack as severe as 9/11 didn't cause intelligence officers to drop their turf-protecting habits says something profound about human nature: we can't expect to change it. A smarter strategy is to finesse and co-opt human nature. Jean Monnet did this by redrawing—as opposed to erasing—tribal boundaries. His great genius was to harness the competitive instincts of Europeans to collectively compete with *non*-Europeans instead of one another.

Our brains are hardwired to make us affiliate with a group of people we define as "we" to work against other groups we define as "they." But long fuse, big bang innovations—such as the European Union—can emerge when we don't try to fight our tribal instincts, but go *with* them, simply redrawing and expanding the "we-they" boundary.

CHAPTER 11

Lighting Fuses as a Way of Life

A MOM AND MOM BUSINESS

As a psychotherapist, Carol Fenster understood the concept of personal boundaries. For three years, even though she'd wanted to get to know her daughter's dance teacher, Hilda Jimenez, better, Carol didn't want to come across as an interfering mother. So Carol gave the teacher space, confining their occasional conversations at dance recitals to polite small talk.

Maintaining the professional distance wasn't easy for Carol because Hilda fascinated her. Hilda exuded energy and enthusiasm. Hilda was creative. Hilda was likeable—just the sort of person who'd make a great friend.

When at last Carol's daughter finished middle school, and would no longer be Hilda's student, Carol felt the time was right to get to know Hilda better. In April of 2004, with the school year ending, Carol approached Hilda and suggested the two of them take the entire graduating class of eighth grade dance students on a celebratory trip to Atlanta to see performances of professional dancers. Hilda quickly agreed, and on a warm, humid south Florida morning, they loaded an excited group of fourteen- and fifteen-year-olds onto a chartered bus for a nine-hour trip from their hometown of Miami to Atlanta.

With a long ride ahead of them, Carol didn't pounce on Hilda immediately, choosing instead to sit away from the teacher and to get the kids settled down (as much as you can quiet teenagers who have an entire summer ahead of them). But a few hours into the trip, Carol got up, sat next to Hilda, and struck up a conversation. Carol is a good listener, so it didn't take long for Hilda to open up, describing her passion for preserving Hispanic culture and her ideas for writing books about Hispanic nursery rhymes and childhood songs. The target audience for the books would be Hispanics who wanted to recapture warm memories and share them with their kids.

Carol was intrigued. She thought back to her own childhood, remembering with great fondness the Yiddish songs her Jewish immigrant parents had sung to her. Carol sensed that Hilda was on to something. The therapist in Carol knew that wanting to relive safe, cozy childhood experiences was not unique to the Hispanic community, but universal. Also universal, Carol realized, was an innate desire to belong to a group and to feel a strong connection to your culture. Products that simultaneously recaptured warm and fuzzy childhood moments while reaffirming cultural roots couldn't lose.

Returning to Miami three days later, Carol was unable to let go of her excitement for Hilda's idea. She started to research how to make the Hispanic nursery rhyme concept work as a business. She had no real business experience, except as a location scout and production assistant in her brother's motion picture business twenty years earlier, but she plunged ahead anyhow. The more she studied the market for Hispanic nursery rhymes, the more enthusiastic she got. The Hispanic market was growing fast in America, but Carol found very few mass-market products that helped immigrants and their children hold on to Hispanic culture as they assimilated into American society.

Hilda's original idea to publish books, however, didn't seem like the right way to start. Carol remembered that her own daughter would go through her children's books once or twice, then they would gather dust on the shelf. Looking for an approach that would have more "legs" with kids, and sell better, Carol wandered through toy stores in search of inspiration. She found it at a Miami JCPenny, in the form of a Beach Boys singing doll. Carol was astonished at the high quality of the music coming out of the inexpensive figure, and realized that technology had advanced to the point where not just the words to nursery rhymes could be delivered in a product, but the music itself.

A little more research into Hispanic traditions revealed that it was common for children to learn nursery rhymes from their grandparents. Carol was seized with an idea. What if kids heard nursery rhymes in the most natural way possible: from grandparent figures? Googling "grandfather dolls" and "grandmother dolls," Carol found there were virtually no grandparent figures on the market, let alone those that sang in Spanish. The field was wide open.

Bubbling with excitement, she went to see Hilda with an idea to market Abuelita (little grandmother) and Abuelito (little grandfather) dolls that would sing nursery rhymes. Hilda was not enthusiastic. She liked the concept in principle, but was a working mother with two children and had little time to start a business. Hilda pointed out that Carol had a full-time job too, and it might be a little crazy to start a business from scratch with no experience.

Carol was undeterred. She located a Cuban-American artist to design the dolls and lined up financing through a distributor with experience in the toy business, overseas manufacturing, and U.S. supply chain operations. In July 2004 Baby Abuelita began life as a company, with Carol and Hilda as owners and partners. The two principals had day jobs that took most of their time, but with $40,000 they managed to manufacture three thousand Abuelita Rosa and Abuelito Pancho dolls and get them into nineteen Navarro drugstores in the Miami area. The kindly looking dolls were unusual. Abuelita wore a traditional *bata de casa,* "housedress," while Abuelito sported a yellow guayabera shirt. Both grandparents smiled warmly out of their packages, from rocking chairs. Abuelita Rosa sang *"Arroz con leche* (Rice Pudding)" and five other traditional songs, while Abuelito Pancho sang *"Campanitas* (Bells)" and four other standbys.

Carol's instincts about the universal appeal of reliving warm memories proved to be spot-on. The dolls flew off the shelves at Navarro, and soon Rosa and Pancho were selling in Toys "R" Us.

Though pleased with the early successes, Carol was frustrated at her inability to get the largest retailer in the world, Wal-Mart, to sell Baby Abuelita dolls. Without the production volumes that sales to the behemoth would provide, it would be hard to transform Baby Abuelita into more than a sideline for the two owners. Buyers at Wal-Mart headquarters had listened courteously to the Baby Abuelita pitch, and even offered helpful suggestions about how to develop the product line, but in the end they passed on the singing dolls.

In her career treating patients, Carol had developed an intuition for when to stop "beating her head against the wall" trying to change someone's mind. She'd learned when to switch tactics and when to quit trying altogether. Carol's intuition told her not to give up on Wal-Mart, but to go "around the brick wall instead of through it." Researching the giant retailer more carefully, Carol found two new avenues of approach. She learned that local Wal-Mart stores had authority to buy unique products that would sell well in their market, and that Wal-Mart had a diversity program that encouraged minority- and woman-owned companies to become Wal-Mart suppliers. Carol fashioned a two-prong attack. She requested a meeting with a local Wal-Mart store manager and also got Baby Abuelita certified as a woman-owned enterprise.

Carol's discussion with the local Wal-Mart manager went well. As the two walked through the store before the meeting, shoppers kept stopping Carol, asking where in the store they could find the unique dolls she was carrying. The store manager took notice and agreed to give Baby Abuelita a try. The toys sold well, paving the way for Carol's next move.

She then made a cold call to Wal-Mart's Supplier Diversity Department and managed to reach the department's director, Anthony Soto. Soto liked both the Abuelita concept and the promising sales numbers coming out of the local store, so he set up a meeting for Carol with a toy buyer at Wal-Mart headquarters in Bentonville, Arkansas.

Baby Abuelita impressed the toy buyer at headquarters, and he agreed to give Pancho and Rosa a test in several Wal-Mart stores. If the dolls outperformed other toys, Wal-Mart would take Baby Abuelita on as a regular supplier. But Carol's elation faded when she learned that the trial would run in the summer, the slowest part of the toy-buying year. When she asked if Wal-Mart could move the trial to the Christmas season, they explained that the real test of a toy's appeal was in off-peak season. The test would go ahead as planned, in summertime.

To Carol's relief Pancho and Rosa did outperform other toys in their class that summer, and her distributor, PTI Toys, signed a supplier agreement that eventually got Baby Abuelita products into 950 Wal-Mart and Sam's Club stores.

The business was on its way.

Carol quit her job as a therapist in 2007 to assume full-time duties as Baby Abuelita's CEO. By 2009, with added financing from a venture that included money from Danny Garcia, Dwayne "The Rock" Johnson's business partner, the company had diversified into books, DVDs, slippers, and three new baby dolls, Andrea, Tita, and Mimi. Baby Abuelita products sold in three thousand stores, with international business growing fast.

With the acquisition of the Wal-Mart account, the long fuse Carol had lit after the bus ride to Atlanta had finally burned to a big bang.

Looking back over the steps Carol took to build a successful business, it's instructive to examine which parts of the brain's playbook she followed. Carol is effective at influencing people because she's a good listener and *likeable*. Also, she provided Wal-Mart *social proof* that other retailers, such as Navarro and Toys "R" Us, liked Baby Abuelita. And when she initially failed to win over Wal-Mart buyers who only had diversity in their peripheral vision, Carol went to company executives whose gaze was locked firmly on Baby Abuelita's strength as a woman/minority-owned enterprise. Finally, Wal-Mart diversity executives *wanted* to find unique companies just like Baby Abuelita. Carol may not have had formal training as a brain scientist, but she'd learned that people only take notice of things they are paying attention to, and only change when they want to.

If the story stopped there, Carol's success would be interesting and inspirational but wouldn't add any new pages to the brain's playbook. However, Baby Abuelita has more to tell us about how to co-opt the brain's hardwired scripts to achieve big bang success.

THE IMPORTANCE OF CULTURE

We take it for granted that people like to feel part of a group with a clear identity. In America, cultural icons such as hot dogs and baseball games arouse feelings of warmth and familiarity. Americans don't like it when someone threatens to change their cherished icons. When I was at Disney Imagineering, we decided to update Pirates of the Caribbean with newer technology and more contemporary themes, such as maids who chased pirates instead of the reverse. After we opened the refurbished, slightly re-themed attraction, irate letters poured in. Why had we tried to improve perfection? Why had we caved to political correctness? Above all, why had we changed something that, like the Washington Monument, should have been an unchanging part of the American cultural landscape? New parents could no longer show their kids exactly what their own childhood was like!

In retrospect, these reactions weren't surprising. Cultural symbols and rituals provide solid foundations for our lives. Imagine how you'd feel if the government decided to change the national anthem, the colors of the flag, or the month that key holidays are celebrated? What if foods like hamburgers and hot dogs were no longer available and you could never hear songs from your teen years again? Suppose historians proved that cherished national heroes never existed and their feats had been made up?

Without strong cultural anchor points, we feel disconnected and lost. We suffer what sociologists call "culture shock."

Evolutionary psychologists such as the husband-and-wife team of Leda Cosmides and John Tooby of the University of California, Santa Barbara, believe that our affinity for cultural symbols, rituals, norms, and shared beliefs is so powerful because evolution has hardwired "Darwinian algorithms" (I call them scripts) into our brains. These scripts predispose us to share cultural information with those we live or work with, especially our offspring.

Such sharing of information enhances human survival in several ways. First, cultural information, such as folktales and legends, carries with it valuable lessons about how to survive. For example, we've all heard Aesop's fable about the boy who cried wolf. Like most such fables, this story has a "moral" useful for surviving (no one will rescue you if you raise false alarms). When such information is passed within and across generations, fewer people die by repeating the mistakes of others.

An Abuelito Pancho song about Puerto Rican woodsmen, *"Asserin, Aserran* (Saw, Saw)," carries a clear moral about the perils of trust. Translated, the song goes:

> *Saw, saw*
> *The woodsmen of San Juan*
> *They ask for bread*
> *They're given none*
> *They ask for cheese,*
> *Even less please*
> *Ask for wine, if they're given some*
> *They get sick and go back home*

A second reason affinity for culture is hardwired into our brains is that common cultures bind individuals into cohesive groups that cooperate for mutual benefit. We're much more likely to help people who share our religion, language, rituals, and values than people who don't. Culture is the glue that binds us together. Groups that internally cooperate warn one another of danger, share scarce resources, and help raise one another's young.

Finally, culture provides what anthropologists call "referents" that make cooperative activities among humans streamlined and efficient. If you're in a budget meeting, and someone says that a pessimistic earnings forecast is just "crying wolf," no further explanation is needed. Everyone in the meeting will instantly know what crying wolf means and why it's a bad thing.

Carol Fenster's intuition that people would buy products that preserved cultural heritage resonated with the latest thinking of evolutionary psychologists. Carol succeeded in part by following the cultural affinity play in the brain's playbook.

We're still not finished with Carol's story, because as it continues, we'll see how healthy cultures not only help us to survive today, but also to thrive tomorrow with consistent big bang successes.

MIND MELD WITH A MEGALITH

After Carol signed the Wal-Mart deal, she had to hire a specialist experienced in Wal-Mart's "supply chain" information technology systems. One of the systems, called Electronic Data Interchange (EDI), lets Baby Abuelita and Wal-Mart efficiently transmit purchase orders and invoices back and forth as if Carol's firm were an integral part of Wal-Mart's internal IT infrastructure. Another system, Retail Link, allows Carol to see, hour by hour, the sales figures for all of her products in each and every Wal-Mart outlet. Retail Link also has historical data that shows when consumer demand for Baby Abuelita waxes and wanes throughout the year in different stores. Armed with this information Baby Abuelita can make very accurate sales forecasts and order just the right amount of products from their own suppliers at just the right times to meet demand in Wal-Mart stores.

Forecasting accuracy in its wholesale supply chain, from companies as large as Procter & Gamble, to those as small as Baby Abuelita, is one of the chief methods by which Wal-Mart beats its competition with "everyday low prices." Accurate forecasting helps Wal-Mart in two ways. First, neither Wal-Mart nor their suppliers will buy more products than Wal-Mart shoppers are likely to want at any given time and place. Thus, money isn't wasted manufacturing, shipping, tracking, and storing unwanted merchandise. Second, by insuring that enough merchandise will be available to meet peak demand, Wal-Mart avoids lost sales from out-of-stock items. Forecasting efficiency thus lowers costs and raises profits at both Wal-Mart and their suppliers, letting Wal-Mart negotiate lower prices with suppliers and pass those lower prices along to their customers.

Pete Abell, retail research director of AMR Research, wrote: "We view Wal-Mart as the best supply chain operator of all times. Efficiency is a key factor in maintaining Wal-Mart's low-price leadership among retailers. Their margins can be far lower than other retailers' because they have such an efficient supply chain. The company's cost of goods is 5% to 10% less than that of most of its competitors."

By connecting to Wal-Mart via EDI and Retail Link, Baby Abuelita sees everything that Wal-Mart sees about Abuelita sales. Carol Fenster's small company has effectively become a seamless part of the largest enterprise in the world.

Wal-Mart made this possible by redrawing the traditional "tribal" boundary that separates retailers from their suppliers. Recognizing that its costs are a composite of all costs in the supply chain, from raw materials to packaged merchandise, Wal-Mart continues to squeeze inefficiencies out of their supply chains by extending we-they boundaries to encompass suppliers' suppliers, and *those* suppliers' suppliers, all the way to ultimate producers of raw materials. Wal-Mart's ultimate goal is to let every participant in their supply chain— from bottom to top—see everything that everyone else sees about sales, improving forecasting accuracy and lowering costs to an irreducible minimum.

To accomplish this Wal-Mart has pioneered a sophisticated supplier forecasting system, Collaborative Planning, Forecasting Replenishment (CPFR), that forecasts merchandise to meet expected demands. Wal-Mart now leads the way with radio frequency identification (RFID) technology that eliminates manual scanning and tracking of merchandise, along with many other IT innovations that smooth out bumps in the long road from raw materials buried in the ground all the way to products sitting on Wal-Mart shelves. Historically, each new wave of IT innovation has turned into a big bang success for Wal-Mart. For instance, Ted Rybeck, CEO of Benchmarking Partners, the consulting firm that helped get CPFR up and running, said that the Internet collaboration system played a big role in letting Wal-Mart double its sales from 1995 to 2000.

Even though Wal-Mart is the largest company in the world, with costs already lower than its competitors, it never stops trying to get costs and prices even lower. The company behaves as if it lives in a perpetual discomfort zone—as if it has a culture of discontent.

DIVINE DISCONTENT

I learned in business school at UCLA that the culture of a company is laid down within the first two to three years of its founding, usually mirroring the personality of its founder. My experiences at companies started by Howard Hughes and Walt Disney reinforced this idea. Both Howard and Walt were risk takers who, in a very non–Wal-Mart fashion, were less interested in what things cost than in what things did. Both innovators wanted to create experiences, whether in airplanes or theme parks, that were astonishing, never-been-done-before innovations. Howard and Walt cared more about bang than buck, and so did successive generations of their employees. At Hughes, our technologies almost always cost more than those of our competitors, but we did well because our extra features were important to our customers. For example, Hughes pioneered spin-stabilized satellites that kept the orbiting communication relays constantly oriented toward Earth. At Disney, our theme parks always cost more than our competitors', but we maintained our market leadership because theme park guests appreciated the extra touches that made Disney's "magic."

However, there's more than one way to succeed in the marketplace, and it's hard to argue with Wal-Mart's impressive results from cutting costs, or the commercial value of the culture that remorselessly drives them to do it.

Wal-Mart's winning culture, like Disney's, started with its founder. Sam Walton was born in 1918 in Kingfisher, Oklahoma. From 1929 to 1931 he traveled with his father, who worked for a mortgage company, on trips to repossess Missouri farms whose crops had blown away in the dust bowl of the Great Depression. Seeing farmers' hardships firsthand made an impression on Sam, as did his parents' frugal ways. Walton wrote in his autobiography: "One thing my mother and dad shared completely was their approach to money: they just didn't spend it."

At a very young age Sam Walton came to appreciate what he called "the value of a dollar."

Then, fresh out of the army after World War II, Walton and his new wife, Helen, bought a Ben Franklin variety store in Newton, Arkansas. Sam learned that it was important to experiment with the new products, promotions, and ways of doing business to beat his competition, the Sterling Store across the street. He wrote of those early days in retail: "It didn't take me long to start experimenting—that's just the way I am and always have been."

In one experiment to increase traffic in his Ben Franklin franchise, Walton overcame his aversion to borrowing money and took out an $1,800 loan to buy a soft-serve ice cream machine that he put in the front of the store to lure customers in. The promotion worked spectacularly, as did a popcorn machine Sam put next to the soft-serve.

The most important experiments, though, were those that tweaked his supply chain. Before Sam and Helen bought it, the Ben Franklin store purchased ribbons and bows from a wholesaler, Butler Brothers. Sam decided to try going around Butler Brothers and buying directly from satin manufacturers. He earned the wholesaler's wrath, but the experiment worked, saving Walton's store 25 percent on ribbons and bows, and enabling it to pass those savings on to its shoppers. Buoyed by this success, and encouraged that his tactics were wooing shoppers away from the Sterling Store, Walton spent several days on the road each week looking for bargains that helped him lower prices on other items. Walton wrote in 1992:

> If you're interested in "how Wal-Mart did it" this is one story you have to sit up and pay close attention to. Harry [a manufacturing agent] was selling panties—two barred—tricot satin panties with an elastic waist—for $2.00 a dozen. We'd been buying similar panties at Ben Franklin for $2.50 a dozen, and selling them at three pair for $1.00. Well, at Harry's price of $2.00, we could put them out at four for $1.00 and make a great promotion for our store.

Walton soon discovered that the lower prices rapidly drove up sales, which in turn allowed him to place larger orders with his suppliers at lower unit costs (due to volume discounting), which allowed him to cut prices further, driving sales still higher and unit costs lower. Sam had discovered a virtuous circle that is preserved to this day in Wal-Mart's approach. Lower costs drive higher sales which enable larger wholesale buys that drive down costs further.

Not everything Sam tried worked out as well as soft-serve ice cream and panties. In his eagerness to get started owning a business, he neglected to get rights to renew the lease on his Ben Franklin store and lost it as a result. Sam later wrote: "Every crazy thing we tried hadn't turned out as well as the ice cream machine, of course, but we hadn't made any mistakes we couldn't recover from."

Sam did bounce back from losing his first store, plowing the profits from the Ben Franklin franchise back into a series of other stores that he continued to experiment with and make ever more profitable.

By 1962, when Sam opened the Rogers, Arkansas, store that would become the first in a vast worldwide chain, he'd developed core beliefs that form the foundation of the present-day Wal-Mart culture. Two of these beliefs were: (1) Customers know the value of a dollar: serve them best by getting prices down as low as possible, and (2) Never stop experimenting.

Kevin Turner, Wal-Mart's chief information officer in 2002, described the company's built-in passion for experimenting as "divine discontent" that drives them to "never be satisfied with where you're at or where you're going" and to know "that you can always improve."

Some of Wal-Mart's most important experiments were in Kevin Turner's part of the company, Information Systems. Wal-Mart's strategy of opening stores in rural areas, where both competition and high-speed data communications were scarce, required them to develop their own data communications network to keep track of sales and inventory in their fast-growing retail empire. So Wal-Mart experimented with a satellite communication system that connected their Bentonville, Arkansas, headquarters with some of their rural stores. Over time, they expanded this network such that, by 1987 it had become the largest private satellite system in the world.

Four years earlier Wal-Mart had pioneered use of bar codes on products to track inventory and speed up checkout, which improved operating efficiency and drove down costs. Together, the bar code system and satellite network let Wal-Mart executives in Arkansas monitor sales on a minute-by-minute basis at every cash register in every store in their system. This up-to-the-minute business intelligence helped them quickly correct problems. For instance, they once offered an aggressive price promotion on HP computers, but in the first hours of the promotion, the bar-code/satellite network showed that the computers weren't selling. Bentonville managers immediately called the stores to see what had gone wrong and learned that the promotional displays didn't make clear that the computer's price included a monitor. The stores swiftly corrected the problem and sales took off the same day.

These kinds of experiences proved that access to timely information offered a huge competitive advantage, so Wal-Mart invested heavily in building a massive data warehouse. By 1990 this system recorded and archived sales, shipping, and inventory of every item of merchandise in every Wal-Mart store. Like their satellite network, this data archive quickly grew to become the largest of its kind in the world.

Access to accurate historical sales data helped Wal-Mart forecast seasonal demand and buy only the amount of merchandise for each store that was likely to sell. Initially, this alarmed many of Wal-Mart's largest suppliers, who soon discovered that they couldn't sell their excess inventory to Wal-Mart simply by cutting prices. With detailed historical sales data in hand, Wal-Mart buyers knew that they couldn't sell that excess inventory at *any* price. Thus vendor sales executives frequently returned from meetings with Wal-Mart buyers without a deal.

Wal-Mart quickly realized that this trend was hurting them as much as their suppliers, because it meant that there were major inefficiencies in the supply chain. Vendors were either overproducing merchandise, driving up their costs for manufacturing, shipping, and storing goods, or underproducing merchandise, costing both Wal-Mart and their suppliers lost sales.

In 1993, Wal-Mart decided to open up their books and show all their suppliers exactly how much merchandise they could expect to sell in every store at different times of the year. This was the birth of the Retail Link system that Baby Abuelita and tens of thousands of other Wal-Mart suppliers use to this day.

The most interesting—and instructive—part of the Wal-Mart IT story is that Sam Walton hated to spend money on anything, especially computers. Wal-Mart is famous for its shabby corporate headquarters, and for requiring senior executives to fly coach and share hotel rooms on business trips. Though the legend isn't true that Sam chose the name Wal-Mart because it had five fewer letters than "Walton Stores" and thus made for cheaper signs, it is true that Sam acted as if damn computers were one word. Sam wrote: "The funny thing is, everybody at Wal-Mart knows that I've fought all these technology expenditures as hard as I could."

But the two parts of Sam's psyche (and Wal-Mart culture)—saving money and constantly experimenting—warred with each other, with the experimenter psyche ultimately winning out. In his heart of hearts, Sam Walton was a mercantile Darwinian who knew that a constantly changing business environment meant that you have to "mutate or die." Thus, he agreed to foot the bill for experiments with IT that might lower prices for Wal-Mart shoppers.

As a research and development (R&D) executive, I always lamented the shortage of R&D funds to help my enterprise "mutate or die," whether at Hughes, Disney, or the government. The need to control operating costs or invest in near-term results took precedence over long fuse, big bang innovations. But when I learned about Wal-Mart's success, I felt guilty for all the whining I'd done about having too little R&D money. Wal-Mart is legendary for pinching pennies, and yet it is a world-class innovator with expensive technology. The company's commercial data warehouse and satellite systems are the largest in the world, but Wal-Mart spends less on IT as a percent of sales than their competitors. When I dug into Wal-Mart's success as part of an R&D benchmarking exercise for a consulting client, I wondered: How does Wal-Mart do so much with so little? How did they rack up one long-term success after another to become the world's biggest company, while keeping a sharp eye on next quarter's profits?

The answers to these questions carry important lessons for lighting long fuses to big bangs.

Wal-Mart, craving next quarter earning as much as the next company, doesn't suppress their hardwired here-and-now instincts, but goes with them. In a quest to continually improve near-term operating results, Wal-Mart managers and associates are encouraged to "fail faster," with a constant stream of new promotional ideas and ways of doing business. If these new ideas don't cost much and can be proven quickly, management provides the resources and recognition for success. If the quick experiments don't pan out, Wal-Mart cuts its losses and moves on. But it doesn't punish the experimenters. Bobbie Baldridge, a twenty-year Wal-Mart employee who moved up through the ranks from hourly employee to corporate director of replenishment (keeping shelves stocked across the vast Wal-Mart empire), said that even when she was a lowly "associate," her bosses encouraged her to continue coming up with new ideas, even when some of her ideas didn't work out.

Wal-Mart's state-of-the-art information infrastructure emerged gradually from just such a "fail fast" process. Wal-Mart's IT Department experimented with new technology on a small scale, then ramped it up as the technology added to profits. This gradual approach to growth is a very cost-effective way of scaling up large IT systems. More ambitious approaches, where enterprises try to modernize in one leap, often generate enormous cost overruns when they try to correct problems that could have been identified earlier with small-scale trials. Large IT projects obey a perverse principle called Brooks' Law (after Fred Brooks, author of the *The Mythical Man-Month*), where pouring extra manpower and money into late, overbudget projects makes them even *more* late and overbudget.

After 9/11, Congress sharply increased funding for large IT programs at the FBI and intelligence agencies to create unified data warehouses and information retrieval systems surprisingly similar to Wal-Mart's massive data repository. The hope was that IT upgrades in law enforcement and intelligence would eliminate problems with data access and sharing that caused early evidence of the 9/11 plot to be overlooked. But many of the massive programs, like the FBI's Virtual Case File—a project that tried to modernize the Bureau's antiquated criminal case management system—failed because they spent massive sums cramming myriad features into fast-track projects. The FBI also attempted what the software industry calls a "flash cut," swapping out their old case management system in one step, as opposed to a gradual migration away from their legacy IT system. Intelligence agencies fared no better with many of their hyper-expensive, too-much-too-soon approaches to IT modernization.

Wal-Mart's more miserly, go-slow approach to IT modernization reaffirmed an old Russian proverb that says: "The slower I go, the faster I get there." Bobbie Baldridge, who worked in Wal-Mart's IT department, said the company's technology development philosophy was to build systems that met the majority, but not all, of the requirements laid out for it. Thus, Wal-Mart's IT team was constantly deploying projects before they hit the point of diminishing returns. The IT projects didn't solve 100 percent of the problems they could have, just enough to help Wal-Mart lower its prices and grab market share from their competitors. In the end, the twin pillars of Wal-Mart's culture—cutting costs and experimenting—didn't conflict at all, but mutually reinforced each other to connect many short-fuse IT projects into long fuse, big bang successes.

Wal-Mart's story adds two more plays to the brain's playbook. The retail giant succeeds not only because it goes with the brain's natural desire for instant rewards, but also because it harnesses the neocortex's enormous capacity to learn and change. And Wal-Mart takes maximum advantage of our brain's affinity for following cultural norms and practicing what anthropologists call "social learning" from experiences of people who preceded us. Sam Walton said: "Most everything I've done I copied from someone else."

CHANGING CULTURE BY THINKING INSIDE THE BOX

The world is changing at an accelerating pace. Therefore many corporate cultures that once worked magnificently sooner or later will become greater liabilities than assets. Lou Gerstner discovered this at IBM and slowly changed his company's culture to conform to the new realities of the IT marketplace.

But what if your organization doesn't have a unique culture like Wal-Mart's or a visionary leader like Lou Gerstner? How do you change an entrenched culture that's no longer working?

Gerstner's experience provides the first clues. He changed IBM's compensation system to reward new behaviors, such as customer focus and agile decision making. These new behaviors were, in the language of evolutionary biology, "adaptive" to their changed environment. Lou knew that he would get the behaviors he rewarded and applied this simple principle of brain function to good effect.

I've seen many such attempts at culture change fail, however, because rewarding "good behavior" is often not enough to get brains to change their ways. When I was training rabbits back in graduate school, I had to pay close attention to punishments as much as rewards. If, through carelessness, when they first engaged in "correct" behaviors, I made a loud noise or sudden movement that was aversive to the rabbits, the animals took much longer to learn the tasks I'd set out for them, or never learned them at all.

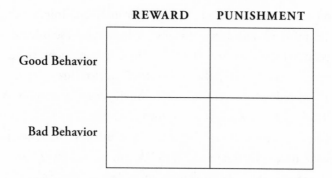

THE BOX

To correct this problem, I developed a simple diagram that I taped to the wall of my lab. I called the diagram "the box" because it was a square with two rows and two columns. The rows were labeled "good behavior" and "bad behavior" while the columns were "reward" and "punishment." I checked the cells in the box for rewarding good behavior and punishing bad behavior, while leaving the other cells blank to remind me that behavior change is a four-way proposition. To get the best results you have to reward "good" behavior, punish "bad" behavior, and avoid at all costs punishing "good" behavior and rewarding "bad" behavior.

I liked rabbits, so I never punished "bad" behavior, and learned that adhering to the remaining three cells of the box worked just fine.

But human brains change fastest when you operate in all four cells of the box. Culture change often fails despite rewards for "good" new behaviors, because the organization simultaneously punishes some types of "good" behavior, while rewarding "bad" behaviors instead of punishing them. I've seen executives advocate risk taking, then turn around and fire managers who took risks that didn't work out. These same executives also continued to promote conservative, risk-averse managers. Finally, I've seen many skilled corporate infighters get promoted, not fired, despite the CEO's advocacy of a "new culture of cooperation."

President Bush's behavior after 9/11 provides a classic example of the pitfalls of a top executive violating the "box principle." On the one hand, the president encouraged greater sharing of intelligence and law enforcement information by signing the Intelligence Reform and Terrorist Prevention Act of

2004. This sweeping new law mandated much greater sharing of information across intelligence, military, and law enforcement lines, and established a single point of accountability in a new direct report to the president, the director of National Intelligence. Bush also set up the Terrorist Threat Integration Center and ordered all law enforcement, intelligence, and military organizations to freely share terrorist threat information there.

On the other hand, Bush actively supported subordinates, like Donald Rumsfeld, who were notorious infighters. Bob Woodward's *State of Denial* describes a 2003 meeting when CIA director George Tenet took David Kay, the new man in charge of finding WMD in Iraq, to see Rumsfeld in the Pentagon. Over lunch, Tenet suggested that Kay report jointly to the CIA and to Rumsfeld. "Absolutely not," Rumsfeld said. Kay could see that Rumsfeld deserved respect as one of the best bureaucratic infighters of all time. Presuming Kay found WMD, it would only validate the CIA's estimates. If he didn't find WMD, no good could come to Rumsfeld from being associated with the unsuccessful search.

As a subordinate of Rumsfeld's (I reported two layers down), I had direct experience with his attitude toward cross-department cooperation. When I decided to send Department of Defense technologists who worked for me to help out at Homeland Security, a Pentagon official advised me, "OK, just don't get caught. The boss doesn't like us helping DHS [Department of Homeland Security] on his nickel."

Bush ultimately sacked Rumsfeld, but not for being uncooperative with intelligence agencies. Republicans had gotten clobbered in the 2006 elections over poor progress in Iraq.

From where I sat, Bush acted far too late. Rumsfeld and others like him were, in my estimation, much better at fighting political opponents than at fighting Al Qaeda. One of the chief reasons I decided to leave the government in 2007 was that even after Rumsfeld's departure, the President continued to promote and support "bureaucratic black belts" who were better at protecting their turf than protecting America.

Some chief executives pay closer attention to all four cells of "the box" and therefore succeed even in changing cultures over a hundred years old. Procter & Gamble had been in operation for 167 years when Alan Lafley took its helm in 2000, in the middle of a string of disappointing financial results. His predecessor, Durk Jager, had tried to transform Procter & Gamble's conservative, inward-looking culture into a much more innovative one, but only managed to disrupt the company's performance.

Lafley's main goal, after narrowing P&G's focus to fewer, more profitable businesses, was to accelerate earnings growth through "organic" innovation. This meant growing not by acquisition, but by developing new products. Like Gerstner, Lafley rewarded behaviors that he thought were critical to P&G growth. These included openness to NIH (Not Invented Here) ideas from P&G's business partners and consumers, and flexibility taking on many different roles at once. Lafley referred to this last quality as being "ambidextrous." Lafley said that some of his managers weren't up to the challenge. In a 2008 interview in *Chief Executive* magazine, he said: "Everybody can't do this, so it helps to filter out some people."

"Filter out" is a euphemism for what I call punishing "bad" behavior. Lafley also understood the importance of *not* punishing "good" behavior. In his book *The Game-Changer: How You Can Drive Revenue and Profit Growth with Innovation*, Lafley lists eleven failures for which he takes personal responsibility. The P&G CEO said those failures taught him valuable lessons that helped him triple his company's profits over a period of eight years. So Lafley avoided punishing managers who took worthy risks that didn't work out. In *Chief Executive* Lafley said: "Did you see the section [in my book] where we list my 11 failures? If you add them up, it was a pretty costly education for A. G. Lafley. We are not a one strike and you're out company. Now, if you swing at the same pitch, and fail in a big way a second time, we start to wonder. That might be the end, but we're a two and three strikes and you're out company."

Although it was a long fuse, multi-year undertaking, Lafley did succeed in changing a 167-year-old culture by thinking inside "the box" and harnessing the brain's natural mechanisms for responding to both rewards and punishments. These incentive mechanisms represent part of the brain's great strength. By paying close attention to cues that lead to either punishment or reward, the brain can quickly adapt to new environments and thrive by moving toward new sources of food or shelter, while moving away from new dangers. Lafley's deft application of rewards and punishments is therefore a classic example of brain judo, where he channeled an "opponent's" natural strength in a direction Lafley wanted it to go.

RECAP

Creating—and Re-creating—Big Bang Cultures

Humans are a herd species. We rely upon—and learn from—one another. This learning occurs both *within* generations (for example, imitation) and *across* generations (through the passing down of cultural information). Folktales that parents read to their kids, such as "The Boy Who Cried Wolf" and "The Three Little Pigs," teach valuable survival lessons. Visionary leaders take advantage of our brain's natural affinity for cultural learning by creating cultures that drive innovation and success. Sam Walton established an early culture of "divine discontent" that ultimately propelled Wal-Mart to become the largest company in the world. A. J. Lafley and Lou Gerstner didn't create the original cultures at Procter & Gamble and IBM, but the two executives managed to transform the cultures of these huge corporations by working with what I call the "box principle." This principle asserts that for all its complexity, the brain will change its behavior when confronted with two simple contingencies: behaviors that are consistently rewarded will be repeated, and behaviors that are consistently punished will not. The "box principle" implies that we can't instill a culture of big bang innovation into an organization by simply rewarding big bang thinkers who succeed, but we must also avoid punishing big bang thinkers who fail. Similarly, we can't transform risk-averse cultures into more adventurous ones if we continue to reward risk-averse conservatives or fail to hold accountable employees who always play it safe.

CHAPTER 12

Keeping Long Fuses Lit

BIG BANG POSSIBILITIES IN MEDICINE

August 1865: Standing in the garden of the building on Lazarettgasse in the Döbling section of Vienna, Dr. Ignaz Philipp Semmelweis realized that his friend and mentor, Dr. Ferdinand Von Hebra, had betrayed him. The facility wasn't a new clinic, as Von Hebra had claimed, but a lunatic asylum.

Ignaz had agreed to make a brief stop in Vienna while traveling with his family from his home in Budapest to a rest spa in the present-day Czech Republic, to see where Von Hebra, a fellow physician, worked. Von Hebra met Ignaz and his uncle at the Vienna train station and escorted the pair to Döbling. But soon after the three men went inside the asylum, Von Hebra and Ignaz's uncle slipped out the door, leaving Ignaz alone with guards.

As the guards approached him, Ignaz realized that he was about to become an inmate at the asylum and tried to escape, but the guards forced him into a straightjacket and locked him in a dark cell.

Two weeks earlier the renowned Hungarian surgeon Janos Balassa and two other physicians had signed a document "referring" Ignaz to the mental institution. The ruse with Von Hebra was necessary because Ignaz never would have voluntarily sought treatment. Ingaz's behavior in the previous months had grown increasingly troubling to his colleagues and family. He suffered extreme mood swings and forgetfulness and drank heavily. He grew obsessed with the idea that doctors in Europe were killing their patients. All of his conversations focused on that one subject, and Ignaz wrote letters attacking individual doctors by name.

Ignaz's physical condition was also deteriorating rapidly. His hair had turned gray, his face was bloated, and he was aging at an alarming rate. These physical changes were so striking that years later, doctors who studied his case speculated that he suffered from a severe case of early onset Alzheimer's or tertiary syphilis (an advanced stage of the disease in which brain damage causes insanity).

In July 1865, fearing that, without help, her husband would spiral irretrievably into madness, Ignaz's wife, Anna, finally decided to act, asking Dr. Balassa to start commitment proceedings.

As it turned out, the involuntary commitment did put an end to her husband's troubles: two weeks after commitment, Ignaz died at age forty-seven. The autopsy ruled the cause of death to be blood poisoning from an infected finger wound, but a later investigation revealed that guards had doused Ignaz with freezing water, force-fed him laxatives, and beaten him severely when he attempted escape. Ignaz almost certainly died from the beatings.

Only a few people attended Ignaz's funeral. Ironically, Dr. Spaeth, whom Ignaz had attacked in his open letter, and another rival, Dr. Braun, were among the small company of mourners. Conspicuous by their absence were any family members. Although Ignaz had belonged to the Hungarian Association of Physicians and Natural Scientists, no member of that group of doctors and scientists acknowledged his passing in a commemorative speech as required by Association rules regarding the death of members.

Ignaz had died alone and in disgrace.

Twenty-six years later Ignaz's remains were dug up and returned to his native Budapest, only to be unearthed again in 1964 and buried in a garden of the house where he was born. That house is now a museum and a monument to Ignaz's achievements. Not far from Ignaz's final resting place, a prestigious medical school bears his name, as do commemorative gold coins, medals, postage stamps, awards, and medical societies.

FROM LUNATIC TO HERO

The story of how Dr. Ignaz Philipp Semmelweis was transformed from shunned lunatic to national hero begins two years after he graduated medical school in 1844. Unable to find a post in internal medicine, Dr. Semmelweis accepted a job as assistant to a professor of Obstetrics, Dr. Johan Klein, at Vienna's General Hospital. Dr. Klein assigned Ignaz to teach medical students, assist with surgeries, and attend patients in one of two maternity wards of the Vienna General Hospital. Viennese authorities had set up the two facilities for the indigent, the First and Second Obstetrical Clinics, to discourage poor mothers and prostitutes from killing their infants.

The First Obstetrical Clinic, where Ignaz worked, trained medical students, while the Second Clinic trained midwives. Having studied medical statistics while earning his doctorate, Ignaz was puzzled and disturbed by differences in death rates from childbed fever at the two clinics. Childbed fever was a collection of ailments where mothers contracted serious infections of the genitalia, cervix, uterus, abdominal cavity, and bloodstream. Victims of the disease developed high fevers and frequently died of septic shock.

Like many "lying in" maternity hospitals in Europe, where approximately one in ten women died of childbed fever, delivering at the First Obstetrical Clinic was a risky proposition for new mothers. Poring over hospital records, Semmelweis learned that the death rate from childbed fever, also called puerperal fever, was more than 11.4 percent at the clinic where he worked. Curiously, death rates at the Second Obstetrical Clinic were only 2.8 percent, and "street births," which occurred when poor mothers elected to avoid the hazards of the notorious First Obstetrical Clinic, resulted in death from childbed fever only 5 percent of the time. The large statistical differences in deaths at the two clinics were persistent; from 1841 through 1846, Semmelweis noted differences in death rates ranging from 3 to more than 7 percent.

Organized and methodical, Semmelweis began a careful comparison of the two clinics to unravel the mystery, but his initial investigation failed to explain why death rates at the two hospitals should be so different. Treatment procedures for mothers were virtually identical at the First and Second Obstetrical Clinics, and the climate at the two facilities was also equivalent. The climate was of special concern because prevailing medical opinion at the time was that "miasmas," or malodorous air, around patients caused puerperal fever. Ignaz also ruled out overcrowding as a cause of higher mortality rates, because the Second Clinic was actually more crowded than the First.

Important new clues surfaced in March 1847, when a close friend of Semmelweis, Jakob Kolletschka, died of blood poisoning after being cut by a scalpel while assisting in an autopsy. The scalpel wound had become infected, causing the blood poisoning and, ultimately, Kolletschka's death. An autopsy revealed that Kolletschka's symptoms were remarkably similar to those of childbed fever. Semmelweis wrote:

I could see clearly that the disease from which Kolletschka died was identical to that from which so many hundred maternity patients had also died. The maternity patients also had lymphangitis, peritonitis, pericarditis, pleurisy, and meningitis, and metastases also formed in many of them. Day and night I was haunted by the image of Kolletschka's disease and was forced to recognize, ever more decisively, that the disease from which Kolletschka died was identical to that from which so many maternity patients died.

The phrase *forced to recognize* was no mere figure of speech, because Kolletschka's death suggested a truth that would be painful for any physician to grasp: that doctors *themselves,* not some mystical miasma, were responsible for the high mortality rates at the First Obstetrical Clinic. Semmelweis reached this conclusion when the death of his friend highlighted a major difference between the First and Second Clinics that he'd overlooked: the First Clinic trained doctors, while the Second trained midwives. Doctors and medical students often performed autopsies before examining or treating maternity patients, whereas student midwives did not. If Kolletschka had gotten a pathogen on his hand from a corpse and died of puerperal fever, then it seemed obvious to Semmelweis that other doctors, after performing autopsies, were carrying this same pathogen to their patients and infecting them. Ignaz's theory that "cadaveric particles" were a vector for puerperal fever also explained why street births, where no doctors were present, produced fewer deaths than deliveries at the First Clinic.

Semmelweis tested his theory by instructing all doctors and medical students to rinse their hands in chlorinated water before touching their patients. The results were immediate and dramatic. The death rate from puerperal fever dropped from 18.2 percent in April 1847 to 2.2 percent in June. The following year, two months went by at the First Obstetrical Clinic without *any* deaths from the disease.

A LONG FUSE SPUTTERS OUT

More interested in treating patients than publishing, Semmelweis let others write up his work. Among the first of his colleagues to do this was Ferdinand

Von Hebra, one of Ignaz's instructors in medical school and editor of a Vienna-based medical journal. Students of Semmelweis, Routh and Wieger, also lectured and wrote about Semmelweis's work.

Although the statistics coming out of the First Obstetrical Clinic were clear-cut, they failed to impress the European medical establishment. The idea that disease could be spread by "cadaveric particles" on doctors' hands ran counter to the established medical "fact" that disease spread through circulation of malodorous atmospheric "miasmas." The miasma theory emerged from observations in medieval times that the air around patients with infections had a foul smell, as did polluted water that made people ill. Therefore, physicians reasoned that contagious diseases must spread through "bad air." Finally, every obstetrician of the mid-1800s knew that puerperal fever was not *one* disease, but many ailments, as its symptoms varied from patient to patient. Some women died of blood poisoning, others peritonitis, still others from gangrene of the uterus. That such diverse symptoms had one cause was preposterous. Even more outrageous was the suggestion that the hands of gentlemen and physicians could be so unclean as to infect their patients.

Semmelweis's reluctance to publish his own work exacerbated the controversy because colleagues' writings left out important details of his research. For instance, Von Hebra's paper implied that the pathogen responsible for puerperal fever was a "septic virus" that was transmitted only from one victim of childbed fever to another, whereas Semmelweis had concluded that *any* decaying organic matter could cause the disease. The confusion over Semmelweis's conclusions allowed critics to attack his work on the grounds that it was nothing new. English physicians such as Oliver Wendell Holmes had already surmised that childbed fever was contagious.

Frustrated by the criticism, and alarmed that the lack of hand washing at maternity clinics was killing thousands of women, Semmelweis finally published his work in 1858 and 1861. But if he'd hoped that publishing his own work would clear up confusion and produce widespread adoption of antiseptic techniques, Semmelweis was bitterly disappointed. Leading medical figures such as the father of modern pathology, Dr. Rudolf Virchow, attacked Semmelweis at medical conferences, while others published point-by-point refutations of his theories. For example, Danish obstetrician Carl Levy wrote in 1848:

A rapidly fatal putrid infection, even if the putrid matter is introduced directly into the blood, requires more than homeopathic [small] doses of the poison. And, with due respect for the cleanliness of the Viennese students, it seems improbable that enough infective matter or vapor could be secluded around the fingernails to kill a patient.

Even though medical science was aware of the existence of microbes, it would be twenty years before the work of Pasteur and others would establish the "germ theory" of disease that proved Levy wrong.

Semmelweis reacted badly to the attacks of contemporaries, responding with attacks of his own. Unfortunately, public attacks on reputable doctors as "murderers" and "ignoramuses" eroded Semmelweis's credibility and made it easier for opponents to paint him as reckless and irresponsible.

Despite replicating the dramatic reductions in patient mortality at clinics he ran in Budapest and later in his own private practice, Semmelweis was ultimately only able to persuade a small circle of obstetricians to believe his theories and to adopt the hand washing practice.

Biographer Sherwin Nuland said that Semmelweis's findings were so obscure, there is no evidence that Louis Pasteur, who is widely credited with proving the "germ theory" of infection, even knew of the Hungarian's work. After Semmelweis died, his successor at the Pest University maternity clinic, Janos Diescher, discontinued the practice of hand washing with chlorinated water, and the death rate from puerperal fever promptly rose from 1 percent to 6 percent. The pronounced increase in death rates was meticulously noted in the clinic records, but no explanation for it was offered, nor any remedy pursued.

Semmelweis had lit a long fuse to a big bang, but the fuse fizzled out long before it could ignite an explosion.

FAST AND FRUGAL DECISION MAKING

It's understandable that medical science in the nineteenth century would reject a theory as vague as "cadaveric particles" that wasn't backed up with hard evidence, such as microscope slides showing that identical microorganisms lived on autopsy corpses, the hands of doctors performing autopsies, *and* infected tissues from patients those same doctors treated. But why did physicians who witnessed Semmelweis's dramatic success reducing deaths from puerperal fever fail to adopt his antiseptic practices, especially at the maternity ward of Pest Hospital, where these methods saved lives? Even if the Hungarian obstetrician's theory was unproven, it was hard to argue with his results.

The answer is that doctors who knew about Semmelwies's theories followed the 80/20 play in the brain's playbook and simply ignored the Hungarian's data as irrelevant. You've probably heard of the 80/20 rule, also known as the Pareto Principle, where 20 percent of all possible inputs are responsible for 80 percent of all outcomes. For instance, management expert Joseph Juran observed that 20 percent of the workforce in a given business often produced 80 percent of that business's output. Twenty percent of a company's customers can account for 80 percent of its revenue. Microsoft found that fixing 20 percent of the bugs in its software eliminated 80 percent of computer crashes. Vilfredo Pareto, the Italian economist for whom the Pareto Principle is named, observed that 20 percent of the Italian population owned 80 percent of Italy's real estate.

The human brain, in its never-ending quest to spend as little energy as possible, has embraced the Pareto Principle that only a small fraction of the information it receives really matters. Thus, our brains don't waste precious time or energy sifting through every bit of sensory data from our eyes, ears, nose, tongue, and skin. Instead our brains automatically filter out data that are unlikely to matter and focus all their energy on the few bits of information that do matter.

Optical illusions result from the brain throwing away information that it believes doesn't matter, but that actually does matter. Here's an example. How much more water is in the left glass than the one on the right?

Most people would say there is about twice as much water in the left glass. But the left glass actually holds *four* times the fluid as the one on the right.

Your brain creates this illusion by making the simplifying assumption that the volume of fluid is proportional to the height of the glass, because the majority of containers, like cups and drinking glasses, have constant widths from top to bottom. Thus, your brain assumes that all containers have equal amounts of fluid in the top and bottom halves and that this half-full martini glass is no exception.

This illusion underscores the importance of expectations in determining what information we let through our sensory filters. We let in information, such as the height of a glass, that we expect to be important, while automatically filtering out information, such as the glass's width, that we expect to not be important.

Semmelweis's contemporaries didn't expect his data on hand washing to be important for two reasons. First, it was widely accepted that atmospheric miasmas caused infections, not invisible particles on hands. Why waste time or energy on theories that weren't grounded in the truth? Yes, the death rate from puerperal fever was lower in Semmelweis's clinics, but that must have been due to better control of miasmas, not extraneous factors such as hand washing. Second, evolution has hardwired an association between bad smells and disease into all of our brains. Harmful bacteria generate noxious odors, which themselves aren't harmful, but which warn us away from contaminated food or water. Just as our brains have an instinctive affinity for high-calorie sweets and fats, they have an instinctive aversion to decaying, malodorous substances. Thus, evolution led nineteenth-century doctors to unconsciously expect that things they could sense, such as bad air, mattered, while things they couldn't sense, like invisible particles, did not matter.

Gerd Gigerenzer and colleagues at the Max Planck Institute, who have researched what they call "fast and frugal" decision-making processes, believe that ignoring information might have benefits that go beyond helping us conserve neural resources to focus only on what matters. In what Gigerenzer calls *ignorance-based decision making,* we actually put our ignorance to work making complex discriminations. For example, when Gigerenzer asked test subjects to sort a long list of cities according to population size, the subjects could achieve about 90 percent accuracy by simply asking themselves whether or not they'd ever *heard* of the city. If subjects had never heard of a city, fast and frugal logic assumed—correctly most of the time—that the city was small.

By this logic, nineteenth-century doctors may well have assumed that the cadaveric particle theory was unlikely to be true because they'd never heard of it before.

Common phrases and idioms underscore the value of emphasizing one vital piece of data while actively ignoring other information. We say, "Just get to the *point*," not "Just get to the points," and "Here's the bottom *line*," not "Here are the bottom lines." A phrase that's popular in the military is KISS (Keep It Simple Stupid). Finally, I once worked for an admiral who said, "Just tell me the time, not how your watch works!"

SEMMELWEIS 2.0

Even though Semmelweis's research was largely ignored, nineteenth-century medicine eventually did embrace both the germ theory of disease and the antiseptic practices that Semmelweis pioneered. Did the chemist who deserves much of the credit for making this transformation do a better job than Semmelweis avoiding the pitfalls of the brain's playbook? Let's see.

A Problem with Beetroot Juice

In 1856, two years into his job as a university professor of chemistry in Lille, an industrial city near the Belgian border, Louis Pasteur met with Monsieur Bigot, father of one of Pasteur's students, to discuss a serious problem at the senior Bigot's manufacturing plant. Bigot produced alcohol by fermenting beetroot, but like other distillers in France, he did not have complete control of the fermentation process. Some batches of fermenting beetroot produced alcohol, while others only yielded lactic acid, the same compound that makes spoiled milk taste sour. Bigot wanted to know if Professor Pasteur would visit the plant, determine what was wrong with the fermentation, and help correct the problem.

Pasteur agreed to help, packed up some lab equipment, including a microscope, and went to the alcohol plant to investigate. Comparing samples of beetroot juice that produced alcohol with those that created lactic acid, Pasteur observed under the microscope that all spoiled samples contained tiny, rodlike figures, while normal samples had only healthy yeast cells. Pasteur suspected that the rodlike organisms were bacteria that were spoiling the brew.

Bigot's son later said that this insight helped his father improve alcohol manufacturing yield by monitoring different batches of fermenting beetroot and discarding those that grew rod-shaped organisms.

During his research at Bigot's distillery, Pasteur also decided that biological processes of living yeast cells converted sugars in the beetroot juice into alcohol. This belief ran counter to widely accepted wisdom of that time that decomposition of organic chemicals, not living yeast cells, caused fermentation.

Mindful of the harsh criticism his research was likely to receive from traditionalists, Pasteur undertook a series of additional experiments to prove beyond all doubt that one class of microbes, rod-shaped bacteria, was spoiling the good work of another class of microbes, yeast.

For example, Pasteur extracted a grayish goo that was only present in infected samples of beetroot juice, and deposited small quantities of the goo in fresh preparations of sugar water. Invariably, more gray goo formed in the new samples. And under the microscope, these samples always had rod-shaped microbes. Pasteur also reasoned that if he could kill rod-shaped organisms, while leaving yeast cells unharmed, he could insure healthy fermentation and reliable production of alcohol. By demonstrating that removal of bacteria invariably prevented spoilage, he could make his theories of yeast fermentation and bacterial spoilage that much harder to attack.

Pasteur expanded his research over the next six years to the wine, beer, and vinegar industries, which also suffered major problems with spoilage. He demonstrated that killing bacteria by heating fluid stocks before introducing healthy yeast prevented spoilage during fermentation. Similarly, heating wine and beer after it had fermented kept them from growing bacteria or going sour. Pasteur also stopped milk from spoiling by a similar heating process, now known as pasteurization. In each of his experiments, Pasteur did not use lack of spoilage as the sole indicator of bacterial death; he verified the lack of bacteria in normally fermented liquids under the microscope.

Pasteur's work proved enormously beneficial to France's alcohol, beer, wine, vinegar, and milk industries, making him what today we would call a superstar. However, meticulous measurement and solid documentation did not prevent Pasteur's work from coming under attack. His demonstration that heated liquids did not harbor bacteria directly contradicted prevailing theories that microbes spontaneously generated themselves, regardless of the sterility of their environment. This something-from-nothing idea was known as the "spontaneous generation theory."

Pasteur had little patience for theories, such as spontaneous generation, that were based on speculation rather than well-designed experiments, but he decided to answer his critics anyhow with a set of experiments to prove that bacteria could not spring into existence from nothing. He had glass-blowers create special flasks with long, bent necks. In one experiment, after sterilizing all the flasks, he left the mouth of one set of flasks open to the air, while he sealed the openings of the others. Flasks with open mouths grew microbes that had been floating in the laboratory air, while closed flasks did not. In a second experiment, Pasteur showed that fluid only grew bacteria in open flasks when the fluid sloshed into the long necks near the openings. Fluids that didn't come in contact with the necks of flasks, where airborne particles settled, never grew bacteria. As in his previous work with fermentation, Pasteur bolstered his findings with direct observation of bacteria under the microscope.

Critics were unable to fault the logic of Pasteur's results, nor were they able to devise experiments to prove conclusively that bacteria created themselves. Pasteur had not only succeeded in killing harmful bacteria, but also killed the theory of spontaneous generation.

The Worm Crisis

France's alcohol and beverage business was not the only industry beset with problems. In 1849 silk production began to decline due to a disease in silk-worms called pébrine, which got its name from small, pepperlike spots on infected silkworms. Impressed with his results in the beverage industry, the French government in 1865 asked Pasteur to perform another miracle, this time resurrecting the silk business. Pasteur was initially reluctant, but Professor Dumas, a friend who lived in a stricken silk producing region of France, eventually persuaded the great man to gather his team of researchers and move to Alès, a city in Southern France twenty miles northwest of Nimes and sixty miles north of the Mediterranean. By 1865 silkworm disease in France had reached crisis proportions, costing silk producers in Alès alone 120 million francs per year.

Using experimental methods he'd developed studying fermentation, Pasteur discovered that the eggs of worms that would eventually develop pébrine all harbored a microscopic parasite, now called *Nosema bombycis*. To prove that the parasites were infectious, Pasteur introduced the suspect microorganism into healthy colonies of worms through several different routes, including placing diseased worms among healthy ones, sprinkling infected worm feces in the cages of healthy worms, and feeding healthy worms mulberry leaves that had been contaminated. In all cases, the healthy worms got sick. Pasteur also demonstrated that healthy worms were free of microbes and that uncontaminated mulberry leaves never infected healthy animals.

Pasteur had evidently solved the silkworm mystery. And indeed, improved hygiene at silkworm farms did reduce illness among the precious worms. But to Pasteur's dismay, eliminating the pébrine parasite did not cure *all* of the worms. This partial failure opened Pasteur up to intense criticisms from the worried silk industry despite his promising early results.

It was difficult for Pasteur to fathom where his careful methods had failed. If infecting healthy worms invariably made them sick, and healthy worms *never* harbored parasites, the presence of pébrine parasites must be sufficient to cause the disease. Upon reflection, Pasteur realized that there was nothing wrong with his logic; the parasites he saw under the microscope were *sufficient* to cause disease. However, these parasites were not also *necessary* for disease to take hold. A second, unrelated organism might also make worms sick, accounting for the incomplete success.

Further careful investigation revealed that, in fact, a second organism, the flacherie virus, caused symptoms closely resembling pébrine.

After five years of painstaking work and numerous heartbreaking setbacks, Pasteur had discovered two diseases that, taken together, were necessary *and* sufficient to sicken worms. The insight that silkworm illness was two diseases, not one, ultimately led to more thorough care and feeding of silkworm litters and saved France's silk industry.

Necessity and Sufficiency Among Sheep

Pasteur's initial setback with silkworms, and his later work investigating cause and effect in spoilage of fermented drinks, caused him to expand his experimental techniques to encompass the twin concepts of necessity and sufficiency. This meant that to prove conclusively that a pathogen (or pathogens) caused disease or spoilage, he had to demonstrate that diseased or contaminated animals or fluids *always* harbored pathogens and that healthy ones *never* did. Without support of the twin pillars of necessity and sufficiency, any theory of disease or spoilage would collapse. As scientists in other fields learned of Pasteur's work, it became clear to them that *any* theory that sought to explain cause and effect in nature, whether in biology, chemistry, or physics, must also stand up to twin tests of necessity and sufficiency. This insight revolutionized science and remains a cornerstone of the scientific method to this day. For example, although the German scientist Alfred Wegener proposed in 1905 that the continents we see today were once a single continent that broke up and drifted apart, it wasn't until geologists proved more than fifty years later that constant lava upwellings between tectonic plates (separate pieces of the earth's crust) were both necessary and sufficient to cause the plates, and the continents on them, to drift apart, that Wegener's controversial theory was accepted.

In an effort to help himself withstand criticisms of detractors, Pasteur had developed a means for all scientists to prove unpopular theories. But in 1881, Pasteur was far from finished proving his own novel ideas using the logic of necessity and sufficiency.

An ardent patriot, Pasteur retained throughout his life a desire to help the French economy. This interest focused his attention on anthrax, which was killing livestock and costing French farmers 20 to 30 million francs per year. Five years earlier, the German physician Robert Koch (whose assistant Petri invented the covered glass dish that still bears the name of its creator) had shown convincingly, with techniques similar to Pasteur's, that the microbe *Bacillus anthracis* caused anthrax.

To tackle anthrax in France, Pasteur knew he had to build on Koch's findings. However, relying on the work of a German must have irked him because Pasteur did not care for Germans in general, or for Koch in particular. Lord Joseph Lister, whom we shall hear more about shortly, did manage to introduce Koch and Pasteur at an 1881 conference in London, but Pasteur had to grit his teeth and force himself to shake hands with his German rival. During the Franco-Prussian War, which had ended just ten years earlier, Pasteur had written: "All my work, to my dying day, will bear as an inscription, 'Hatred towards Prussia! Revenge! Revenge!'"

Patriotic fervor ultimately did not stop Pasteur from taking advantage of Koch's research, and going one up on Koch by *preventing* anthrax instead of just diagnosing it. Pasteur was aware of Edward Jenner's success in 1796 vaccinating against smallpox using a weakened form of the virus, which conferred immunity to humans. The French were early adopters of Jenner's vaccination technology, with Napoleon ordering the inoculation of French troops as early as 1805. Pasteur speculated that inoculating livestock with a weakened form of *Bacillus anthracis* might immunize them against anthrax.

Experimenting with different ways to weaken anthrax bacteria with both heat and chemical preparations, by the late spring of 1881 Pasteur was confident that he had a workable vaccine.

Not everyone shared his confidence. Although Pasteur by this time was a popular figure in France, like any pioneer, he had a number of powerful enemies, one of whom was an editor of a veterinary journal, a horse doctor named Rossignol. Rossignol saw in Pasteur's brash claims about anthrax an opportunity to discredit him. He baited Pasteur, saying:

"Pasteur claims that nothing is easier than to make a vaccine that will protect sheep and cows absolutely from anthrax. If that is true, it would be a great thing for French farmers, who are now losing 20 million francs a year from this disease. Well if Pasteur can really make such magic stuff, he ought to be able to prove to us he has the goods. Let us get Pasteur to consent to a grand public experiment. If he is right, we farmers and veterinarians are the gainers; if it fails, Pasteur will have to stop his eternal blabbering about great discoveries that save sheep and worms and babies and hippopotamuses."

Pasteur, who saw this as a huge opportunity for publicity, not a trap, accepted the challenge. With Rossignol's help, the Agriculture Society of Melun, a farming district southeast of Paris, raised funds to buy fifty sheep for the demonstration. Under Pasteur's guidance, the society then placed the animals in special holding pens at a farm at Pouilly-le-Fort. Pasteur specified that the sheep be divided into three groups: one that would receive no treatment, one that would be infected with a virulent strain of anthrax bacteria, and a third that would be infected with the same virulent strain *after* being inoculated with the vaccine containing weakened anthrax.

Pasteur set up these three groups so that he could demonstrate that vaccination was both necessary and sufficient to confer immunity. If only inoculated sheep survived infection, and uninoculated, uninifected sheep developed no illness, then Pasteur could claim with confidence that the disease the sheep developed was in fact anthrax and that animals would be protected from infection if, and *only* if, they were vaccinated.

Due to the importance of the demonstration and the publicity surrounding it, hundreds of locals as well as dignitaries and politicians from the rest of France also attended. Alarming his staff, Pasteur hyped the event, publicly predicting that all infected sheep who had the benefit of inoculation would live, whereas all infected sheep who were not vaccinated would die. After the brash announcement, Pasteur tried to calm his anxious team: "What worked with fourteen sheep in our laboratory," he assured them, "will work with fifty at Melun."

With great fanfare and press coverage, the demonstration commenced on May 5 with the inoculation of the sheep. In a second, well-attended ceremony twelve days later, Pasteur showed that the earlier inoculations had not harmed any sheep, and instructed his assistants to administer a second dose of vaccine, this time with a less weakened version of the bacteria.

On May 31, at a third show, both inoculated and uninoculated sheep got injections of lethal doses of virulent anthrax microbes, while the third group went unmolested. The next night, on the eve of the final demonstration, where both Pasteur and a large crowd would see whether the vaccines had worked, Pasteur did not sleep well. He tossed in bed and got up more than fifty times. Perhaps he was just excited at the next day's spectacle, or perhaps he finally began to fear that he'd walked into a trap.

If the latter possibility was agitating him, Pasteur needn't have worried. The next day, all of the inoculated sheep were healthy, while all but two of their uninoculated counterparts had died. And the two survivors did not look well, wobbling about in their pen and exuding dark, ominous fluid from their snouts. Before the large crowd had dispersed, even these two survivors died.

The famous journalist Adolphe de Blowitz, of the *London Times,* who witnessed the final demonstration, immediately cabled his editors, "The experiment at Pouilly-le-Forte is a perfect, unprecedented success." One detractor exclaimed, "It's true that I have made jokes about microbes, but I am a repentant sinner." Dr. Biot, a veterinarian and vocal Pasteur critic, was so moved by the demonstration that he pleaded, "Inoculate *me* with your vaccine."

This last observation underscored what had become obvious to all but the most conservative physicians of that time: that Pasteur's compelling demonstrations proved that germs caused disease in more than just animals.

Three years before the spectacle at Pouilly-le-Fort, Pasteur himself told the

French Academy: "If I had the honour of being a surgeon, not only would I use none but perfectly clean instruments but I would clean my hands with the greatest of care."

Across the Channel

Pasteur published a paper in 1861 demonstrating that airborne microbes, not spontaneous generation, caused contamination of open flasks, and in 1863 released another paper, in which he speculated that fermentation of beverages and suppuration of wounds had a common cause, microbes.

Joseph Lister, a surgeon in Edinburgh, Scotland, read these papers with great interest. The discovery of anesthetic in the 1840s had greatly expanded the scope of ailments that surgeons could treat, but almost half of major surgery patients died from infection following surgery. Lister realized that, taken together, Pasteur's two papers suggested that airborne microbes could infect open wounds.

Lister later said: "When it had been shown by the researches of Pasteur that the septic property of the atmosphere depended not on the oxygen or any gaseous constituent, but on minute organisms suspended in it, which owed their energy to their vitality, it occurred to me that decomposition in the injured part might be avoided without excluding the air, by applying as a dressing some materials capable of destroying the life of the floating particles."

In 1865, Lister directed that surgeons treating patients in the Male Accident Ward of Edinburgh Hospital sterilize their instruments with carbolic acid, wash their hands before surgery, and wear gloves during surgery. Lister also instructed his surgeons to dress wounds after surgery with bandages soaked in antiseptic. Over the next four years, post-surgical death rates in the Male Accident Ward fell from 45 percent to 15 percent.

These impressive results failed to convince the majority of surgeons in Great Britain and the United States to adopt Lister's antiseptic methods. Despite the successes of younger surgeons who had embraced Lister's ideas in regional centers such as Birmingham and Manchester, influential surgeons in London, who tended to discount findings at provincial hospitals, took a wait-and-see attitude for more than ten years. Lister realized that antiseptic surgery would have to gain acceptance from thought leaders in London before it was universally adopted.

Lister decided to move to London in 1877, to become chairman of surgery at the prestigious Kings College. In October of that year, he performed a radical new procedure successfully repairing a fractured kneecap by binding it together with a sterilized silver wire. Kneecap operations had, up to that point, been notorious for causing infection, and the much publicized results of Lister's success tipped the balance of opinion on the value of antiseptic surgery in his favor.

Within a few years aseptic surgery had become the accepted norm for surgeons worldwide.

REVIEWING THE PLAYBOOK

Unlike Semmelweis, Pasteur (with help from Lister) lit a long fuse that stayed lit all the way to a monumentally big bang. We've already seen that the "ignore what you don't expect" play in the brain's playbook hurt Semmelweis by causing nineteenth-century doctors to treat his statistics as irrelevant. Let's now explore how the playbook helped Pasteur succeed where Semmelweis failed.

Both Semmelweis and Pasteur were meticulous scientists who carefully constructed experiments to rule out alternative explanations for the disease phenomena they observed. There were key differences to their approaches, however. There is no evidence that Semmelweis anticipated the nearly universal skepticism that would greet his startling findings. He had a logical and methodical mind and seemed to have assumed that other doctors did as well. His initial surprise and anger at the rejection of his solid statistics connecting hand washing to lowered maternity death rates suggests that he didn't understand people very well. In particular, he didn't anticipate that doctors could be so wedded to accepted ideas that they'd ignore compelling scientific evidence contradicting their beliefs.

In contrast, Pasteur's writings suggest that he was acutely aware that his research on microbes would create controversy. Some of his papers address what potential critics might say, before these critics actually attacked him. Pasteur's anticipation of criticism may have been one reason he went to such great lengths to bolster his arguments with hard, visual evidence of microbes obtained through his microscope. Visual evidence was a far more compelling way to shake doctors out of their complacency than an undocumented theory such as "cadaveric particles." Similarly, after his initial setbacks with the silkworm research, Pasteur addressed the twin issues of necessity and sufficiency to provide unassailable proof of cause-and-effect relationships between microbes and disease. Pasteur was also a natural showman, with a flair for dramatic demonstrations—like those at Pouilly-la-Forte—that were capable of converting even hardened skeptics. Lister's showmanship as well proved instrumental in selling Pasteur's germ theory of disease. Semmelweis, on the other hand, preferred to stay in his clinic and let his data speak for itself. When his compelling statistics did not convince critics, Semmelweis violated the number one rule of brain judo by losing his balance and attacking his detractors with emotionally charged letters.

Pasteur, on the other hand, kept his balance when attacked. Instead of just getting mad at critics, he got busy, returning to his lab to find hard evidence to back up his theories and disprove those of his adversaries. Another factor in Pasteur's success was that he was a chemist who set out to solve business problems for patrons who knew they were in trouble, not a doctor trying to convince other doctors they were killing their patients. Thus, his job wasn't to push people out of deeply entrenched comfort zones, but to help them escape *discomfort* zones.

Discomfort zones are fertile places to plant new ideas because people in trouble are acutely aware of here-and-now problems. As a result, their brains let in information that might otherwise get filtered out, if that information promises to resolve immediate problems. The play in the brain's playbook goes something like this: "Ignore everything that you don't expect to matter, except when you're in deep trouble. Then, pay close attention to anything that might solve your problem."

The lesson here is that long fuses to big bangs lie inside people's discomfort zones. Instead of willfully ignoring unexpected opportunities, brains in trouble will actively look for them.

In *The Innovator's Solution, Creating and Sustaining Successful Growth,* Clayton Christensen and Michael Raynor acknowledge the difficulty of getting entrenched, successful organizations to embrace revolutionary or "disruptive" changes. Christensen and Raynor believe it's far easier to introduce radically new products or ways of doing business when these innovations "serve the underserved." For example, Christensen and Raynor observed that when radios built with transistors instead of vacuum tubes first came on the market in the 1950s, they did not immediately displace vacuum tube radios despite being much more compact and power efficient. However, the low cost and portability of battery-operated transistor radios appealed to teenagers who wanted to listen to music anytime, anywhere. Most teenagers couldn't afford a vacuum tube radio, and couldn't easily carry it with them even if they could afford it, so transistor radios admirably served an underserved teenage market. Ultimately, as the sound quality of transistor radios improved, the smaller size, lower cost, and greater portability of transistor technology made vacuum tubes obsolete in all radios. Unlike their parents, who were content to stay in the comfort zone of vacuum tube radios, teenagers, before transistor technology came on the market, occupied a *discomfort zone*. Like Pasteur's patrons in the silk, beverage, and livestock businesses, these teenagers saw that there was more to gain by action than inaction, and therefore embraced a radically new idea.

When I volunteered at a community mental health center in Manhattan Beach, California, throughout most of the 1980s, the therapists at the center liked to tell a joke:

QUESTION:

How many psychologists does it take to change a lightbulb?

ANSWER:

Only one, but the lightbulb really has to want to change.

CHAPTER 1

5 *placed study of the Human Terrain at the top of the list*: Office of the Undersecretary of Defense for Acquisition, Technology, and Logistics. *Report of the Defense Science Board Task Force on Understanding Human Dynamics*, March 2009.

6 *most significant development in past six months*: Testimony before Congress, General David Petreus, September, 2007.

7 *Consider Honda*: Honda Corporate Web Site, http://world.honda.com/history/challenge/index.html#1960s.

7 *"Taco Bell tried to turn around a steep decline in sales"*: Hammer, Michael, and James Champy, *Reengineering the Corporation*, Harper Collins, New York, 2001.

7 *IBM's "inbred and ingrown" culture*: Gerstner, Lou, *Who Says Elephants Can't Dance?*, Harper Collins, New York, 2002.

8 *The difficult is what takes a little time*: Pratt, David, *The Impossible Takes Longer: The 1,000 Wisest Things Ever Said by Nobel Prize Laureates*, Douglas & McIntyre, Vancouver, BC, 2007.

11 *future eaters*: Flannery, Tim, *The Future Eaters: An Ecological History of the Australasian Lands and People*, Reed Books, Melbourne, Australia, 1994.

12 *"delaying a reward by a year"*: Laibson, David, *Impatience and Savings: BER Reporter: Research Summary*, National Bureau of Economic Research, Fall 2005, http://www.nber.org/reporter/fall05/laibson.html.

CHAPTER 2

22 *That is what I am and who I am*: Malone, Andrew, "Face to Face with Stone Age Man", 2007, http://www.dailymail.co.uk/news/article-469847/Face-face-Stone-Age-man-The-Hadzabe-tribe-Tanzania.html.

23 *"more than 1 billion adults world wide are overweight*: World Health Organization, *Obesity and Overweight*, 2009, http://www.who.int/dietphysicalactivity/publications/facts/obesity/en/.

23 *"so I don't have to walk that extra fifty feet"*: Horgan, John, "How the Peacock Got Its Feathers and Other Tales of Nature's Spendthrifts," 2004, http://www.incharacter.org/article.php?article=6.

24 *Perceptual psychologist Denny Proffitt*: Proffitt, Denny. "Embodied Perception and Economy of Action," *Perspectives on Psychological Science*, Association for Psychological Science, May 23, 2006, *Vol. 1, No. 2*, pp. 110–122.

28 *"I only made it a novel"*: Dr. XX, personal conversation with author, 2009.

29 *"There are three gynecologists and thirty-nine veterinarians at NIH"*: Greenberger, Phyllis and Jennifer Wider, *The Savvy Woman Patient: How and Why Sex Differences Affect Your Health*, Herndon: Capital Press, 2006.

33 *"a black belt who wrote this about coping with stronger adversaries"*: Judo Tom, 2005, http://www.elitefitness.com.

40 *Paula Goode, a former IBM executive*: Goode, Paula. 2004. Personal conversation with author.

CHAPTER 3

45 *Bill Haseltine recognized the impact of HIV-1*: Lever, Andrew, "Science—A Life Fully Lived: Joe Sodroski Wins the 2006 Retrovirology Prize," 2006, http://www.retrovirology.com/content/3/1/45.

46 *Barry Werth wrote in 1988*: Werth, Barry, "The AIDS Windfall." *New England Monthly*, June, 1988.

CHAPTER 4

60 *Eventually, Randy gathered detailed data*: Pausch, Randy, et al., *Disney's Aladdin: First Steps Toward Storytelling in Virtual Reality*, International Conference on Computer Graphics and Interactive Techniques Proceedings of the 23rd Annual Conference on Computer Graphics and Interactive Techniques, 1996.

63 *Clayton Christensen's new book*: Christensen, Clayton, *The Innovator's Dilemma*, Harvard Business School Press, Cambridge, Massachusetts, 1997.

CHAPTER 5

79 *Dean Burch, director general of Intelsat said*: Andrews, Edmund, "Tiny Tonga Seeks Satellite Empire in Space," August 28, 1990, http://www.nytimes.com/1990/08/28/business/tiny-tonga-seeks-satellite-empire-in-space.html?pagewanted=all.

80 *I believe God intended us to do this work*: Lee, Peter, "China as Collateral Damage in the Tongan Crisis," 2006, http://chinamatters.blogspot.com/ 2006_11_01_archive.html.

82 *Winston Churchill*: Plugge, Bob, http://www.quotationsofwisdom.com/view/ Winston_Churchill/12002.html.

83 *The Tony Award–winning producer observed*: David Merrick, David Merrick Quotes, http://thinkexist.com/quotation/it-s-not-enough-that-i-should -succeed-others/534134.html.

CHAPTER 6

89 *"It's not jour job"*: Babcock, Elizabeth, *Magnificent Mavericks*, China Lake Museum Foundation, China Lake, 2008.

91 *Dr. Howie Wilcox, a lead engineer*: Westram, Ron and Howard A. Wilcox, "Sidewinder," http://www.americanheritage.com/articles/magazine/it/1989/2/ 1989_2_56.shtml.

108 *Both Don and Sean were what author Malcolm Gladwell*: Gladwell, Malcolm, *The Tipping Point*, Little Brown and Company, London, 2000.

110 *Twenty-three people at*: Calabresi, Massimo, "Wikipedia for Spies: The CIA Discovers Web 2.0," April 8, 2009, http://www.time.com/time/nation/ article/0,8599,1890084,00.html.

111 *enabled experts from different disciplines*: DiGiammarino, Frank and Lena Trudeau, "Virtual Networks: An Opportunity for Government," *The Public Manager*, Vol. 37, No. 1, Spring 2008.

111 *There are people who describe*: Fingar, Thomas, speech before the DNI's information sharing and technology expo, Denver, Colorado, 2006, http://www.dni.gov/speeches/20060821_2_speech.pdf.

CHAPTER 7

115 *The Chandler town car, in blue*: Theobald, Mark, Harley Earl 1893–1969, 2004, http://www.coachbuilt.com/des/e/earl/earl.htm.

116 *"Unfortunately," he said*: Theobald, Mark, Harley Earl 1893–1969, 2004, http://www.coachbuilt.com/des/e/earl/earl.htm.

120 *For example, when college students in the labs*: Szpunar, Karl and Kathleen McDermott, "Remembering the Past to Imagine the Future," 2007, http:// www.dana.org/news/Cerebrum/detail.aspx?id=5526.

122 *Consumers could be prepared by measured steps*: Mroz, Albert, Why the Y-Job, Harley Earl and the Buick Dream Car, http://www.prewarbuick.com/ features/why_the_y_job.

124 *"I'd rather try crossing a river on a path"*: Mroz, Albert, Why the Y-Job, Harley
     Earl and the Buick Dream Car, http://www.prewarbuick.com/features/why_
     the_y_job.

126 *You could drop the barometer from the roof*: Ferren, Bran, conversation with
     author, 2009.

135 *You know how you see a show car*: Grossman, Lev., "How Apple Does It,"
     October 16, 2005, http://www.time.com/time/magazine/article/0,9171,
     1118384,00.html.

136 *But there are a lot more hearts out there*: Personal conversation between author
     and John Hench (sixty-five year Disney employee and Walt Disney confidant,
     who quoted Walt directly).

136 *The best way to predict the future is to invent it*: Personal conversation between
     author and Alan Kay, 2000.

CHAPTER 8

139 *Barbara Fredrickson, head of*: Fredrickson, Barbara, Research, http://www
     .unc.edu/peplab/research.html.

144 *Psychologist Daniel Goleman*: Goleman, Daniel, *Primal Leadership*, Harvard
     Business School Publishing, Boston, 2002.

152 *Neurologist Antonio Damasio says*: Damasio, Antonio, *Descartes' Error*,
     Putnam and Sons, New York, 1994.

156 *what Harvard business professor Clayton Christensen calls*: Christensen,
     Clayton, Anthony Scott, and Erik Roth. *Seeing What's Next*, Harvard
     Business School Publishing, Boston, 2004.

156 *says that in the past, new technologies always "trickled down" from*: Prahalad,
     C. K., *The Fortune at the Bottom of the Pyramid*, Wharton School Publishing,
     Upper Saddle River, New Jersey, 2010.

CHAPTER 9

165 *I had lost my passion and excitement for liquid crystal*: Heilmeier, George, "A
     Moveable Feast," acceptance speech for Kyoto Prize, 2004.

166 *Thirty years later, when these ultra-classified silver bullets*: Heilmeier, George,
     "A Moveable Feast," acceptance speech for Kyoto Prize, 2004.

169 *"that laid out basic principles for estimating how much electromagnetic"*:
     Ufimtzev, P. Y.a., *Method of Edge Waves in the Physical Theory of Diffraction*,
     U.S. Air Force publication FTD-HC-23-259-71, 1971.

174 *or what Richard Dawkins calls "memes"*: Memes, http://en.wikipedia.org/wiki/
     Meme.

176 *"addicted to novelty"*: Cruse, Amy, personal conversation with author, 2009.

CHAPTER 10

185 *"There are two kinds of people in this world"*: Monnet, Jean and George Ball, *Memoirs*, Fayard, Paris, 1976.

186 *Monnet said of those early years*: Monnet, Jean and George Ball, *Memoirs*, Fayard, Paris, 1976.

186 *"Take my horse," the man said*: Yergin, Daniel and Joeseph Stanislaw, *The Commanding Heights*, Simon and Schuster, New York, 1998.

187 *Monnet told Vivani*: Roussel, Eric, *Jean Monnet 1888–1979*, Fayard, Paris, 1996.

189 *"When ideas are lacking"*: Duchene, Francois, *Jean Monnet: The First Statesman of Interdependence* Norton, New York, 1994.

189 *"People only accept change"*: Monnet, Jean, http://www.newworldencyclopedia.org/entry/Jean_Monnet.

190 *"During the war, the pooling"*: Duchene, Francois, *Jean Monnet: The First Statesman of Interdependence,* Norton, New York, 1994.

191 *By early June, DeGaulle, Churchill, and Monnet*: Jean Monnet FAQ, http://www.jean-monnet.net/menu06/page1us.html.

191 *Shortly after the war, de Gaulle observed*: Jean Monnet, http://www.encyclopedia.com/doc/1G2-3404704528.html.

191 *This expansion prepared America for war to such*: Jean Monnet, http://en.wikipedia.org/wiki/Jean_Monnet.

191 *Pleased that Roosevelt had gotten*: Arsenal of Democracy, http://www.search.com/reference/Arsenal_of_Democracy.

193 *There will be no peace in Europe*: Jean Monnet, http://en.wikipedia.org/wiki/Jean_Monnet.

194 *"Peace must be based upon equality"* : Monnet, Jean and George Ball, *Memoirs*, Fayard, Paris, 1976.

196 *In his memoirs, Monnet wrote*: Monnet, Jean and George Ball, *Memoirs*, Fayard, Paris, 1976.

200 *One of Monnet's favorite quotes*: Brinkley, Douglas, and Clifford Hackett, *Jean Monnet: The Path to European Unity*, St. Martin's Press, New York, 1991.

201 *In a letter to Monnet in 1963, John F. Kennedy*: Kennedy, John F., Letter to Jean Monnet Commending His Achievements on Behalf of European Unity, January 23, 1963, http://www.presidency.ucsb.edu/ws/index.php?pid=9365.

202 *Towards the end of his life, he wrote*: Monnet, Jean and George Ball, *Memoirs*, Fayard, Paris, 1976.

CHAPTER 11

210 *evolutionary psychologists such as the husband-and-wife team*: Cosmides, Leda, and John Tooby, Evolutionary Psychology: A Primer, http://cogweb.ucla.edu/ep/EP-primer.html.

212 *Peter Abell, retail research director of AMR Research wrote*: ICMRINDIA, Wal-Mart's Supply Chain Management Practices (B): Using IT/Internet to Manage the Supply Chain, http://www.icmrindia.org/CaseStudies/catalogue/Operations/Wal-Mart-Supply%20Chain%20Management%20Practices-IT-Internet.htm.

213 *Walton wrote in his autobiography*: Walton, Sam, and John Huey, *Sam Walton: Made in America*, Doubleday, New York, 1992.

214 *He wrote of those early days in retail*: Walton, Sam, and John Huey, *Sam Walton: Made in America,* Doubleday, New York, 1992.

214 *Walton wrote in 1992*: Walton, Sam, and John Huey, *Sam Walton: Made in America,* Doubleday, New York 1992.

215 *Sam later wrote*: Walton, Sam, and John Huey, *Sam Walton: Made in America*, Doubleday, New York, 1992.

215 *"divine discontent"*: Turner, Kevin, Kevin Turner: Potomac Officers Club Executive Business Breakfast, 2007, http://www.microsoft.com/Presspass/exec/turner/09-21poc.mspx.

216 *Sam wrote*: *"The funny thing is"*. Walton, Sam, and John Huey, *Sam Walton: Made in America*, Doubleday, New York, 1992.

221 *Kay report jointly to CIA and to Rumsfeld*: "Absolutely not," Woodward, Robert, *State of Denial*, Simon and Schuster, New York, 2006.

222 *In a 2008 interview with* Chief Executive *magazine*: Donlon, J. P. "Lafley's Law: If You Want to Win Become a Game-Changer", 2008, http://www.chiefexecutive.net/ME2/dirmod.asp?sid=&nm=&type=Publishing&mod=Publications::Article&mid=8F3A7027421841978F18BE895F87F791&id=8B79F0D0B7394691B7F544FF938DAB76&tier=4

CHAPTER 12

226 *Semmelweis wrote*: Semmelweis, Ignaz, *The Etiology, Concept and Prophylaxis of Childbed Fever*, trans. K. Codell Carter (reprinted by permission of University of Wisconsin Press, 1983) in *Medicine: A Treasury of Art and Literature*, Vol. 136.

228 *For example, Danish obstetrician Carl Levy wrote*: Contemporary reaction to Ignaz Semmelweis, http://en.wikipedia.org/wiki/Contemporary_reaction_to_Ignaz_Semmelweis.

231 *In what Gigerenzer calls ignorance-based decision making*: Gigerenzer, Gerd,

Todd, Peter, and ABC Research Group. *Simple Heuristics That Make Us Smart*, Oxford University Press, New York, 1999.

236 *During the Franco-Prussian war, which had ended just ten years earlier*: Lehrer, Steven, *Explorers of the Body: Dramatic Breakthroughs in Medicine from Ancient Times*, Universe Books, Lincoln, Nebraska, 2006.

237 *Pasteur claims that nothing is easier*: De Kruif, Paul, *Microbe Hunters*, Harcourt, Orlando, Florida, 1926.

238 *What worked with fourteen sheep*: King-Thom, Chung and Deam Ferris, Louis Pasteur (1822–1895) The True Master of Microbiology, http://highered. mcgraw-hill.com/sites/dl/free/0072320419/20534/pasteur.html.

238 *One detractor exclaimed*: De Kruif, Paul, *Microbe Hunters*, Harcourt, Orlando, Florida, 1926.

239 *Pasteur himself told the French Academy*: Cohn, David V., The Life and Times of Louis Pasteur, http://www.labexplorer.com/louis_pasteur.htm.

239 *Lister later said*: Joseph Lister, http://www.whonamedit.com/doctor.cfm/3367 .html.

241 *In* The Innovator's Solution: Christensen, Clayton, and Michael Raynor, *The Innovator's Solution,* Harvard Business School Publications, Boston, 2003.